Generation Disaster

EMERGING ADULTHOOD SERIES

Series Editor
Larry J. Nelson

Advisory Board
Elisabetta Crocetti
Shagufa Kapadia
Koen Luyckx
Laura Padilla-Walker
Jennifer L. Tanner

Generation Disaster

Coming of Age Post-9/11

Karla Vermeulen

OXFORD
UNIVERSITY PRESS

OXFORD

UNIVERSITY PRESS

Oxford University Press is a department of the University of Oxford. It furthers
the University's objective of excellence in research, scholarship, and education
by publishing worldwide. Oxford is a registered trade mark of Oxford University
Press in the UK and certain other countries.

Published in the United States of America by Oxford University Press
198 Madison Avenue, New York, NY 10016, United States of America.

Library of Congress Cataloging-in-Publication Data
Names: Vermeulen, Karla, author.
Title: Generation disaster : coming of age post-9/11 / by Karla Vermeulen.
Description: New York, NY : Oxford University Press, 2021. |
Includes bibliographical references and index. |
Identifiers: LCCN 2021015165 (print) | LCCN 2021015166 (ebook) |
ISBN 9780190061630 (paperback) | ISBN 9780190061654 (epub) |
ISBN 9780190061661
Subjects: LCSH: Coming of age—United States. | Disasters—Social
aspects—United States. | Young adults—United States. |
Generation Y—United States. | Generation Z—United States. |
United States—Social conditions—21 century.
Classification: LCC HQ799.7 .V47 2021 (print) | LCC HQ799.7 (ebook) |
DDC 305.242—dc23
LC record available at https://lccn.loc.gov/2021015165
LC ebook record available at https://lccn.loc.gov/2021015166

DOI: 10.1093/oso/9780190061630.001.0001

1 3 5 7 9 8 6 4 2

Printed by Marquis, Canada

For my beloved nieces and nephews, Max (plus Edith), Bridget, Rachel, Sam, Ethan, and Marisa. And to all of the other emerging adults out there, doing your absolute best with the complicated hand you've been dealt. I'm counting on you all to save the world.

And for Michael, always.

Each generation imagines itself to be more intelligent than the one that went before it, and wiser than the one that comes after it.

—George Orwell

Change is coming, whether you like it or not.

—Greta Thunberg

Contents

Series Foreword

The *Emerging Adulthood Series* examines the period of life starting at age 18 and continuing into and through the third decade of life, now commonly referred to as emerging adulthood. The specific focus of the series is on flourishing (i.e., factors that lead to positive, adaptive development during emerging adulthood and the successful transition into adult roles) and floundering (i.e., factors that lead to maladaptive behaviors and negative development during emerging adulthood as well as delay and difficulty in transitioning into adult roles) in the diverse paths young people take into and through the third decade of life.

There is a need to examine the successes and struggles in a variety of domains experienced by young people as they take complex and multiple paths in leaving adolescence and moving into and through their twenties. Too often the diversity of individual experiences is forgotten in our academic attempts to categorize a time period. For example, in proposing his theory of emerging adulthood, Arnett (2000, 2004) identified features of the development of young people including *feeling in-between* (emerging adults do not see themselves as either adolescents or adults); *identity exploration* (especially in the areas of work, love, and world views); *focus on the self* (not self-centered, but simply lacking obligations to others); *instability* (evidenced by changes of direction in residential status, relationships, work, and education); and *possibilities* (optimism in the potential to steer their lives in any number of desired directions). Although this is a nice summary of characteristics of the time period, the scholarly examination of emerging adulthood has not always attempted to capture and explain the within-group variation that exists among emerging adults, often making the broad generalization that they are a relatively homogeneous group. For example, emerging adults have been categorically referred to as "narcissistic," "refusing to grow up," and "failed adults." While there certainly are emerging adults who fit the profile of selfish, struggling, and directionless, there are others who are using this period of time for good. Indeed, there is great diversity of individual experiences in emerging adulthood. Hence, there is a need to better examine various beliefs/attitudes, attributes, behaviors, and relationships during this period of time that appear to reflect positive adjustment, or a sense of flourishing, or conversely those that lead to floundering.

For example, recent research (Nelson & Padilla-Walker, 2013) showed that young people who appear to be successfully navigating emerging adulthood tend to engage in identity exploration, develop internalization of positive values, participate in positive media use, engage in prosocial behaviors, report healthy relationships with parents, and engage in romantic relationships that are characterized by higher levels of companionship, worth, affection, and emotional support. For others who appear to be floundering, emerging adulthood appears to include anxiety and depression, poor self-perceptions, greater participation in risk behaviors, and poorer relationship quality with parents, best friends, and romantic partners. Thus, while various profiles of flourishing and floundering are starting to be identified, the current work in the field has simply provided cursory overviews of findings. This series provides a platform for an in-depth, comprehensive examination into some of these key factors that seem to be influencing, positively or negatively, young people as they enter into and progress through the third decade of life and the multiple ways in which they may flourish or flounder. Furthermore, the series attempts to examine how these factors may function differently within various populations (i.e., cultures and religious and ethnic subcultures, students vs. nonstudents, men vs. women, etc.). Finally, the series provides for a multidisciplinary (e.g., fields ranging from developmental psychology, neurobiology, education, sociology, criminology) and multimethod (i.e., information garnered from both quantitative and qualitative methodologies) examination of issues related to flourishing and floundering in emerging adulthood.

It is important to make one final note about this series. In choosing to employ the term "emerging adulthood," it is not meant to imply that the series will include books that are limited in their scope to viewing the third decade of life only through the lens of emerging adulthood theory (Arnett, 2000). Indeed, the notion of "emerging adulthood" as a universal developmental period has been met with controversy and skepticism because of the complex and numerous paths young people take out of adolescence and into adulthood. It is that exact diversity in the experiences of young people in a variety of contexts and circumstances (e.g., cultural, financial, familial) that calls for a book series such as this one. It is unfortunate that disagreement about emerging adulthood theory has led to a fragmentation of scholars and scholarship devoted to better understanding the third decade of life. Hence, although the term "emerging adulthood" is employed for parsimony and for its growing familiarity as a term for the age period, this series is devoted to examining broadly, from a variety of perspectives and disciplines, the complexity of pathways into and through the third decade of life. In doing so, it is my hope that the series will help scholars, practitioners, students, and others better understand, and thereby potentially foster, flourishing and floundering in the lives of young people in the various paths they may take to adulthood.

Generation Disaster: Coming of Age Post-9/11

Without a doubt, every generation of young people in the United States has grown up within a context of challenges and adversity. In particular, war and economic hardship seem to be challenges that human beings repeatedly bring on themselves, shaping the development of those coming of age during events like the Great Depression and a series of wars with various names, fought for a variety of reasons, occurring on a variety of continents, and spanning numerous decades. Racism, inequality, and injustice have been the context in which far too many young people from ethnic and racial minorities have made the transition to adulthood for countless generations. The journey from childhood to adulthood for girls has occurred in a landscape that has been far different for them than for their male peers. About the only commonality across time, race, and gender has been that traumatic events have been part of the context of young people's development that has shaped their lives, especially affecting the important process of becoming adults. Thus, Dr. Karla Vermeulen has not written this book to suggest that today's young people have had it worse than any prior generation in the challenges they have faced in growing up (it certainly is not a competition!), but rather to analyze how the unique challenges facing this generation have shaped who *they* have become.

In particular, in *Generation Disaster: Coming of Age Post-9/11*, Dr. Vermeulen examines how the context for development of today's young people has been shaped by the events of 9/11 (and other acts of terror, constant threats thereof, and the wars in Iraq and Afghanistan that followed 9/11), mass shootings, the effects of climate change in the form of natural disasters, a major economic recession, political divisiveness, protest movements brought on by continued inequity and injustice, and, most recently, a worldwide pandemic. Furthermore, Dr. Vermeulen paints a vivid picture of how the development of technology during the lifetime of this generation has brought these events right into their lives. For this generation, news of events no longer came hours or even days later in print (e.g., daily newspaper, magazine), still life photography, or via the evening news on one of just a handful of television stations. For them, the events were often captured on video and, often, delivered in real time via numerous media platforms. Thus, some of the disasters not only are unique to this generation (e.g., 9/11) but also their real-time exposure (often including graphic, brutal, and disturbing images) to so many of the events is unarguably something no other generation has ever experienced.

Thus, how have the events of this generation, and their direct and immediate exposure to them via technology, shaped the beliefs, perspectives, behaviors, and relationships of this generation? Dr. Vermeulen undertakes the task of addressing these important issues in this volume in a way that does not try to paint a broad picture of an entire generation of people. Instead, she takes a very nuanced look at how the same events have influenced individuals so differently depending on complex factors such as gender, race, and social class. She does this by drawing on a wealth of existing empirical literature, her own research conducted throughout her career, and data collected specifically to address some of these questions for this book. A particularly powerful aspect of the book is the way in which Dr. Vermeulen brings the empirical evidence to life by employing the actual "voices" of young people collected via interviews with young people. Taken together, Dr. Vermeulen does a masterful job of taking a macro-level look at the context in which today's generation of young people has grown up in order to better understand individuals' beliefs, perspectives, behaviors, and relationships as they make their way toward adulthood.

References

Arnett, J. J. (2000). Emerging adulthood: A theory of development from the late teens through the twenties. *American Psychologist, 55*(5), 469–480.

Arnett, J. J. (2004). *Emerging adulthood: The winding road from that late teens through the twenties*. New York, NY: Oxford University Press.

Nelson, L. J., & Padilla-Walker, L. M. (2013). Flourishing and floundering in emerging adult college students. *Emerging Adulthood, 1*(1), 67–78.

Acknowledgments

This book is the culmination of several years of research that began out of my personal sense of cognitive dissonance after I started teaching college students around 2010. I never meant to get into academia, but a close encounter with the events of 9/11 inspired me to change careers from journalism to applied developmental psychology, with a focus on disaster mental health. I suddenly found myself working closely with people in the early part of emerging adulthood, and once I starting really getting to know them, I was amazed at how lovely they were. Their energy, passion, and willingness to work hard was so contrary to the way they were being depicted in the media, I could hardly believe it. I grew increasingly defensive on their behalf when I heard older adults blithely and reductively dismissing them and decided I needed to do something to counter those negative and belittling messages. In the words of Toni Morrison, "If there's a book that you want to read, but it hasn't been written yet, then you must write it." So, I started doing research on emerging adults a decade or so ago, and here we are.

This book would not have been possible without the ongoing support of the Oxford Emerging Adulthood Series editor, and current president of the Society for the Study of Emerging Adulthood, Dr. Larry Nelson. Larry responded immediately and enthusiastically when I first reached out to him to pitch this book topic back in 2017, and he has helped steer me through the process from proposal to delivery. His insightful feedback has clearly improved the final product, and I'm grateful for his guidance. I received further support over time from my editors at Oxford University Press: Andrea Zekus, Courtney McCarroll, and especially Abby Gross, who gracefully brought the project across the finishing line, ably assisted by Katie Pratt.

I'm also grateful for the practical and moral support from my colleagues at the State University of New York at New Paltz. That includes my fellow Psychology Department faculty members; my Institute for Disaster Mental Health colleagues, including Dr. Amy Nitza, Rebecca Rodriguez, Kelsey Valencia, Andrew O'Meara, and Ethan Yake; and my long-time mentor, collaborator, and friend, Dr. James Halpern. I also thank the SUNY New Paltz administration for the sabbatical leave that allowed me to focus fully on writing the manuscript, and our president, Donald P. Christian, for creating such a broadly supportive environment for faculty and students alike—especially throughout the pandemic.

While I'm the sole author of the book and any shortcomings are my responsibility alone, an enormous team of emerging adults contributed to its development. Thanks to

all of the emerging adults who have participated in my research studies over the years and shared their perspectives on the challenges and opportunities they face. Their words have never failed to move me, and I really hope I've done justice to their stories in the way I've chosen to incorporate them here.

the students who have worked on my evolving research team, whose perspectives helped inform the various studies leading up to this book: Melinda Campo, Erin Einhart, Anggie Estrella, Danielle Finer, Emily Kramek, Tristien Perez, Becky Shea, Kelsey Valencia, and especially Jack Salend and my OG (Original Grad student) Melissa Blankstein. They all contributed invaluable insights as we developed and analyzed the surveys that provide the backbone of this book.

the hundreds of students in my Disaster Psychology courses over the past decade, who really planted the seeds that grew into this project; the students in my Senior Seminars in the spring 2019 and 2020 semesters who graciously allowed me to use them as first readers for early versions of the manuscript; and the awesome Student Resilience Advocates I've been blessed to work closely with through a campus-based Student Psychological Resilience Project I'm fortunate to manage. Their collective appreciation of the counternarrative to the usual "kids today" message confirmed that I was on to something and kept me going through the long process of researching and writing.

I could not have done this, or so many other important things in my life, without the support and encouragement of my husband, the amazing Michael Frank, who I've loved since we were emerging adults ourselves. Thank you for saying yes.

Finally, thanks to my families by birth and marriage, especially my wise and loving parents, Barbara and David Vermeulen. I still think you were a little nuts to bring a child into the hectic world of 1969, but I'm sure glad you did!

1

Introduction

Perhaps [9/11] did not influence my life directly, but everything from the way that the government viewed foreign relations to airport security was changed as a result of the attacks. It's impossible to be alive in the U.S. today and not have the attacks influence one's life, whether they realize it or not.

—**Female, born 1999**

I was in fifth grade and feel that witnessing such a state of human suffering, as well as the suffering it caused adults in my life, has desensitized me to shootings and terrorism. They have been a part of my life from a young age making them almost normal. It upsets me that I don't often feel much sadness in relation to these events.

—**Male, born 1991**

Everything changed. Security changed, economy changed. Everything. Changed.

—**Male, born 1992**

Do you remember where you were when you first heard about airplanes crashing into the World Trade Center, the Pentagon, and a Pennsylvania field in 2001? If, like me, you're now somewhere in the vague stage of life referred to as "middle age" or older, you almost certainly can recall that moment, and it's likely that you divide at least some aspects of your adult life story into before versus after that day. At the very least, your experience of air travel drastically changed. Perhaps it also impacted your life in more existential ways, like shaping your views about security and risk, even if you weren't directly affected by the attacks themselves.

But if you're an emerging adult, somewhere between 18 and 29 years old, your perceptions of the events of that day may be a lot more variable. If you're

Generation Disaster. Karla Vermeulen, Oxford University Press. © Oxford University Press 2021.
DOI: 10.1093/oso/9780190061630.003.0001

at the younger end of that age range, like most of my current undergraduate students, you were a baby or toddler and have no direct memory of the attacks themselves. Those at the older end of the group may recall learning about the attacks soon after they occurred, when the first images were broadcast on television. Some heard about the disaster while they were still at school that Tuesday through an announcement by a teacher or principal. According to recollections I've heard from many young people, a lot of these authorities delivered the news in ways that were presumably well intentioned, but that often inadvertently confused or distressed children who were far too young to understand what was happening or to grasp whether they were in danger personally. Many of my students who came from the New York City area recall being picked up at elementary or middle school and brought home early by a caregiver or sibling—and then in some cases spending hours waiting to hear the fate of a parent or other relative who worked in the city and who couldn't be contacted. Most of those stories had happy endings as the parent eventually made their way home, but some did not.

Obviously the impact of losing a caregiver had profound developmental consequences for the more than 3,000 children whose parent was on one of the planes, in the buildings, or killed in the response. Plenty of research also recognizes lasting effects among those young people who were directly exposed to the event, like the children who lived in lower Manhattan and were displaced from home or the adolescents at nearby high schools who heard the planes crash into the World Trade Center and may have witnessed people falling from the burning buildings. Children whose parents participated in the rescue and recovery efforts or served in the resulting wars experienced other types of acute and chronic trauma due to their caregivers' emotional and physical injuries and sometimes due to parents' serious illnesses and premature deaths years later because of the environmental toxins they were exposed to during the response.

While I discuss some of the literature about outcomes for children with that kind of direct exposure to 9/11 in Chapter 3, that relatively small group is really not my primary focus throughout this book. Instead, I argue that the effects of 9/11 and many other subsequent disasters and societal forces—now including a global pandemic that has impacted everyone alive to varying degrees—have significantly shaped the lives of all of today's emerging adults in multiple ways, even if they lived far from the crash sites and they or their families had no firsthand connection to the attacks.

That's hardly a controversial thesis: Of course major world events and social norms shape each generation's environment, and the developmental impact of stressors like the Great Depression, major wars, previous pandemics, and other disasters has long been recognized and studied. I can see evidence of this among recent generations in my own family: My grandparents' experiences during the Great Depression of the 1930s permanently shaped their values regarding money and self-sufficiency, creating a habit of fiscal conservatism and a dedication to saving for uncertainty that lasted throughout their lives. Then they started their own families as the world was heading into the Second World War, so they were raising young children amid all of the political and social turmoil that wars always produce. My maternal grandfather was deployed to the South Pacific shortly after my grandmother got pregnant, and apart from a 3-day leave immediately after the birth, he didn't even get to know his first child, my mother, until he returned home for good when she was already 3 years old—a not uncommon pattern for families during a war when men were subject to being drafted regardless of marital or parental status and women were left behind to raise children alone, often while working outside the home to make ends meet.

My parents were born in 1942 and 1943, so they grew up during the early Cold War era, with its much-mocked "duck-and-cover" drills that instructed schoolchildren to take shelter under their desks to protect themselves during a nuclear attack. Today we can look back and scoff at the absurdity of that practice, but they remember that the threat of attack seemed very real to them at the time—just as the threat of school shootings is intensely real to today's students, despite the very slim odds they'll ever actually experience an attack firsthand. Some 70 years later, my mother recalls being told as a third grader (the most senior grade in her school) that she would be responsible for looking after the kindergarteners in the event of a nuclear attack by the Soviet Union (which in retrospect was pretty unlikely in her small Ohio town), and she worried about how her 8-year-old self would be able to protect and feed dozens of 5-year-olds. My father grew up in a New Jersey suburb with a distant view of the Manhattan skyline, and he says as a child he frequently thought about how quickly the fallout would reach his town if the city were bombed. These threats shaped them, without ever touching them directly.

For me and my Generation X peers (born 1965–1980), our Reagan era fears focused on the lingering preglasnost threat of nuclear war with Russia and worries about how we'd survive the apocalyptic conditions we watched in horror in the 1983 television miniseries *The Day After*. More saliently, we also entered adolescence during the growth or height of the AIDS epidemic, before transmission routes were really understood and long before effective treatments were developed. That meant an end to the post-Pill sexual freedom enjoyed by many of the Baby Boomers who preceded us. Instead, we faced our initiation into sexual activity knowing that unprotected sex might not only lead to unwanted pregnancy or stigma but also could outright kill us.

So, yes, external forces that drive childhood and adolescent anxiety about the world are not a new phenomenon, and there's no winning in a competition over which generation had it worse than others. However, I make the case throughout this book that no past American generation has faced the *cumulative load of multiple simultaneous stressors* that today's emerging adults grew up with. That load may center on the attacks of 9/11 and their aftermath as a critical cultural turning point for the nation, but it's by no means limited to that single event's direct impact. (*Note*: This point about multiple stressors clearly does not apply to earlier cohorts in other regions of the world, like Germans in the 1930s, growing up amid crippling financial and political instability and the rise of the Nazis. Nor does it apply to those currently growing up in developing nations or regions plagued by wars, corrupt governments, famine, and forced migration. I absolutely don't mean to ignore or downplay the challenges those groups have faced, but this book focuses on current cultural dynamics in the United States.)

In fact, I propose that today's emerging adults share a uniquely stressful cohort effect based on an unprecedented combination of challenges, which I elaborate in each chapter throughout the book:

- Whether or not they remember the actual events of 9/11, they can't clearly recall a time when Americans were not conscious of the risk of another terrorist attack at home or a time when we weren't at war abroad.
- Many have seen peers or older relatives enter military service or have done so themselves (in some cases because they had no other employment options), perhaps to return with physical or psychological wounds.
- Throughout their lives, they've been exposed to increasingly dire reports about how climate change may affect them personally, and they've experienced its impact, directly or via the media, in a series of major hurricanes, tornadoes, wildfires, droughts, and other natural disasters.
- They also have been exposed to reports of a relentless series of mass shootings in schools and other public settings, often committed by—as well targeting—members of their own generation.
- Their childhood and adolescence occurred during a period of serious economic recession and slow recovery that may have robbed their family of assets and limited their expectations for their own future careers, while they watched the income and wealth gaps grow between the rich and everyone else.

- They entered into adulthood during a period of extreme political strife and internal conflict within the nation—and for some, within their own families—and they've lived through the election and reign of a highly divisive president, as well as witnessed and often participated in developing protest movements like #BlackLivesMatter and #MeToo.
- Setting today's emerging adults even further apart from past generations, all of these events are shown and discussed nonstop in mass and social media, amplifying political conflicts and distorting perceptions of disasters' actual frequency and the degree of personal risk of exposure.
- In addition to all of those external stressors, older adults and members of the media regularly accuse the group of alleged character flaws that are supposedly shared by the entire generation, judging them as "entitled," "lazy," and "narcissistic"—and as we'll see in Chapter 5, many of them appear to have internalized these harmful labels.

On top of all that, the Covid-19 global pandemic that started spreading through the world in 2020 has thoroughly disrupted every aspect of life and caused multiple new losses for emerging adults. Those impacts, which are still evolving as this book goes to press, include upending traditional educational experiences, preventing opportunities like jobs and internships, limiting typical developmental experiences like dating and traveling, disrupting marriage plans, and for some, causing serious personal illness or the deaths of family members and friends.

It's a lot to have dealt with as the group moved through childhood and started taking on the responsibilities and privileges of adulthood, but what does it mean for their current and future functioning and expectation? As psychological and sociological literature on cohort effects has demonstrated, like Elder's classic 1974 study of children of the Great Depression, the environment a generation grows up in shapes numerous aspects of their adult lives, including practical matters like their professional ambitions, as well as more philosophical matters like their beliefs about justice and safety. Again, I'm not proposing a competition about which generation has faced the most challenges in their respective times, but I've spent my career wondering about two key questions: How has this particularly complex combination of disasters, social conditions, and omnipresent media influenced this cohort of emerging adults? And what does that mean for America's future as they pursue career and life goals and move into positions of power in society? Those are the primary themes that I explore throughout the book, examining not only those directly impacted by 9/11 and other disasters but also the broader cohort whose entire world has been shaped by this distinct combination of conditions.

* * *

I begin this book, which strives to describe a generation, by saying I dislike books and theories that claim to describe a generation. Or rather, I dislike the books, almost always written by older academics or journalists about younger people, which seem to rest on simplistic, knee-jerk assumptions about the inferiority of "kids today." (More on this phenomenon in Chapter 5 and elsewhere.) It doesn't require much self-analysis to trace my hostility back to youthful indignation over my Gen X peers and I being dismissed as alienated slackers lacking in the ambition of our Baby Boomer predecessors, who claimed we would doubtless be responsible for the downfall of productive society as we moved into adulthood. Fortunately, those prognosticators were mostly wrong, and I believe the current critics of Millennials (generally defined as those born between 1981 and 1996) and what's increasingly being called Generation Z (born between 1997 and 2012) are equally wrong when they blithely dismiss these young people as narcissistic, entitled, and fragile. That is not what I see in my students, in my nieces and nephews, or in the thousands of emerging adults I've surveyed over the last decade.

Rather than using those common generational groupings of Millennial and Gen Z (though I will occasionally refer to external research on those groups), this book focuses specifically on the cohort who were emerging adults while I was writing it in 2019–2020. As *emerging adulthood* is generally defined as the period between ages 18 and 29, that includes people who were born between 1989 and 2001, which comprises the younger half of the Millennials and the older portion of Generation Z. I refer to this group throughout as *Generation Disaster*—a name I chose not because they *are* a disaster (far from it, as we'll see), but because their lives as they move into adulthood have so clearly been shaped by the societal impact of 9/11 and all of the other acute and chronic threats that shaped their developmental environment.

Let me make it clear from the start that I'm not testing any tidy hypotheses about this group's character or trying to demonstrate a linear relationship between disaster exposure and psychological distress, though I do examine correlations among many demographic and experiential variables throughout the book based on my own and other scholars' research. Instead of generating a reductive description of an incredibly diverse group of people living in a sometimes overwhelmingly complex world, my goal was to create a platform for today's emerging adults to describe themselves and to provide their direct perspectives on why they sometimes demonstrate the negative reactions they're criticized for by older people. In some cases that means I highlight voices of a particular subset of the generation who may not be representative of the entire cohort, but whose experiences are worth noting for their intensity or because they shed light on an often-overlooked problem or phenomenon. As you'll read throughout each chapter, members of Generation Disaster have legitimate cause to feel stressed, anxious, and frustrated at times, yet their very real problems don't prevent them from engaging in political activism, seeking romance and satisfying work, and pursuing many of the other positive markers of flourishing in early adulthood.

The book consists of three sections, in chronological order. The first section examines the formative experiences and environments the cohort were exposed to in their childhood and adolescence, including how their parents felt and behaved in the wake of the 9/11 attacks and their own early exposure to the threat of school shootings throughout their years of primary and secondary education. The second section explores the current impact of those cumulative stressors as the group moves through the period of emerging adulthood, with chapters that examine their perceptions about personal safety, their attitudes toward politicians and other authorities, their concerns about climate change, and their very mixed emotions about the value of a college education. The final section discusses how their expectations for the future may shape U.S. society moving forward, including their plans for pursuing careers and starting families—plans that have now been further derailed for many by the pandemic, on top of previously existing economic barriers to typical markers of adulthood that many already grappled with, like settling into a stable career and buying a home.

Each chapter draws on published academic literature and demographic statistics, as well as my own research on the topic, including results from numerous studies I've conducted over the past decade. Some of that research has been with students at my institution, the State University of New York at New Paltz. For context, we're a small liberal arts college located about 100 miles north of New York City. Students come from a mix of urban and rural backgrounds, and while the majority are politically on the liberal side, there are also many with more conservative views. One quarter are the first generation in their families to attend college. These students have been extremely generous in sharing their views about their experiences in various studies I've conducted over the years.

However, research on emerging adults is often rightfully criticized for focusing on college students to the exclusion of the views of people from other backgrounds. I elaborate more on this methodological issue in Chapter 5, but in order to avoid the problem and to capture a broader perspective, in spring 2019 I commissioned a nationally representative survey of 1,000 emerging adults using the Qualtrics panel service. To be sure I could capture the views of people who did not attend college, I intentionally oversampled those with a high school diploma as their highest level of education. Participants provided information about a range of topics, including their disaster experiences, political views, economic and family expectations, and perceptions about their own generation. Unless identified as coming from a different sample, all quotations and original data I describe throughout the book came from this large study.

Some key demographics of this national sample are as follows:

- **Year of birth**: Ranging from 1990 to 2001, skewed slightly toward the older end.
- **Gender**: 49.6% female; 48.7% male; remainder "prefer not to answer" or "other" (trans, nonbinary, agender).
- **Race/ethnicity**: 60.3% White; 17.5% Latinx; 12.5% Black or African American; 5.5% Asian; remainder "prefer not to answer" or "other." This closely mirrors the U.S. national population distribution according to 2019 U.S. Census Bureau estimates.
- **Highest level of education**: 51.9% high school diploma; 14.4% associate's degree; 22.8% bachelor's degree; 5.6% master's degree; 2.0% doctorate; remainder "other" (including less than high school; trade school).
- **Political affiliation**: 39.6% Democratic; 19.3% Independent; 18.8% Republican; 15.4% no affiliation; 2.8% Libertarian; remainder Working Families, Green, Constitution, and other.
- **Sexuality**: 81.1% straight; 7.2% bisexual; 6.2% gay or lesbian; 1.1% queer/fluid; remainder "prefer not to answer" or "other" (asexual, pansexual).
- **Current relationship status**: 50.5% single; 22.6% married/in a domestic partnership; 17.7% in a long-term partnership; 8.7% in a casual relationship; 0.5% other.
- **Current family socioeconomic status**: 8.2% below or close to poverty line; 26.3% lower middle class; 45.4% middle class; 13.4% upper middle class; 2.1% wealthy; 4.6% don't know/ prefer not to answer.
- **Current employment status** (participants could select more than one, so this total exceeds 100%): 32% fully employed; 22.3% full-time student; 19.7% employed part-time; 17.7% unemployed; 2.3% underemployed; 1.8% on disability; 3.9% other.

- **Level of religiosity**: 32.8% not at all religious; 50.8% a little or somewhat religious; 16.4% very religious.
- **Level of spirituality**: 21.2% not at all spiritual; 54.8% a little or somewhat spiritual; 24% very spiritual.

I present empirical findings from this survey throughout the book, along with many excerpts from the qualitative responses I've collected in order to let the generation describe their own experiences and views. As you'll see from the thoughtfulness and passion of some of these write-in responses, many participants seemed to appreciate having the opportunity to express their views about their generation's challenges and opportunities. I find their voices incredibly powerful, and I hope I've done them justice in the ways I've presented their comments. In Chapter 3, I also include excerpts from a smaller survey I conducted of the parents of emerging adults to collect their perspectives on raising children in the complicated post-9/11, post-Columbine world.

Overall, my goal has been to challenge the negative and reductive stereotypes that are so often used to smear today's emerging adults as somehow globally inferior to their elders and to replace that narrative with a richer analysis that addresses the following questions:

- What is the developmental impact of the cumulative load of stressors whose number and complexity appear to outweigh any previous American generation's experiences during childhood and adolescence?
- How have those formative experiences shaped this cohort's worldviews and expectations for their futures—and how will those expectations drive or limit their pursuit of education, family, career, and other forms of societal involvement?
- Do they perceive the "American dream" of upward mobility as open to them, or do they feel trapped by their economic circumstances?
- How will the current political climate inspire or discourage civic engagement?
- How might American society change as this group moves into power?

The following 10 chapters attempt to address those topics and much more, using both quantitative and qualitative data to explore how growing up in an unprecedented environment of threat and stress has influenced this group, Generation Disaster. I hope I've served them well by presenting this detailed profile that acknowledges the very real challenges they face—and if I've failed them in any way, I hope they'll let me know by sharing their stories with me at https://www.generationdisaster.com. I also sincerely hope that reading about these young people's perspectives in their own words opens a dialogue between this group and the older Americans who have been so quick to dismiss them. As we'll see throughout the book, intergenerational conflict is certainly nothing new, but today it seems to have achieved a level of vitriol in both directions that really concerns me.

I end here with the words of one survey participant who captured both the challenges and the promise of her generation, which are explored throughout the book:

> I think [we] are misrepresented. We are the generation of a new turning. We were raised in a time of crisis (9/11, dot-com bubble, 2008 housing bubble) and we weren't given a fair chance at adult life like previous generations. We have a positive outlook on life even though times might be personally hard for us. We're never taken seriously and that's a sad realization as an adult. I think my generation is capable of great things, the world just needs to give us a chance.
>
> —**Female, born 1990**

SECTION 1

GENERATION DISASTER IN THEIR YOUTH

Formative Experiences

The first section examines the formative experiences and environments the cohort were exposed to in their childhood and adolescence, including how their parents felt and behaved in the wake of the 9/11 attacks and their own early exposure to the threat of school shootings throughout their years of primary and secondary education.

2

Meet Generation Disaster

> After we found out, I remember being scared. I have a lot of family that lives and works in the city. I had no idea where they were. Soon after we heard, kids started to leave early and we stayed in one class. When I went home that night and watched the news, I cried. I was only 9. I was horrified, and terrified. I still am, and now I understand it more. But I don't understand how anyone could do something like that. I'll never forget that day.
>
> —A recollection of September 11, 2001, written by a SUNY New Paltz student in 2011 for the 10th anniversary of the attacks

Who decides what characterizes a generation?

The first widely used label, Baby Boomers, initially simply described a demographic phenomenon (i.e., "lots of babies being born between 1946 and 1964!"). The traits that supposedly define the group were ascribed later, partially by its own members, who liked to perceive themselves as distinctly different from their parents (Jones, 1980). Names for the subsequent U.S. cohorts, including Generation X, Millennials, and Generation Z, have fuzzier origin stories. Gen X was sometimes described as the "Baby Bust Generation" as postwar birth rates fell, and some researchers placed its boundaries at different points than the commonly accepted 1965 to 1980 (e.g., Foot, 1996; Gordinier, 2008; Strauss & Howe, 1991). This indicates that the chronological grouping is arbitrary, as is the label. And that criticism can be made about all attempts to capture an entire peer group—including this book's concept of Generation Disaster. These are not biological boundaries but human-imposed names and time frames, so they are subject to debate. Still, it would be difficult to deny that sharing a transformative experience or notable societal condition at a particular developmental stage creates at least some commonalities across people of a similar age. That's the basic premise of a "cohort effect."

Generation Disaster. Karla Vermeulen, Oxford University Press. © Oxford University Press 2021.
DOI: 10.1093/oso/9780190061630.003.0002

I was fascinated by generational effects, especially the impact of the wider environment on cultures and individuals, long before I became a developmental psychologist. Perhaps this was because I was born in 1969, a tumultuous moment in American and world history. I was conceived about a year after the assassination of Martin Luther King and a few months after Richard Nixon became president. I was in utero during the moon landing, Woodstock, and the Stonewall uprising, and on the day the U.S. death toll in Vietnam surpassed that of the entire Korean War. My birth fell 1 week after the launch of ARPANET, the precursor to the Internet, and 1 week before the first episode of *Sesame Street* aired on television. Of course I have no memory of any of those events, but as with every generation, what happened before and after my birth shaped the environment I grew up in. Those events influenced my family, my community, and my broader culture; therefore, they shaped me.

I'd always sensed that influence intuitively, but didn't fully appreciate its mechanism until encountering the work of Urie Bronfenbrenner in graduate school, which gave me a framework for understanding my own generation and, I hope, Generation Disaster. Other classic developmental models by Freud, Piaget, Erikson, Vygotsky, and others focus on the stages an individual moves through over time and the skills they acquire or tasks they must accomplish at each point. These models each have their merits, but always struck me as incomplete because they pay little or no attention to the context (at least beyond the immediate family) in which that development progresses.

On the other hand, Bronfenbrenner, a Russian-born psychologist who lived from 1917 to 2005 and spent most of his career at Cornell University, was all about context. His "Ecological Systems Theory," first outlined in the 1970s, proposes (in one big mouthful of a sentence) that

> The ecology of human development is the scientific study of the progressive, mutual accommodation, throughout the life span, between a growing human organism and the changing immediate environments in which it lives, as this process is affected by relations obtaining within and between these immediate settings, as well as the larger social contexts, both formal and informal, in which the settings are embedded. (Bronfenbrenner, 1977, p. 514)

In other (and far fewer) words, people's development is directly and indirectly impacted by the environment in which it occurs. In turn, individuals change that environment, thereby impacting the developmental context of others around them, like a pool table full of moving balls all knocking each other in new directions.

Bronfenbrenner's perception of environments began with, but was by no means limited to, the immediate family. Think of it as a bullseye that is unique to every person: At the center, the individual bears certain characteristics (e.g., their sex, age, intelligence, and quality of health) that influence how they're treated by and interact with the other levels. Moving out from that center, they first encounter the *microsystem*, which consists of direct influences on the individual. That begins with family and home, but as a child matures, this system expands to include other influential immediate forces, like peers and school. These direct microsystem exchanges then expand into the *mesosystem*, which includes interactions between microsystems that can support or impede healthy development. For example, a toddler's access to high-quality day care or a Head Start program may help to compensate for a resource-poor home environment. On the negative side, imitating peers' risky behaviors in high school can expose a youth to adverse academic and social consequences.

The next level out is the *exosystem*, which Bronfenbrenner described as the forces that indirectly affect the individual's development, including "the world of work, the neighborhood, the mass media, agencies of government (local, state, and national), the distribution of goods and services, communication and transportation facilities, and informal social networks" (1977, p. 515). The final level is the *macrosystem*, the "overarching institutional patterns of the culture or subculture, such as the economic, social, educational, legal, and political systems" (1977, p. 515). As we'll see, the attacks of 9/11 had a major impact on the American macrosystem (and that of many other parts of the world), which in turn shaped the broad environment Generation Disaster grew up in, even if they had no direct exposure to the attacks themselves. The Great Recession of 2008 had even stronger effects at multiple levels for many people, as it impacted the national macrosystem as well as the exosystem and microsystem for those whose family members lost work or wealth. Clearly, the Covid-19 global pandemic will impact everyone, at every level, in ways that will unfold for an unforeseeable length of time.

Bronfenbrenner later added a *chronosystem*. This refers to sociohistorical circumstances like wars and technological developments, as well as the impact of environmental changes and transitions, like a young adult leaving home for college or to begin a career. These chronosystem changes will have a different effect depending on the developmental stage of the individual at the time of the shift. For example, your nation going to war has a very different potential personal significance if you're a child, of military service age, or retired at the time. Or, perhaps more relevant for today's emerging adults, the impact of smartphones and social media is likely to vary if it's all one has ever known versus a later addition that may change social interaction practices rather than forming them initially. It's not that one version of this timing is intrinsically better or worse than another, they're just different. (But that doesn't stop each generation from thinking their way is the right one!)

This chapter focuses on the contexts that are most likely to be shared across members of any society: the exosystem, macrosystem, and chronosystem. Then the next two chapters in this section of the book move further inward to examine major formative influences during this generation's childhood: the parenting they received in the post-9/11 world and the threat of school shootings they perceived directly, starting for some in early childhood. After that we move into these various forces' developmental effects now that those in the cohort are emerging adults, but first I want to establish what the broader world looked like before Generation Disaster reached emerging adulthood, using Bronfenbrenner's Ecological Systems model as a framework. This book is not a history text, so it may seem strange that this chapter goes into detail about the pre-9/11 world, but given the contextual approach it takes, it's important to understand the forces that shaped this group's childhood and adolescent environment in the years leading up to, and following, the major transitional point of the attacks of 9/11. Again, future sections elaborate on the developmental and psychological aspects of these early influences now that the cohort individuals are emerging adults as that's the book's real focus, but first readers need to understand what the broader systems were like, including the media environment, as they entered the world.

Generation Disaster's Starting Point: 1989

Looking back from the chaos of our current political and social environment, the period spanning the years when members of Generation Disaster were born, 1989 to 2001, seems relatively idyllic. But of course it did not always feel that way at the time, and in fact, it was a period of many conflicts and transitions. Here's a snapshot of major events in 1989 alone.

World Events: Globally, 1989 was the year the Berlin Wall fell and the Solidarity Party won elections in Poland, events seen as important first steps toward the dissolution of the Soviet Union in 1991 (but only after the opening of a McDonald's in Moscow in 1990, viewed at the time as a triumph of capitalism). A 1989 meeting between the heads of the United States and the former Soviet Union was instrumental in ending the decades-long Cold War between the two nations. That year marked the beginning of the end of the apartheid era in South Africa, but it also saw the Chinese government's violent suppression of protesters in the Tiananmen Square demonstration. Denmark became the world's first nation to legally recognize same-sex civil unions. The Dalai Lama won the Nobel Peace Prize.

U.S. Events: Domestically in 1989, Republican President George H. W. Bush took over from Ronald Reagan and began his single term. President Bush nominated the first Black chairman of the Joint Chiefs of Staff, General Colin Powell, while U.S. voters elected New York City's first Black mayor, David Dinkins, and first Black governor, Douglas Wilder of Virginia. At the same time, strict drug laws and "broken windows" policing policies were instituted that punished people who committed petty crimes, which led, in turn, to disproportionate incarceration of people of color nationwide—an injustice that remains prevalent today. The Supreme Court ruled that burning the U.S. flag was protected speech under the First Amendment, and it granted states both the power to restrict access to abortions and the right to execute murderers who were mentally retarded (the terminology in use at the time) or as young as 16.

Economically, the year was generally positive, though not without its hiccups. The U.S. had suffered through its part in a global recession in the early 1980s, which then-President Reagan had addressed with major tax cuts whose benefits were intended to "trickle down" to the middle class. This had mixed effects, delivering short-term gains but substantial long-term costs: By the end of Reagan's time in office, average household income grew, while unemployment fell from 7.5% in 1981 to 5.4% in 1989. However, these tax cuts also tripled the national budget deficit between 1980 and 1990 and drastically increased wealth inequality in the United States. Throughout 1989, the Dow Jones Industrial Average grew steadily, hitting multiple record high closes and recovering rapidly from a minicrash in October. That economic growth largely continued until the collapse of the market and ensuing Great Recession of 2008, compounding post-9/11 distress for many Americans.

In terms of media and technology, 1989 was a much simpler time. Mobile phones the size and weight of bricks existed but were far from common, so most people had no expectation of being constantly in touch while out of the home or office. Use of the Internet was largely limited to scientists and academics. There was certainly no social media; for news and entertainment, the public relied on what we now call "mainstream media" but was then simply "the media" including newspapers, magazines, radio, and television. Probably the biggest technology news of the year was the release of the Nintendo Game Boy portable video game system—exciting for many, but hardly a cultural game changer like the release of the iPhone 18 years later. Reality television had yet to be invented; TV viewers in 1989 watched the premiers of *Seinfeld* and *The Simpsons* and the finale of long-running nighttime soap *Dynasty*. And they only saw these programs when the networks chose to air them. If you wanted to rewatch a favorite show, you had to remember to record it on your VCR. The idea of streaming video on demand would have seemed like pure fantasy.

The year also saw some high-profile troubling or confusing cultural events. The young Menendez brothers murdered their wealthy parents in their Beverly Hills home in order to inherit their fortune. A young woman was brutally raped and beaten while jogging in New York City's Central Park, and five Black and Latino teenagers were wrongfully convicted, each serving to 6 to 13 years in prison for a crime they didn't commit. The Ayatollah Khomeini of Iran issued a fatwa ordering Muslims to kill author Salman Rushdie for the allegedly blasphemous content of his novel, *The Satanic Verses*. This triggered numerous attacks on bookstores and forced Rushdie to live under police protection for the next 9 years, while fueling negative stereotypes about Islam. Famous Christian televangelist Jim Bakker was convicted of fraud and conspiracy to cover up hush money paid to victims of his sexual misconduct—a bit of foreshadowing of numerous sex scandals involving powerful people that would unfold over the next three decades. (And in March 2020, Bakker was out of prison, back on television, and in the midst being sued by the state of Missouri for hawking fake Coronavirus cures on his website (Connor, 2020).)

Disasters: The United States was struck by many disasters in 1989. In September, Hurricane Hugo caused severe damage in the Caribbean and Puerto Rico before making landfall in South Carolina as a Category 4 storm with winds over 100 miles per hour. The hurricane caused more than 70 deaths and some $8 billion in damage. A month later, the West Coast was struck by a magnitude 6.9 earthquake. Its effects were felt throughout the region, including in San Francisco, where it was powerful enough to liquefy the ground in coastal neighborhoods. A portion of the freeway in Oakland collapsed, as did many buildings, but fatalities were believed to be reduced because the quake struck during a game of the World Series, so fewer people were on the road at the time than would normally be expected. Still, there were 63 deaths and an estimated $6 billion in property damage.

In addition to those natural disasters, a number of human-caused disasters also occurred in 1989. Readers are probably familiar with the March 1989 *Exxon Valdez* oil spill, when negligence by the crew of an Exxon oil tanker caused the ship to hit an underground reef in Alaska's Prince William Sound, tearing open the hull and spilling 10.8 million gallons of crude oil into what had been a pristine habitat for local wildlife. The floating oil contaminated some 1,300 miles of coastland, necessitating a cleanup operation that lasted for years. You may be less familiar with another industrial catastrophe that occurred in October of that year, an explosion at a Philips Petroleum Company plant in Pasadena, Texas. Mishandling of a routine maintenance procedure led to the release of a cloud of highly flammable gas throughout the facility, which ignited and set off a series of explosions of chemical and fuel tanks. Twenty-three employees were killed, and 314 were injured. An Occupational Safety and Health Administration investigation found the plant owner guilty of hundreds of workplace safety violations. In both of these cases, the companies paid financial damages, but executives faced no criminal consequences for their negligence despite the human and environmental harm they caused.

There were also at least two mass shootings that year, both sharing many characteristics of today's all-too-frequent attacks. In January in Stockton, California, a 24-year-old local man with a lengthy criminal record, wearing what news reports described as battle attire, opened fire with an AK-47 into a schoolyard where more than 400 first to third graders were playing outside at recess. He killed five children and wounded 30 people before fatally shooting himself. All of the murdered children were from Vietnam or Cambodia. This was not a new variety of crime: Media coverage of the event at the time mentioned other shootings in schools the previous year in Illinois, South Carolina, Virginia, and Arkansas. The other mass shooting in 1989 was a workplace event where a 47-year-old former worker killed eight and injured 12 before committing suicide in a Louisville, Kentucky, factory. This perpetrator had a history of personal problems and psychiatric issues and had repeatedly threatened violence against his employer, but the threats were not taken seriously. Police searching his home after the attack found several more guns and a *Time* magazine issue featuring an article on the Stockton shooting, possibly suggesting a copycat element—rare then, but a common factor in today's attacks, where many perpetrators strive to outdo each other.

This is by no means a comprehensive list of U.S. disasters and crises in 1989. Disasters have always been part of life and always will be, causing death and loss for those directly impacted. What has changed from 1989 to today is our level of exposure through media to events outside of our communities, and I can't emphasize the psychological and emotional significance of this change enough as a core experience for Generation Disaster. I return to this point later in the chapter.

1989 to 2001

Of course, time did not stand still from our complex starting point of 1989 until the attacks of 9/11, but the 1990s in America was a period of relative stability, though certainly not perfection. The structural racism that would later become the center of the #BlackLivesMatter movement, and the endemic sexism and casual harassment of women that the #MeToo movement would expose, went largely unchallenged—which is definitely not the same as saying this abuse was not recognized by the people of color and the women suffering through it at the time. Still, there was less collective activism during this period than there had been in the 1960s and 1970s, as we'll see in Chapter 6. Gay rights activists were increasingly vocal, but homophobia was still rampant in both popular culture and public policy, including passage of the 1994 Clinton administration's "Don't Ask, Don't Tell" policy that barred openly gay, lesbian, or bisexual people from serving in the U.S. military, and the 1996 Defense of Marriage Act, which federally defined marriage as the union of one man and one woman. The LGBTQ (lesbian, gay, bisexual, transgender, queer/questioning) community was also still reeling from the effects of HIV/AIDS, which peaked in annual death tolls during the mid-1990s.

Younger readers may not be aware that we also experienced a pair of terrorist attacks on U.S. soil during this period. In 1993, four Kuwaiti terrorists, who wanted to punish the United States for supporting Israel against Palestine, detonated a truck bomb in the underground parking garage of the North Tower of the World Trade Center in lower Manhattan. They failed to achieve their goal of destroying both towers, but the explosion killed six people and cut off power to the buildings, trapping hundreds of people in elevators for hours and forcing thousands to evacuate through dark, smoky stairwells. Lessons learned during that response were later used to improve evacuation planning and training processes in the buildings, which is believed to have saved many lives during the 2001 attacks. However, the 1993 attack also marked the towers as high-value terrorist targets, and many first responders presciently expected them to be attacked again (Tramontin, 2019).

The 2005 Oklahoma City bombing, in contrast, was an act of domestic terrorism. Two local White men who were angry at the U.S. government detonated a truck bomb in front of the Alfred P. Murrah Federal Building in downtown Oklahoma City, Oklahoma. The blast destroyed one third of the targeted building as well as destroying or damaging hundreds of surrounding buildings. It killed 168 people, including 19 children who were attending a day care center in the building, and injured 680 others (Tassey, 2019). The perpetrators were captured, and one was executed in 2001. It was the deadliest act of terrorism in the United States until 9/11—yet it appears that 9/11 has thoroughly overshadowed this event in history, especially for those too young to actually remember it. When I ask undergraduate students in my classes each semester how many people are familiar with this bombing, I'm usually met with blank stares by all but a small minority, and the students are often stunned when I describe the enormity of its impact. In fact, among my class of seniors who read a draft of this chapter in 2020, just one out of 20 had ever even heard of the event.

Other major disasters during this time included Hurricane Andrew in 1993, the 1994 Northridge earthquake near Los Angeles, and the Columbine High School shooting in 1999, which is discussed in the next two chapters. Politically, the nation shifted to a Democratic presidency when Bill Clinton (the first Baby Boomer president) took over from George H. W. Bush in 1993, before control moved back after two terms to Republican George W. Bush at the beginning of 2001. The 1990s began with a period of recession, but the economy recovered into a period of persistent—but ultimately unsustainable—growth. Clinton's administration was marked by several personal and professional scandals and an impeachment, but he also presided over an extended period of economic expansion, culminating in a budget surplus during the last years of his presidency. The stock market continued to rise to record heights throughout the decade.

Culturally, the most dramatic development of this period was the rise in digital technology and the accompanying growth of the Internet. Numerous home computer models were released throughout the 1990s, steadily decreasing in cost and size and increasing in speed and power. Equivalent improvements in software made it easier for the average consumer to actually use a computer. Video games increased in complexity. Perhaps most influential, in 1993 the first graphical web browser was released, making the Internet accessible to the general public. That same year America Online (now called AOL) offered user-friendly Internet access and branded email addresses, opening up access to millions of customers. By 2000, of all adult Americans, 50% used the Internet (Perrin & Duggan, 2015), and both personal and work email use was common. Cell phone ownership also grew rapidly as phones became smaller and more affordable. All of this new technology allowed people to be in contact more frequently and in unprecedented ways, setting the stage for the constant connectedness of the smartphone and social media era that would follow.

This period, from 1989 to 2001, was the evolving world that Generation Disaster was born into and that their parents and older readers of this book lived in. It was far from perfect, but it was largely stable and predictable, at least relative to the tumult of the 1960s and early 1970s. People may have been more or less satisfied with many of these societal conditions, but one aspect it seems in hindsight that most of us were oblivious to at the time was our general sense of security in the world. At that point, many people had limited awareness of the threat of climate change (or global warming, as it was usually called at the time), or it was seen as a vague future issue, not something to really be concerned about. Research on its psychological impact was just beginning: A PsycINFO database search finds a single article about climate change or global warming in 1989, while seven were published in 2001—and in 2019 there were 400. It was also largely a time of domestic peace. During the 1990s, the United States had briefly been involved in combat activities during the first Gulf War, and even more briefly in Bosnia and Kosovo, but because these battles were time limited and fought by all-volunteer service members, they lacked the direct impact of the Vietnam War or earlier world wars, when draft policies meant many more families experienced a member's service firsthand.

So, yes, disasters, crimes, and conflicts all occurred in our pre-9/11 lives, and we'd even had two recent demonstrations of terrorism within the United States, but most of us went about daily life free from acute concerns about global threats—and certainly free from policies that impacted our ability to travel or that impinged on our civil rights, at least for documented residents. (My husband and I can recall not only checking in for airline flights without taking our shoes off pre-2001, but also carrying on a bottle of wine and a corkscrew for long flights!) But that was about to change, transforming the world for older Americans and shaping the only world Generation Disaster would know.

September 11, 2001

Which brings us to that actual day. My description of the attacks themselves will be very brief as there are countless books, websites, documentaries, and other resources providing full details about the sequence of events for readers who would like a lengthier account (but *please* beware of the many conspiracy theorists presenting harmful and inaccurate versions). Mitchell Zuckoff's *Fall and Rise: The Story of 9/11* (2019) is particularly detailed and credible for those wanting a meticulously researched account of that day. This History Channel description sums up the events as concisely as possible:

On September 11, 2001, 19 militants associated with the Islamic extremist group al-Qaeda hijacked four airplanes and carried out suicide attacks against targets in the United States. Two of the planes were flown into the twin towers of the World Trade Center in New York City, a third plane hit the Pentagon just outside Washington, D.C., and the fourth plane crashed in a field in Pennsylvania. Almost 3,000 people were killed during the 9/11 terrorist attacks, which triggered major U.S. initiatives to combat terrorism and defined the presidency of George W. Bush. (History Channel, 2018)

Immediate victims included the plane passengers and crew members, people who were working in the buildings in New York and Washington, D.C., and the first responders who rushed in to try to evacuate survivors and were caught when the towers collapsed. Miraculously, no children were killed in the attacks, but nationwide they immediately began to experience its effects. Because the first crash occurred at 8:46 a.m. Eastern time on a Tuesday and the full sequence of events unfolded across that morning, many East Coast adults were at work and children were at school when information about the attacks started to be broadcast via television, radio, and website.

 This meant that school administrators found themselves faced with a terrible decision: Should they inform children about what had occurred or try to shield them from the news so they could learn about it from their caretakers? This was particularly anguish filled in regions where students' parents might work in New York City or Washington, D.C., so they could have been in the destroyed buildings themselves. Some administrators tried to protect students from the information while they remained at school, which was far easier to do in a time when no child had a smartphone pushing alerts or social media commentary directly to them. Others turned on CNN or network news in auditoriums and classrooms, exposing children and adolescents to imagery they struggled to understand. For many on the older end of Generation Disaster, it was an unforgettable day, even if they didn't fully grasp its significance at the time.

Throughout my first years of teaching, starting around 2007, I heard countless stories from college students who were old enough during the attacks to have conscious memories of that day. Many described their confusion and distress at the time. A desire to capture those memories led to my first wave of qualitative data collection on the topic. It was very basic: At the start of the fall 2011 semester, as the 10th anniversary of the attacks was approaching, I simply set up a notebook in the entryway of my campus library where students could record their experiences. The instructions read, "What are *Your* Memories of September 11, 2001? What do you remember from that day? How has it shaped you since then—for better or worse?" There was also an option to submit stories online.

Dozens of students and some faculty and staff members responded, with many writing lengthy descriptions. These are subject to the usual limitations of accounts that are retrospective (in this case, written a full 10 years after the event) and self-reported. They're certainly not intended to be representative of all young people's memories, especially for those who didn't live in the region of one of the crash sites, as most of these New York–based students did. Still, I find it particularly compelling to read the reflections of these young people who were writing as emerging adults, trying to recapture their childhood memory from a decade previously, of an event that was incomprehensible to most adults and far beyond the cognitive and affective understanding of children.

Here are some examples. These are unedited, with only identifying details like names removed as indicated by square brackets, and spelling errors corrected for clarity. (That same policy of minimal editing applies to all of the quotations included throughout the book.) These were submitted completely anonymously, so I don't have any information on the authors' age, gender, or other characteristics. As you'll see, many of the accounts include deeply personal connections to the World Trade Center site since my college draws a lot of students from the New York City area. Many descriptions reflect the fractured nature of memories recalled after a decade. They also intersperse memories of confusion and intense fear with more mundane anxieties and priorities like math quizzes and loose teeth, reminders of how young the authors were at the time of the event. A selection of their memories, in their words:

I was in 6th grade, and honestly, I don't remember much. The teachers wouldn't let us walk across the parking lot to the cafeteria. I remember being mad. When I got to math class, our teacher had us take a multiplication quiz. The speaker above the classroom door called my name. "Please go down to the main office, her sister is here to pick her up," it said. Something was wrong. I grabbed my saxophone case and walked the maze of [my] Middle School to the main office. My sister was tapping her foot and swaying back and forth waiting for my arrival. "Come on, let's go," she said. When I got into the backseat of our Plymouth Sundance, I asked what was going on. "Planes hit the fucking twin towers, [Name]. Don't they fucking tell you anything in school," she yelled. My dad was a cop. We didn't get in contact with him until 4:30 p.m. I was an orphan for over 8 hours, and I couldn't feel anything.

I waited with my classmates to hear from one of our friend's parents. After 6 hours his older sister came in to the classroom said, "Mom's okay." He burst into tears. That memory never goes away.

My dad was on the 71st floor of the South Tower. He survived. I am forever grateful. I love you, Dad.

I was sitting in my seventh grade English class when an administrator voiced on the loudspeaker that an airplane had hit the World Trade Center Buildings. She advised students who were concerned to call their parents if need be. I was in seventh grade; I had no idea what this meant. My friend Dan was taken out of school that day; his father worked in the World Trade Center and had not called. In the following days Dan and our friends kept ourselves "busy." We went to the movies, ate at McDonalds, played outside; Dan vomited the entire time. His father was one of 658 Cantor Fitzgerald employees that died on September 11th. He never called.

All I can remember (my mom sheltered me from it so much that it was years before I realized what really happened) was how dangerous whatever was happening was—and how scared I was for my dad, who was working in the city that day. All I knew was that there was a monster in NYC, and I didn't know if my daddy was strong enough to get away.

It was horrible . . . repeated imagery, fire, death, people jumping out, repeated imagery, tears, fear, fire, explosion.

I was in 4th grade and I remember everyone was leaving throughout the day. I had no idea why everyone was being picked up but I remember being worried that no one was coming to get me. At home I sat on the floor of my parents' bedroom and we watched the footage on the news playing over and over again. I really had no idea what had happened and couldn't comprehend the severity of the situation. I remember sitting there absent-mindedly wiggling my loose tooth, and I remember my dad saying, "This is something that will be talked about for the rest of your life." 10 years later I still think back to that day and thank God my family was not affected by it, but God bless the people that were affected by 9/11—you are so strong.

As these memories suggest, even grade-school children perceived the magnitude of the attacks at the time, though most of us of any age failed to foresee the broad societal consequences they would rapidly lead to. The rest of this chapter summarizes those political and societal reactions, along with the other stressors Generation Disaster, and the rest of us, have faced since 2001. Again, there are many articles and books that elaborate on these shared macrosystem factors, so this is a general overview to establish context for the rest of the book. Many of these changes were rooted in political actions, so it's impossible to describe them in an apolitical way; my point here is not to criticize or validate the decisions of the Bush administration at the time but to establish how those decisions have impacted U.S. and global society.

The United States Post-9/11

I think the terrorist attacks have had an influence on everyone's lives, even those who weren't old enough or even born yet when they happened. The attacks and the way they were dealt with have had a ripple effect across many different aspects of life. Namely, homeland security, the treatment of Middle Eastern people (especially those who are Muslim), and allowing a space for racist and conservative hate-mongers to justify their beliefs.

—**Female, born 1990**

It was the first time in my life America had looked weak and beaten. Not saying it in a negative way. We learned from it, it was the closest America has been in my lifetime.

—**Male, born 1991**

While not directly impacting me, since the attacks an environment breeding hate for non-white Americans, immigrants, and family members of immigrants has developed in the time since. This culture of hate indirectly influences different aspects of my life, how I'm treated and how my family is treated.

—**Male, born 1995**

People often refer to the unification of Americans in the wake of this incomprehensible attack as a silver lining and a source of pride and patriotism. That is true in many ways, but efforts to make meaning of the event—and sometimes to capitalize on it for political or economic gain—also sowed various forms of divisiveness that continue to this day. This is a common pattern in times of societal stress: As in-group bonding and cohesion increase in the face of perceived threat, so does hostility toward the perceived out-group (e.g., Solnit, 2010). In this case, the in-group consisted of victims, broadly defined as ranging from those killed, to the United States as a whole, to the entire world (Ristau & Rozin, 2016). The out-group may have started with the actual perpetrators (all of whom died in the planes they'd hijacked, so no direct form of justice or punishment was possible), but in many cases the hostility and suspicion was soon overgeneralized from terrorists and Islamist extremists to all Muslims, and sometimes to anyone who even looked Middle Eastern or generally "foreign" (Panagopoulos, 2006).

The first divide that I noticed at the time was a kind of hierarchy of victimhood. (Let me clearly acknowledge that this observation is based on my own firsthand impressions as a resident of lower Manhattan at the time of the attacks; others may disagree, and I'm not sure how this point could be quantified or disproven empirically at this point.) Of course, the nearly 3,000 people who died that day were the true victims, followed closely in impact intensity by their family members and loved ones. Then there were the direct survivors, like those who managed to evacuate from the Pentagon or the Twin Towers before they collapsed. Many of them went on to suffer post-traumatic stress disorder (PTSD) and other post-traumatic reactions at high rates because of their experienced threat to their lives.

The directly impacted also surely should include the first responders who lost so many colleagues and who often experienced survivor guilt in addition to PTSD, depression, and other reactions to the horrible images they were exposed to during their response and recovery work (Greene, Kane, Christ, Lynch, & Corrigan, 2007). In New York City, the death toll included 343 firefighters and paramedics, 23 New York Police Department officers, and 37 Port Authority police officers who were killed on the spot, plus the hundreds of first responders who are now dying from cancers and respiratory disease as a result of toxic air they breathed during the rescue and recovery efforts. We also must count the thousands of casualties of the "post-9/11 wars," Operation Iraqi Freedom and Operation Enduring Freedom, as victims—and not only the enlisted American and allied service members, but the civilian residents of areas where the fighting occurred. More on this later in the chapter.

Then the hierarchy becomes a lot more subjective and divisive, even among residents of New York and Washington, D.C. I was part of this problem, I can see in hindsight. I lived in lower Manhattan at the time, 10 blocks north of the World Trade Center site. As I was getting ready to leave for work that Tuesday morning, I heard the first plane zoom low over my apartment building and crash into the north tower, and I went outside and saw the gaping hole where the plane was lodged. Like many witnesses, my initial assumption was that this was just a terrible accident. Then the second plane hit and the buildings collapsed, and there was no question it was all intentional. My TriBeCa neighborhood was transformed overnight into a literal militarized zone, with armored vehicles rolling down the cobblestone streets. The acrid smell of burning plastic, crushed concrete, and jet fuel was a constant reminder of the tragedy, as was the sight of a nonstop flow of trucks removing debris, including human remains, as workers deconstructed the pile of rubble. It was a hazardous environment for mental as well as physical health for everyone in proximity to the site, even if, like me, they weren't involved in the cleanup process. I felt fortunate that I didn't know anyone who was injured or killed, and I don't really consider myself a survivor, but I had a front row seat to the catastrophe—and believe me, that was traumatic enough.

For some time, I felt a tremendous divide between those of us who experienced the event in real life, with all of the attendant sights, sounds, and smells, and those who experienced it only through media images—though that mediated exposure was strong enough to cause traumatic stress reactions among many television viewers (Neria & Sullivan, 2011). I recognize now that for at least several months after that day I was highly intolerant about the impact on people who seemed to be reacting irrationally intensely to something that I felt didn't really affect them, like when my Seattle-based sister-in-law described how frightened she'd been when she heard the news on the radio on her way to work that morning, 3,000 miles away. It was *my* disaster, not hers, and it made me furious to hear her talk about it. (Sorry, Randie!) In short, I was a jerk for a while, and I can only imagine how a real survivor would have judged me for my self-centered response. Time and therapy helped me come to terms with my experience, and in fact it's the entire reason I'm now a psychologist since it motivated my return to graduate school and decision to focus on disaster psychology.

I've tried to remain mindful of my own judgmental response at the time as a cautionary tale about how easily and arbitrarily those in-group/out-group divides can arise and how harmful they can be, and I hope that because of that painful lesson, I'm now more open to accepting how variable and unpredictable people's reactions are to collective tragedies like 9/11 and other disasters. That memory also keeps me conscious of how generally irrational we can all be while we're in the throes of strong emotions—and, at the macrosystem level, how easily public emotion can be used to advance an agenda or to suppress dissent or evade simple questioning about motives. That influence can be difficult to recognize for those who are old enough to have a comparison point between the way things were and the way they became, but I believe it's particularly hazardous for younger people with no personal experience to contrast current policies to.

So, as the next step in setting the stage for the rest of the book, here are some of the key political and societal changes that resulted from the 9/11 attacks— the "after" for older readers and the "always" for Generation Disaster.

The USA PATRIOT Act: On October 26, 2001, President George H.W. Bush signed into law the USA PATRIOT Act, a much snappier acronym than the act's full title, "Uniting and Strengthening America by Providing Appropriate Tools Required to Intercept and Obstruct Terrorism." Before reaching the president, it had received near unanimous bipartisan support in the Senate, with just one Democrat opposing it. Support was somewhat more divided in the House, with 66 opposing votes (mostly by Democrats) and 357 supporting votes across both parties. According to the U.S. Department of Justice (n.d.), the goal of the act was to "arm law enforcement with new tools to detect and prevent terrorism."

Supporters said that the act essentially just combined existing legal tools for fighting drug trafficking and organized crime in order to make them more available as counterterrorism measures. That included allowing law enforcement to increase use of electronic surveillance techniques; increasing penalties for those who commit terrorist crimes; and implementing measures to improve information sharing across government agencies to detect terrorist plots during the planning stages, as the failure to do this sooner was a major cause for criticism of the Central Intelligence Agency, Federal Bureau of Investigation, and other agencies after 9/11 who were accused of failing to connect dots that should have allowed them to detect the plot before it was activated.

Critics of the act, like the American Civil Liberties Union, the American Library Association, and the Electronic Privacy Information Center, said it gave law enforcement excessive power to search email, telephone, library, and financial records without a court order, and it allowed indefinite detentions of immigrants. These critics accused politicians of capitalizing on the attacks to increase their power at the expense of citizens' rights, while those in favor of the act argued that any infringement on individual rights to privacy was worth it to improve the detection and prevention of future terrorist attacks. That fundamental debate between proponents of civil rights and those emphasizing security above all else wove through many post-9/11 government actions and resulting public reactions, polarizing those with different views and inserting a wedge between those on the political right and those on the left. This anxiety-based divide has only widened in recent years, stoked by politicians and pundits who advance conspiracy theories and xenophobic rhetoric as ways to justify strong government powers (Summers, 2017).

Travel Restrictions: According to the Bureau of Transportation Statistics, airline travel decreased dramatically after 9/11, taking a full 3 years to return to preattack levels. Many people chose to drive because they now perceived air travel as too dangerous—perhaps not a rational choice in hindsight. As we all probably know, road travel is riskier than flying per mile traveled, and one analysis (Gigerenzer, 2004) estimated that an additional 1,595 Americans above the expected norm died in motor vehicles in the year after the attacks. That's more fatalities than the number of passengers on the four planes that crashed in the attacks.

Those who do continue to fly have had to adapt to a progressively more restrictive experience. Even prior to 2001, airport security measures have always been largely reactive rather than preventive. The first screening procedures were established in the 1960s after a wave of armed hijackings, but until 9/11, measures usually remained limited to passing through a metal detector meant to prevent passengers from carrying guns on board. After the attacks (where the terrorists used box-cutter knives that *were* permitted in carry-on baggage at the time), the Transportation Security Administration (TSA) was created to federalize airport security practices. Then, over the following several years, measures in the United States became increasingly invasive and disruptive in reaction to three subsequent terrorist attempts, all unsuccessful. First, the failed "Shoe Bomber" in December 2001 led to the TSA requiring passengers to remove their shoes and pass them through a metal detector. In 2006, the discovery of a plan to smuggle liquid explosives onto planes led to limits on carrying on more than tiny amounts of liquid. Then 2009's "Underwear Bomber" attempt inspired the next security measure—thankfully not a ban on underwear, but the increased use of body-scanning machines intended to detect items concealed under all clothing.

Have these measures worked? Unfortunately, we can't really be certain because we can't know how many hypothetical attacks they've actually prevented. It does seem worth remembering that different countries use different airport security practices, indicating there's no established best practice in the field, but even without that consistency it's difficult to prove whether any of these measures are necessary or effective as deterrents. Psychologically, they're sometimes referred to as "security theater," or practices that are meant to create an *illusion* of safety even if they don't actually reduce threats. This emphasis on optics is understandable, according to one security expert:

> Security is both a feeling and a reality. The propensity for security theater comes from the interplay between the public and its leaders. When people are scared, they need something done that will make them feel safe, even if it doesn't truly make them safer. Politicians naturally want to do something in response to crisis, even if that something doesn't make any sense. (Schneier, 2009)

It's likely that these visible security practices really do have some deterrent effect on potential perpetrators who don't want to risk getting caught, and perhaps they also provide some comfort to travelers who assume their benefits actually outweigh their costs. On the other hand, security theater may *increase* anxiety for some people as it's a constant reminder of the existence of threat. (A similar effect is explored in Chapter 4 as it relates to armed guards, metal detectors, and other security measures in schools.)

Necessary or not, these practices are certainly inconvenient and resource intensive, resulting in higher plane ticket prices. Long lines to get through security add an additional hour or more at the airport for most travelers. Some people are racially profiled and subject to additional bag searches and pat-downs. Some travelers and airport workers are concerned about radiation exposure from the body scanners. Overall, these unavoidable but perhaps unnecessary security elements mean that air travel may be the part of life where 9/11's legacy is most directly experienced for many Americans—but not for those who participated in the post-9/11 wars.

Operation Enduring Freedom and Operation Iraqi Freedom: Whether or not they make us safer, the costs of the PATRIOT Act and travel security changes can be somewhat abstract and difficult to quantify—making them all the more difficult to protest and try to overturn for critics. That is not the case for the two wars the United States initiated in the wake of the attacks, whose costs can be directly measured.

Our rapid entry into war in the Middle East could be seen as another example of security theater writ large: Everyone in the United States felt attacked and frightened, and by God, we were going to do something about it (Summers, 2017). Of course, the actual perpetrators, the 19 hijackers, were dead, and we couldn't pursue justice against them, so we needed to redirect our anger elsewhere. This is a phenomenon that's often seen after human-caused disasters when the perpetrator is dead or otherwise outside the reach of justice, like in many mass shootings where the perpetrator is killed by their own hand or by law enforcement (Halpern, 2019). When those responsible can't be punished through the legal system, survivors may redirect their need for retribution to a positive force, like advocating for policy changes to prevent a similar event from occurring again, or to a negative one, like scapegoating a tangentially related person or group.

This is not a new phenomenon. The term *scapegoat* literally comes from the Old Testament, where a passage in Leviticus describes the practice of transferring the sins of the people onto an actual goat, who would carry its burden into the wilderness, thereby cleansing Israel of sin for the year. Today, the term implies unfairly blaming someone for a problem that's not really their fault. Pioneering social psychologist Gordon Allport described human vulnerability to this tendency back in 1944 in a publication intended to reduce American scapegoating of Jews in the wake of World War II:

> Though an ever present and universal phenomenon, it is especially during times of stress—of war, famine, revolution, depression—that the motivations to scapegoating are strengthened and scapegoating increases. If in ordinary times we have an impulse to "take it out on the dog," in times of severe social tension, this impulse is so greatly magnified that deeds of incredible savagery may result. (p. 5)

Allport went on to acknowledge that those selected as scapegoats are not always entirely disconnected from the original sin:

It is not necessary to assume that in every case of persecution the victim himself is lily-white in his innocence. History often records provocative acts (or at least defensive and retaliatory conduct) on the part of the victim. But there is in scapegoating always an element of projected, excessive, and unwarranted blame. . . . And so it turns out that there are many degrees of scapegoating. It is sometimes added to justified blame, though often its victim is wholly innocent of the crime of which he is accused; it is often the exaggerated expression of common prejudices, occurring in times of abnormal social tensions and personal frustration; it is always due to muddled and pre-logical thinking; but fortunately it is capable of being partly or wholly checked in minds that possess adequate sentiments of justice and fair play. (Allport, 1944, pp. 5–6)

Regrettably, the American public's state of mind immediately after the attacks appeared to tick all of Allport's boxes, apart from the very last one about the power of justice and fair play to check the impulse to find someone to punish. Some of this took the form of anti-Muslim and anti–Middle East bias and abuse within the United States, including a number of overtly violent attacks, as well as lower level hostility and discrimination, like the biases described in some of the quotations at the start of this section.

Judging whether the Bush administration was in the throes of the same irrational thought patterns or they took advantage of the country's distress to advance a preexisting goal is beyond the scope of this book, as are detailed descriptions of the wars in Afghanistan and Iraq. Regardless of underlying motivation, the immediate outcome of our post–attack need to retaliate was rapid entry into combat in Afghanistan to take down Osama bin Laden and al-Qaeda, the group responsible for the attacks. That war, dubbed Operation Enduring Freedom, would last from October 2001 to December 2014, and it took an entire decade for U.S. forces to capture and kill bin Laden.

That initial military action was quickly followed by entry into a second war in Iraq—a country that had nothing to do with the 9/11 attacks. However, Bush administration claims (later debunked) that Iraqi ruler Saddam Hussein was developing weapons of mass destruction retriggered the public's fears about additional attacks against the United States. Enough people were either unaware of the difference between threat sources or chose to ignore it—or they were shut down by implications that dissent or questioning was unpatriotic (Mayer, 2008)—that the administration's case for invasion was successfully made, and in early 2003, U.S. troops entered a war, Operation Iraqi Freedom, that would last until the end of 2011.

The costs of these wars were immense. U.S. casualties in Afghanistan included 2,438 deaths, and in Iraq there were 4,491 U.S. service member deaths.

Both wars also caused hundreds more deaths among allied coalition forces, mostly British soldiers. Injuries—both physical and psychological—are more difficult to track, and counts depend on the nature and timing of the conditions included, but these wars were notable for high numbers of traumatic brain injuries and limb amputations. Both are life-changing wounds with permanent effects, though many survivors do find ways to adapt to them over time.

It's also difficult to find reliable rates of PTSD and other psychological effects, in part because military culture still stigmatizes any acknowledgment of mental health problems, so service members and veterans often underreport their distress. The National Center for PTSD, a branch of the U.S. Department of Veterans Affairs, estimates prevalence rates of 11% to 20% among Iraq and Afghanistan war veterans. With about 2.5 million veterans of these wars, that means a range of some 275,000 to 500,000 PTSD sufferers. Suicide rates among service members and veterans are also appallingly high: In the final years of both wars, deaths due to suicide among U.S. troops exceeded combat-related fatalities, and at an average of 17 per day, the overall suicide rate for veterans remains about double the general population's. Other ripple effects like homelessness, divorce, substance abuse, and un- or under-employment have compounded suffering and adjustment issues for many veterans.

And let's not overlook the impact on the Iraqis and Afghanis in the areas where fighting occurred. While some of those killed were combatants, the majority were civilians with the misfortune to live in the wrong place when their countries were invaded. Reliable numbers are impossible to locate because of poor record-keeping and conflicting accounts, but the Watson Institute of International & Public Affairs at Brown University in 2019 estimated the following human costs (I discuss the financial costs in Chapter 6):

- Over 800,000 people have died in the post-9/11 wars due to direct war violence, and several times as many have died from indirect causes like illness or starvation.
- More than 335,000 civilians have been killed as a result of the fighting.
- There are 21 million refugees and displaced persons who were forced to leave their homes because of the wars.

Time will reveal how the experience of growing up in a combat zone or an occupied country will shape these nations' own children and emerging adults.

Most members of the American Generation Disaster were too young to serve during the height of the Iraq and Afghanistan wars, though some at the older end of the group were involved, and many had older siblings or parents who served. The key point for now is that this group grew up during wartime, though fortunately for those residing in the United States the actual fighting occurred far away so they faced no risk of becoming collateral damage. Still, media reports about these protracted and politically divisive wars formed part of the macrosystem of their formative years, creating another chronic stressor likely to shape their general perceptions of security and threat, in addition to any personal connections they had to involved service members.

It also should be pointed out that the Bush administration's focus on the military response to terrorism resulted in a shift in attention and resources away from domestic disaster preparedness. Soon after the administration created the Department of Homeland Security in 2002, that new umbrella department absorbed the Federal Emergency Management Agency (FEMA), the main organization charged with disaster preparedness and response. This essentially demoted FEMA from its earlier cabinet-level status (meaning its head reported directly to the president) and reflected a devaluing of the agency's domestic work relative to military and counterterrorism agencies. This was not just a symbolic shift. As the terribly flawed federal response to Hurricane Katrina in 2005 demonstrated, the lower status and appointment of an incompetent agency leader had very real consequences for those impacted by that storm and other natural and human-caused disasters. It was another unforeseen ripple effect of 9/11, and one whose impact continues to shape domestic disaster preparedness and response capacity.

The Great Recession: The next contextual element to remind readers about is the economic climate that formed the backdrop for Generation Disaster's childhood and youth. Returning to our Bronfenbrennerian bullseye analogy, children, nested at the center of the concentric circles, may largely be buffered by their caregivers from forces at the macrosystem level. That likely was the case for many in terms of the attacks themselves and the post-9/11 wars: Unless a child's family was directly exposed to or involved in these events, their impact was generally indirect. Children may have been aware of these forces through media, school discussions, or other sources, but didn't necessarily feel their impact themselves.

The economy, though, is different. While Bronfenbrenner (1977) located the economy in the macrosystem along with social, educational, legal, and political systems, he placed the world of work closer to the center in the exosystem, and the direct influences of home and family closer still in the microsystem. In other words, the broader economy shapes the world of work for parents, who directly shape the home environment for children. The boundaries across levels are far more porous for economic influences than for most other societal forces.

As I wrote previously, the economy in the United States enjoyed a period of fairly steady and sustained growth from the early 1990s into 2007. At that point, the U.S. real estate market collapsed. Wall Street–fueled speculation on home values had created a bubble that encouraged many people to take out enormous mortgages on properties they really couldn't afford to buy, and many homeowners were borrowing even more against the fantastically overvalued assessments of their property as well. When that vastly inflated bubble burst, it sparked an economic meltdown that spread from the United States through much of Europe and the rest of the developed world, plunging these nations into the worst downturn since the Great Depression of the 1930s. The resulting period, roughly from December 2007 to June 2009, is often referred to as the Great Recession.

At the corporate level, many well-established commercial and investment banks experienced major losses and required colossally expensive bailouts by the U.S. government, which feared even worse consequences if these institutions were not rescued. At the personal level, the biggest impact was on employment. According to the U.S. Bureau of Labor Statistics, the civilian unemployment rate spiked from 5% in January 2008 to 7.8% in January 2009, and then to a high of 10% in October 2009 (U.S. Bureau of Labor Statistics, n.d.). It hovered close to that double-digit rate until January 2011, when it began a gradual descent, but it took until September 2015 to return to the pre-recession 5% level. That recovery was temporarily undone by the early impact of the Covid-19 pandemic shutdown, which increased unemployment to an all-time high of 14.7% in April 2020, though the rate had decreased again to just above 6% in Spring 2021 as conditions stabilized.

In addition to recession-related unemployment for many adults, a significant secondary blow for many families was the loss of their home's value as the housing market struggled to recover. The number of potential purchasers decreased as the newly unemployed couldn't afford to buy a new home, so many sellers were forced to settle for less than they owed, if they could manage a sale at all. Those who had borrowed further against their home's inflated value were in even worse circumstances as they now owed large debts above and beyond the mortgage payments they could no longer keep up with. And many homeowners couldn't pay their mortgages at all and lost their homes to foreclosure, forcing them to walk away from what for many had been their main financial asset.

Members of Generation Disaster ranged from about age 6 to 18 at the start of the Great Recession, so many were old enough to grasp the impact on their parents, and for it to shape their own choices about whether and where to go to college, the amount of student loans they needed to take out, career expectations, and other direct influences. For some, the lingering impact of the recession and the near impossibility of closing the wealth gap essentially killed their ability to pursue the so-called American Dream of upward mobility, with financial and personal consequences that are examined throughout the book.

Media Coverage Then and Now

The final historical factor I elaborate on in this chapter is the dramatic shift that has occurred throughout Generation Disaster's lives: technology's impact on media access and consumption patterns. Back in 1989 and into the 1990s, we might have read a newspaper account or watched an evening broadcast news story about a disaster or other distant event, but then the news cycle moved on and reminders of that event faded away for most people. For example, the *New York Times* ran one Associated Press article ("Five Children Killed," 1989) about the Stockton school shooting the day after it occurred, followed by an article the next day that discussed the reactions to the new event among residents of Winnetka, Illinois, a Chicago suburb that had been targeted the previous year by a shooter who killed one student and wounded five in an elementary school. That article, "Illinois Town Suffers With Stockton," included passages that could have come from reporting on any school shooting in the past three decades:

> Donald Monroe, the Schools Superintendent in Winnetka . . . called school administrators in Stockton. "We know what you're going through," he said he told them. "It hurts. If we can be of any help, we'll be available."
>
> After the Winnetka shooting, a team of counselors, psychiatrists and nurses worked with the students and staff through the end of the school year to help them cope with the trauma. This year school officials have been watching for signs of emotional trouble.
>
> Students in Winnetka will soon be given a questionnaire devised by psychiatrists at nearby Evanston Hospital aimed at discerning whether students need special help. "We had expected that there might be more anxiety, marked by sleepless nights, lack of ambition, and so forth," said Dr. Robert McSay, vice chairman of the Department of Psychiatry at Evanston Hospital. "And those are, in fact, the kinds of things some of the children have been experiencing." (Johnson, 1989)

A brief follow-up piece ran a few weeks later in the *Times* stating that the killer's half-brother had been arrested on related weapons charges, and that appears to be the last time the newspaper mentioned the event until it was included in a 2019 article summarizing the escalating frequency and intensity of school shootings in the United States since 1970 (Cai & Patel, 2019). Not surprisingly, the Stockton shooting did receive more ongoing attention in the *San Francisco Chronicle*, published closer to where the event occurred, but even there the follow-up coverage was limited—and it certainly wasn't being pushed out to people's computers or phones 24/7, which brings us back to my point about the drastic change in media coverage between 1989 and today.

Even as someone who lived through the pre-Internet era as an emerging adult at the time, it's almost hard to recall how limited and delayed—by current standards, at least—access to news was then. Remember, until web-based publishing rose in the 1990s, we all lived in a world where newspapers and magazines were only available as physical editions, which meant delays of at least several hours between when an article was first reported by a journalist and when it actually reached readers. In the meantime, it went through steps like editing, fact-checking, being typeset, and getting printed in actual ink on actual paper, along with all of the other articles that had gone through the same process that day. It was then delivered to your home (often by a kid on a bicycle, in what I thought today would probably be considered outrageously dangerous child labor, but which the New York State Department of Labor (n.d.) still considers to be a fine job for 11-year-olds, provided they have a permit) or trucked to a newsstand or store where you physically went to purchase it before you could actually consume the paper or magazine content. With some exceptions, most newspapers printed a single edition a day, so you received your dose of news from your favored local paper once in the morning or the evening, and that was it from that source until the next day.

Breaking news could be reported more rapidly on the radio or on network television news programs, but even in these media there were generally discrete periods dedicated to reporting the latest updates. Television viewers might have found more information at the time on CNN's 24-hour cable news channel, created in 1980, but CNN and its sister channel, Headline News, had little competition until Fox News and MSNBC were both launched in 1996. Without the need to compete for audience share, early cable TV coverage was far less sensationalized and personality driven than today's multiplatform media, and even network-affiliated evening broadcasts in different regions generally didn't devote as much airtime to the news as they do today.

I emphasize this change in media practices to make two main shifts clear. Neither one is intrinsically positive or negative; like everything related to technology, what matters is how we choose to use it. But I want readers to really understand two things that have changed significantly since 1989.

First, nothing was available on demand then—but nothing ever had been available that way before, so this situation was just the norm for everyone. We were accustomed to having news doled out in established doses at certain points during the day. With the exception of major events that might justify special coverage, in between scheduled updates we might have wondered what was going on with an unfolding situation, but at least as I recall it, we mostly accepted that we'd learn more when the next dose was available at its regularly scheduled time. Until then, we'd focus on other things.

Second, professional journalists, editors, and producers controlled the content of all reporting on disasters and other news events, including selecting any photographs or victim interviews the public had access to. While that could be perceived as giving media professionals the ability to censor or skew the news they disseminated, it also meant that journalists could take the time to confirm information before making it public rather than rushing to publish to scoop the competition.

Even more important on the psychological level, these journalists and editors could apply their professional judgment to decide what images and interviews were appropriate to publish given the audiences that might encounter them. That kind of filtering isn't guaranteed in today's era of "citizen journalists," who can use social media platforms to broadcast their experiences without any intermediary. Now, I do not deny that in many ways these technologies give members of the public an incredibly powerful tool to draw attention to issues of interest, to document problems like police violence against citizens of color, and to mobilize protest movements. We examine their positive use by activists in Chapter 6, but we also need to recognize that the lack of professional journalistic standards can unintentionally lead to media recipients being exposed to distressing information they regret seeing. At worst, these platforms can even be used to intentionally spread dangerous information and images, like mass shooters who publish hateful manifestos or, in a horrifying recent trend, livestream their attacks.

I return to these effects throughout the book as a major amplifier of public anxiety around shootings and other disasters. The main point for now is that prior to today's 24/7, on-demand media climate, the public's exposure to news about upsetting events was generally limited and compartmentalized in terms of the sheer amount and timing of information that was available, and it was entirely mediated by professional journalists who were (theoretically, at least) trained to consider the impact of the information they released. Again,

I'm in no way denying that there are many positive aspects to increased access to information from more diverse sources, but that may well be offset by the additional stress this constant, unfiltered access adds to our lives today, whether that takes the form of lowered self-esteem from comparing ourselves to celebrities' Instagrams or it results in fueling our anxiety through constant "doomscrolling" for updates throughout the pandemic, election, or other stressful period.

* * *

So there is a portrait of the broader environment today's emerging adults were born into between 1989 and 2001 and an overview of the substantial societal shifts that occurred as a result of the attacks on 9/11. Regardless of microsystem differences—like whether an individual young person directly experienced any kind of disaster, or their family felt the effects of the Great Recession, or they feel paralyzed by student loans, or they know someone who was changed by military service or opioid addiction, or they worry about climate change or mass shootings—this is the macrosystem that shaped this group's childhood and adolescence and that now forms the backdrop as they move into adulthood.

Of course, there are many, many positive aspects to their world which will be discussed as well—openness about LGBTQ issues, more gender equality, acknowledgment if not resolution of racial discrimination, connectivity to the entire world through technology, and so on. But, especially with everything intensified 24/7 in the echo chamber of social media, members of Generation Disaster live in an unprecedentedly complex world, with what I believe is an unprecedented burden of cumulative stressors. As a result, it's no wonder this group feels concerned about the future. To me, their anxiety seems more like a rational response to an irrational world than a sign of fragility or entitlement—a case I hope to make in future chapters.

With that contextual background established, the next chapter moves on to the more immediate, microsystem experiences that shaped the cohort, starting with the care they received from parents who were grappling with their own reactions to 9/11, the rise in school shootings, climate change, and other contemporary threats.

References

Allport, G. (1944). *ABC's of scapegoating*. Central YMCA College, Department of Psychology, Harvard University.

Cai, W., & Patel, J. P. (2019). A half-century of school shootings like Columbine, Sandy Hook and Parkland. *New York Times*. Downloaded from https://www.nytimes.com/interactive/2019/05/11/us/school-shootings-united-states.html

Connor, T. (2020). Televangelist Jim Bakker sued by government over bogus Coronavirus "cure." *The Daily Beast*. Downloaded from https://www.thedailybeast.com/televangelist-jim-bakker-sued-by-government-over-silver-sol-bogus-coronavirus-cure

"Five Children Killed As Gunman Attacks A California School." (January 18, 1989). *New York Times*. Downloaded from https://www.nytimes.com/1989/01/18/us/five-children-killed-as-gunman-attacks-a-california-school.html

Foot, D. (1996). *Boom, Bust & Echo*. Macfarlane Walter & Ross.

Gigerenzer, G. (2004). Dread risk, September 11, and fatal traffic accidents. *Psychological Science, 15*(4), 286–287.

Gordinier, J. (2008). *X saves the world: How Generation X got the shaft but can still keep everything from sucking*. Viking Adult.

Greene, P., Kane, D., Christ, G., Lynch, S., & Corrigan, M. (2007). *FDNY crisis counseling: Innovative responses to 9/11 firefighters, families, and communities*. Wiley.

Halpern, J. (2019). Human-caused disasters section introduction. In J. Halpern, A. Nitza, & K. Vermeulen (Eds.), *Disaster mental health case studies: Lessons learned from counseling in chaos* (pp. 71–76). Routledge.

History Channel. (2018). September 11 attacks. Downloaded from https://www.history.com/topics/21st-century/9-11-attacks

Johnson, D. (1989). Illinois town suffers with Stockton. *New York Times*. Downloaded from https://www.nytimes.com/1989/01/19/us/illinois-town-suffers-with-stockton.html

Jones, L. Y. (1980). *Great expectations: America and the baby boom generation*. New York: Coward, McCann & Geoghegan.

Mayer, J. (2008). *The dark side: The inside story of how the war on terror turned into a war on American ideals*. Doubleday.

Neria, Y., & Sullivan, G. M. (2011). Understanding the mental health effects of indirect exposure to mass trauma through the media. *JAMA, 306*, 1374–1375.

New York State Department of Labor. (n.d.). Worker protections: Special occupations. Downloaded from https://www.labor.ny.gov/workerprotection/laborstandards/workprot/specoccs.shtm

Panagopoulos, C. (2006). Arab and Muslim Americans and Islam in the aftermath of 9/11. *Public Opinion Quarterly, 70*(4), 608–624.

Perrin, A., & Duggan, M. (2015). Americans' Internet access: 2000–2015. Pew Research Center. Downloaded from https://www.pewinternet.org/2015/06/26/americans-internet-access-2000-2015

Ristau, C. A., & Rozin, P. (2016). The aftermath and after the aftermath of 9/11: Civility, hostility, and increased friendliness. *Peace and Conflict: Journal of Peace Psychology, 22*(2), 168–171.

Schneier, B. (2009). Beyond security theater. *Schneier on Security*. Downloaded from https://www.schneier.com/essays/archives/2009/11/beyond_security_thea.html

Solnit, R. (2010). *A paradise built in hell: The extraordinary communities that arise in disaster*. New York, NY: Penguin Group.

Strauss, W., & Howe, N. (1991). *Generations: The history of America's future, 1584 to 2069*. Morrow.

Summers, F. (2017). Fear and its vicissitudes. *International Forum of Psychoanalysis, 26*(3), 186–192.

Tassey, J. (2019). 1995 bombing of the federal building in Oklahoma City. In J. Halpern, A. Nitza, & K. Vermeulen (Eds.), *Disaster mental health case studies: Lessons learned from counseling in chaos* (pp. 77–85). Routledge.

Tramontin, M. (2019). 2001 World Trade Center attack in New York City. In J. Halpern, A. Nitza, & K. Vermeulen (Eds.), *Disaster mental health case studies: Lessons learned from counseling in chaos* (pp. 86–95). Routledge.

U.S. Bureau of Labor Statistics. (n.d.). Civilian unemployment rate. Downloaded from https://fred.stlouisfed.org/series/UNRATE. Accessed July 25, 2019.

U.S. Department of Justice. (n.d.). The USA PATRIOT Act: Preserving Life and Liberty. Downloaded from https://www.justice.gov/archive/ll/highlights.htm

Watson Institute of International & Public Affairs at Brown University. (2019). Costs of war. Downloaded from https://watson.brown.edu/costsofwar/

Zuckoff, M. (2019). *Fall and rise: The story of 9/11.* Harper.

3

Parenting Post-9/11

My mom is overly concerned about safety and things like school shootings so she is a helicopter parent.

—**Female, born 2001**

I love my kids so much but I think I have done them a real disservice by creating them. The world they have to go into is not the world I would have chosen for them or did in fact envision. . . . I think they will refrain from having children out of fear for the habitability of the world when those hypothetical children would become adults.

—**Female, born 1975, parent of two emerging adults**

Now that we've reviewed the broader societal macrosystem of Generation Disaster's formative years, this chapter looks inward to examine the environment their parents created within the family microsystem throughout their childhood and adolescence. That's generally the most direct and important developmental influence for children, especially before their world starts to widen to include school and other experiences outside the immediate family, which are discussed in the next chapter. (Of course, many children now attend day care outside the home from an early age, but parents still typically remain the primary source of influence at that stage, even for those who are also exposed regularly to nonfamily caregivers.) This means it's important to consider how this cohort's parents were impacted by 9/11 and all of the subsequent societal changes since, as we'll see throughout the chapter, children's response to stressful and traumatic events is closely correlated with their caregivers' reactions. Ideally, caregivers can provide a protective layer of support that buffers children from experiencing external threats, but if they're unable to do so, their children are likely to echo and even amplify the parents'

Generation Disaster. Karla Vermeulen, Oxford University Press. © Oxford University Press 2021.
DOI: 10.1093/oso/9780190061630.003.0003

stress reactions (Pfefferbaum, Noffsinger, Wind, & Allen, 2014; Sprague et al., 2016). This was often the case for members of Generation Disaster in their childhood and adolescence, as their parents were forced to juggle multiple serious stressors above and beyond the attacks of 9/11.

Just as today's emerging adults are often criticized for being coddled or sheltered, the adults who raised them are sometimes vilified in the popular media as "helicopter parents" who are unwilling or unable to let their children develop their independence. But is this alleged shift in parenting style from earlier, more hands-off approaches real, or is this another trumped up and oversimplified charge, like the pop culture accusations that reduce all Millennials to "entitled snowflakes"? As we'll see throughout the chapter, there's no simple answer to that question, and methodologically it's very difficult to demonstrate any direct causal relationship between an event like 9/11 and subsequent changes in parenting behaviors. However, it seems plausible that at least some increases in protective behaviors were driven by parents' concerns about raising kids in what for some suddenly felt like a dangerous world after the terrorist attacks in 2001. And remember, those attacks were swiftly followed by the initiation of two wars that were justified politically through constant messaging that Americans were in danger. Adults were essentially being told by authorities and the media to be hypervigilant at all times (Summers, 2017), possibly keeping their awareness of danger disproportionately elevated.

Given those pervasive threat reminders, it would be natural for many parents to experience increased concern about keeping their kids safe. *Time* magazine summed up the resulting shift in a 2003 article, "Goodbye, Soccer Mom. Hello, Security Mom," that described women in particular as newly focused on protecting their families from danger in the unsettled postattack environment:

> Since 9/11, polls suggest [the American Soccer Mom] has morphed into Security Mom—and that development is frightening to Democrats, who have come to count on women to win elections. She used to say she would never allow a gun in her house, but now she feels better if her airline pilot has one. She wanted a nuclear freeze in the 1980s and was a deficit hawk in the 1990s, but she now believes the Pentagon should have whatever it wants. Her civil liberties seem less important than they used to, especially compared with keeping her children safe. She's someone, in short, like Debbie Creighton, a 34-year-old Santee, Calif., mother of two who voted for Bill Clinton twice and used to choose the candidates who were most liberal on abortion and welfare. "Since 9/11," Creighton says, "all I want in a President is a person who is strong." (Tumulty & Novak, 2003)

Despite this vivid example attributing some mothers' early twenty-first-century anxiety directly to 9/11, that surely wasn't the sole influence on parenting at the time even for the most alarmed, and many of the parents I've surveyed said in retrospect that they really didn't feel the attacks alone had much direct impact on their families or their own behavior. We need to remember that these parents were experiencing a combination of other chronic stressors as they raised their children, in the grownup versions of the numerous challenges that shaped the early environment for Generation Disaster. What's more, the parents were experiencing these stressors with the full awareness of adulthood, unlike their children, who were largely exposed to these issues only indirectly. That includes but is by no means limited to forces like the personal impact of the post-9/11 wars for those who served in the military or had a family member serve, the Great Recession, and parental fears about school shootings, all of which I explore throughout this chapter. The impact of technology, particularly cell phones that allowed parents to remain constantly connected to children, also seems to play a significant part in altered parent-child relationships, as we'll see later in the chapter.

To return to Bronfenbrenner's model that essentially places kids in the center of a concentric bullseye of systems of influence, children and adolescents in the 2000s and 2010s had varying degrees of direct exposure to numerous macrosystem stressors, but their caregivers generally weren't so buffered from these broader external forces. Many of them were taking it on the chin, at least through media exposure to a newly threatening political and social environment after 9/11, and they were trying to support their families in an increasingly precarious economic situation. And let's remember more broadly that many parents of Generation Disaster became mothers and fathers while they themselves were still emerging adults: In 1988, the median age at first marriage was 25.9 years for men and 23.6 years for women, and just over half (51.5%) of married couples had their first child by age 25 (U.S. Bureau of the Census, 1989). This means they were confronting these era-specific macrosystem challenges on top of the usual microsystem challenges of adjusting to parenthood, while they were also grappling with the same general developmental transitions each cohort experiences as they move through emerging adulthood.

Of course, raising children has never been easy, but modern parents are doing it in a uniquely complex environment. Media and technology have radically reshaped some aspects of parenting in ways that have required constant readjustment over the past couple of decades. (I'm willing, though, to speculate that parents from earlier ages might happily accept the challenge of coping with the emotional impact of Instagram on their kids in exchange for knowing they won't die of smallpox.) Like their children, parents during this era rapidly increased their use of social media and omnipresent news feeds, heightening their awareness of all of these perceived threats to their family's well-being, while forming tech-based connection habits that many have found difficult to adjust as their children matured. Notably, this is the first generation where access to mobile phone technologies has allowed parents to track their children's movements and remain in constant contact throughout the day. How did that connection fuel or mollify parents' fears when their kids were young, and how do they learn to let that connection go when the kids move into adulthood?

This chapter explores how technology, 9/11, school shootings, and other societal forces impacted Generation Disaster's parents themselves and whether their own reactions resulted in any changes to their parenting behaviors. That includes how much they felt a need to protect their children while the children were young, and how that evolved—or didn't—into encouraging independence as those children moved toward emerging adulthood.

Immediate Post-9/11 Reactions

> I recall thinking that my generation felt traumatized by 9/11 in a way that my parents' generation did not. While they'd already experienced Pearl Harbor, WWII, etc., my generation—or at least those of us on the tail end of the Baby Boomers—always felt insulated from the violence we'd see on the news from around the world. When 9/11 happened, it felt like the world had been turned upside down. The journalist Thomas Friedman famously summed it up months later when he said that the failure to prevent 9/11 was not a failure of intelligence, but one of imagination. A different impact, of course, on my kids' generation, who have grown up in the shadow of 9/11, with an awareness on some level that bad things can and do happen.
>
> **—Female, born in 1962, parent of three emerging adults**

Let's start by going back to 2001 and considering whether the attacks actually did have any direct effects on parent-child interactions—a research topic that is very difficult to capture empirically from the present moment in time. (As a reminder, the age range I've established for Generation Disaster as current emerging adults means they were born between 1989 and 2001, so at the time of the attacks they were roughly infants to 12 years old.) After the dust started settling, many psychological studies were initiated to explore the attacks' emotional impact across ages. However, those data are largely cross-sectional, reflecting only one point in time. That can tell us that, for example, post-traumatic stress symptoms (not to be confused with clinical-level Post-Traumatic Stress Disorder) were higher among residents of New York City and Washington, D.C., than in the rest of the country in the 2 months after the attacks (e.g., Schlenger et al., 2002; Schuster et al., 2001).

Of course, it's important to recognize that pattern of heightened distress, at the very least as a tool for directing mental health resources toward those who most needed support at the time. However, there's nothing terribly surprising or enlightening about those particular findings. It's generally recognized in the disaster mental health field that those with more direct exposure to a traumatic event are likely to experience more intense negative reactions, in what's referred to as a "dose-response relationship"—the bigger the dose of disaster one receives, the worse the reaction is likely to be, predictably enough (Halpern & Vermeulen, 2017). (To be fair, much of what is now considered common knowledge about patterns of postdisaster mental health reactions came out of the vast body of literature on 9/11, so I'm definitely not dismissing the relevance of this source of data.) These cross-sectional studies can provide a useful snapshot of one group at one point in time, but they don't provide much insight about things like gradual recovery processes or the developmental impact of experiences over time.

Other research—including, admittedly, much of my own—asks participants to recall their experiences, emotions, or behaviors from the past in order to compare them with the present. For example, one study conducted shortly after 9/11 asked 99 parents who worked very close to the World Trade Center to reflect on how the attacks had changed their perceptions of various parenting characteristics, like providing children with discipline, education, and general welfare and protection (Mowder, Guttman, Rubinson, & Sossin, 2006). The researchers asked the parents to reflect on the importance and frequency of these characteristics in their interactions with their child before 9/11, shortly after the attacks, and at the time of data collection, which occurred between April 2002 and February 2003.

Mowder et al. (2006) found that the majority of parents reported a lasting increase in perceived importance of sensitivity, a change that continued through the time of data collection. That contrasted with a temporary increase in bonding and loving, an increase in providing for and protecting children, and a decrease in emphasizing discipline. The parents believed that these behaviors had all changed immediately after the attacks, but had returned to around pre-9/11 levels by the time of the survey, while their increased attention to being sensitive to their child's needs remained elevated. This kind of retrospective self-report (meaning it relies entirely on participants' memories about the past, and only captures what they're willing to acknowledge) can provide some insights into participants' perceptions, but we need to be careful not to overgeneralize this kind of data as the date are very subject to distortion. Memories can be faulty; people may provide socially desirable responses; and parents may over- or underestimate their children's distress or their own reactions to it.

There were also numerous studies that tracked post-9/11 reactions longitudinally over time, many of them using large national samples. These "prospective" studies did not ask participants to recall memories from the past, but they chose the then-current starting point as their baseline and then monitored participants repeatedly over time, at some number of data collection points (often called "waves") moving forward. This approach removes concerns about recall errors as they're capturing responses about each wave as it occurs, but it does not necessarily eliminate inaccurate self-report responses depending on the measures used. These longitudinal studies are also extremely resource intensive, as researchers need some way to keep in touch with participants throughout the study and to motivate them to not drop out (referred to as "attrition"). And, by definition, these studies take time, often many years, to carry out, so the insights they yield can't benefit the field for a long time. Still, they can help us understand how things like symptoms and behaviors evolve, providing a much richer picture than the one-time, cross-sectional snapshots.

For example, one well-designed study (which did not specifically address parenting behaviors, unfortunately) surveyed a nationally representative sample of 1,613 U.S. residents every year for 3 years beginning in 2006 to explore 9/11-related post-traumatic stress and fear and worry regarding future terrorism (Garfin, Poulin, Blum, & Silver, 2018). The authors found that 5 years post-attack, at the start of their study, rates of ongoing post-traumatic stress symptoms were relatively low for most of the participants. Those who continued to experience significantly higher stress symptoms generally had suffered more exposure to the event back when it occurred, either directly or through live television, or they had a history of previously diagnosed mental health difficulties. Again, this is consistent with typical disaster mental health patterns of recovery over time for most people; exceptions generally have had higher exposure levels or other preexisting vulnerabilities like mental health issues that make their recovery more challenging (Halpern & Vermeulen, 2017).

Interestingly, Garfin et al. (2018) also found that people with ongoing stress symptoms 5 years after the attacks expressed higher rates of anxiety about future terrorist attacks in the later part of their 3-year study, reflecting how negative reactions not only can linger over time, but also can even be projected into fear about the future. That's just one example of the insights these longitudinal studies have to offer, along with reinforcing our understanding of the typical patterns of adjustment among the public.

These types of postattack longitudinal studies are valuable, but they share a major limitation in that the researchers all began collecting data from a starting point *after* what was assumed to be the most important influence, without any baseline data on participants before the relevant experience of 9/11. That's a common problem in research on disasters: Since these events usually aren't expected in advance, studies of their effects are generally reactive rather than proactively planned, so researchers rarely have predisaster baseline data to compare to. It's as if a medical study were to examine levels of people's mobility as they recovered from back surgery without comparing it to the mobility they experienced before the surgery: We may be able to detect improvements over time as the patient recovers from the procedure, but how do we know how much restriction the surgery itself caused or how patients' ultimate mobility level at the end of the study compares to what they could do before the surgery?

Avoiding this limitation by chance, a number of researchers who had been collecting longitudinal data on children and parents before 9/11 recognized the attacks as a "natural experiment"—something that could not have been intentionally manipulated, but nevertheless offered potential insight into the attack's impact. Because these researchers had baseline data on their variables of interest prior to the attack, they were then able to isolate the effect of the change and to make claims about causality that are not possible when one only examines behavior after the fact. In other words, if they knew how their participants were functioning before 9/11 and they could control for the effects of any other variables that might also influence that functioning (e.g., a parent's simultaneous layoff, divorce, illness, or other stressor), they could then attribute any change in functioning to the disaster. In this case, it's like the medical researchers had data about patient mobility before the back surgery so they could disentangle the preexisting problem from that resulting from the procedure.

Here are some highlights from a few of these natural experiments in terms of parent and child reactions by child developmental stage. Note that all of these studies addressed many more input and outcome variables than are summarized here, but these are the most relevant points in terms of how parental emotional responses to the attacks appeared to influence children's reactions, even if parenting behaviors didn't directly change or those changes were not recorded as part of the research.

One study examined mothers' anxiety and depression and the development of their children's self-regulation in the first 3 years of life (Conway, McDonough, MacKenzie, Follett, & Sameroff, 2013). Not only were the researchers engaged in an ongoing longitudinal study at the time of the attacks, but also they were in the midst of a wave of data collection at that exact time. They had previously collected data on 194 Midwestern mothers and their babies at 7 and 15 months old, and they were collecting follow-up data at the 33-month mark when the attacks occurred. That allowed them to compare parent and child functioning over time and also to compare distress symptoms between the 169 33-month-old babies and their mothers who were interviewed shortly before 9/11 with the 22 pairs assessed within 3 months afterward. The difference between group sizes was controlled for statistically, and there were no demographic differences between the groups assessed before and after the attack.

Conway et al. (2013) found that mothers interviewed after 9/11 expressed marginally more anxiety than those interviewed shortly before the attacks, though self-reported maternal depression rates didn't differ. Regardless of interview timing, results for the children were statistically significant for both measures used as indicators of distress: All of the participating children had an increase in time crying and a decrease in time sleeping between the 15- and 33-month measurements, suggesting that's a normal developmental pattern at this age. However, those changes were much more pronounced between the 33-month-olds assessed post-9/11 and those assessed just before the attacks. Most notably, the children measured before the attacks cried an average of 60.4 minutes per day, while those assessed after the attacks cried far more, 102.7 minutes per day.

Obviously at less than 3 years old these children were too young to understand what was going on in the world, so the authors suggested the child's distress may have been a reaction at least in part to maternal anxiety—and one can imagine how a distressed child's increased crying and decreased sleeping could further fuel parental stress, creating a negative feedback loop that continues to build for both parties. The authors (Conway et al., 2013) acknowledged that the small size of the group assessed post-9/11 and the overall reliance on maternal reporting limits reliability of their findings, but it's still a compelling example of the indirect impact of societal trauma even on very young children with no direct exposure. In fact, these children's distress was even more extreme than their mothers' anxiety or depression, suggesting they somehow internalized and intensified the mothers' negative reactions, though the study design didn't provide any insight into how the mothers' actual parenting behaviors did or didn't change post-9/11.

Going up a bit in child age, another study (Wilson, Lengua, Meltzoff, & Smith, 2010) focused on how two specific parenting behaviors impacted preadolescent children's responses to news about 9/11 among 137 children and their parents who lived in the Seattle area, far from the crash sites. They were part of an ongoing longitudinal study of child, family, and contextual influences on children's development that included three annual assessments. Participants in the post-9/11 data collection point had already been assessed either once or twice, so the researchers had baseline data on parenting behaviors and child temperament for comparison. These children ranged from 9.1 to 13.7 years at the time of the last interview, with a mean age of just under 11. For this wave, mothers and children completed phone interviews between 2 weeks and 2 months after the attacks.

The parenting behaviors of interest were parental acceptance, which Wilson et al. (2010) defined as a parent's level of warmth and affection for the child, and consistency, defined as a parent's level of predictable discipline responses to children's behaviors. As they put it, "An accepting parent–child relationship may provide security that is protective in times of stress, and a history of consistency may buffer children from the effects of disruption that can accompany traumatic events" (p. 446). They also noted two important influences parental behavior can have. First, caregivers can limit children's media access to reduce the indirect exposure they receive to information about a distressing event. Second, parents can shape discussions about the event in a reassuring manner that helps children process the news constructively. We'll see more evidence of this point in the next chapter in a study about the important role caregivers can take in helping young people process information about distressing events, like the Boston Marathon bombing.

For the post-9/11 wave, the authors (Wilson et al., 2010) interviewed mothers and children separately about, among other things, how much parents restricted children's media exposure to the attacks, how helpful they perceived themselves/were perceived to be, and their "explanatory response type," meaning how they communicated with the child about the event, with types described as passive, fact based, emotional, reassuring, or self-focused. Comparing pre-9/11 parenting behaviors to post-9/11 child traumatic stress symptoms, the authors found that a prior history of maternal acceptance was related to lower levels of child stress post-9/11, but earlier discipline consistency did not influence child stress. The authors suggested that a pattern of accepting parenting may help children process and regulate their emotions about disturbing news. In contrast, maternal reports of a "self-focused" explanatory style, described as those who didn't know what to say or who were too upset to explain anything about the attacks to their child, were associated with worse child symptoms, indicating that children's distress is increased when caregivers fail to communicate openly with them about traumatic news. Again, this study didn't examine 9/11-specific changes in parenting behavior, but it does suggest important ways parents can strive to support children as they process future disasters.

Looking at slightly older children, the next study (Hendricks & Bornstein, 2007) examined mothers and adolescents in the Washington, D.C., area. While it often receives less attention than New York City as the epicenter of the 9/11 attacks, D.C. was the site of the plane crash into the Pentagon, killing 125 on the ground and 44 on the airplane, so the day had a very direct effect on that community. The relevant wave of data collection was the fifth round in a longitudinal study that began when the participating children were just 5 months old. During the post-9/11 data collection point, the children (43 girls and 54 boys) had a mean age of just under 14 years, and their mothers' average age was just under 45 years. Among other topics, the authors were interested in how maternal characteristics and parenting behaviors influenced adolescents' distress symptoms, including arousal, avoidance, and intrusive thoughts. Results varied widely across the mother-child dyads, but a key point was that adolescents whose mothers reported more overall stress symptoms also reported more stress themselves. The adolescents also mirrored their mothers' avoidance symptoms when it came to discussing 9/11—yet more evidence that young people take their cues about how to react to distressing information from their caregivers, regardless of how those caregiver reactions are expressed through parenting behaviors.

Research like this is informative, and I wish we had more pre-/post-disaster longitudinal data to draw on, but like every empirical investigation, these studies all have limitations:

- Most focus on the children's reactions more than the parents' actions or behaviors. That's important, but child responses are only part of the story when we're viewing development from Bronfenbrenner's Ecological Systems perspective, which assumes that the context is key so we must consider interactions between caregivers and children.
- When considering caregivers, many studies include only maternal behaviors, ignoring the role of fathers, siblings, peers, teachers, and other important microsystem influences.
- Responses are generally either self-reported or rely on caregiver reports of child functioning, leaving them subject to distortion.

Above all, most of the "natural experiment" research that began before the attacks focused on changes during the period immediately after 9/11. That makes sense as that was such a traumatic and disruptive time, and as noted above it's very difficult to sustain this kind of study over more than a few years. However, that early focus fails to capture how caregivers behaved as their children matured and everyone struggled toward a "new normal"—one that soon included not only the threat of further terrorism, but also the other major stressors outlined in Chapter 2, which aren't generally taken into consideration in the analyses of parent-child interactions post-attack. Here's an overview of some of these other key influences many parents experienced while they raised Generation Disaster.

The Post-9/11 Wars

Some parents, and/or their partners or other immediate family members, served multiple military deployments during the post-9/11 wars. (Also note that adults who publicly opposed the wars at the time often faced accusations of being unpatriotic or naïve, fueling the growing partisan divide between conservatives and progressives that continues today.) Many of these individuals chose to enlist after the post-9/11 wars began out of patriotism or a desire to defend their nation, so they were aware they were likely to be sent into the field. However, there were also pre-existing active duty service members as well as members of the reserves and National Guard who had signed up during peacetime and then unexpectedly found themselves deployed to war zones, forcing them to leave behind families, jobs, and lives. The number of family members impacted varied by year and declined as the wars wound down, but as of 2017 the total military force (including all service branches, both active duty and reserve) of 2.1 million people had dependents that included about 978,000 spouses and 1.7 million children (Department of Defense, 2017).

Between the reliance on volunteers rather than a draft system, and the unexpectedly protracted nature of the wars in Iraq and Afghanistan, military ranks were often stretched thin as recruiting efforts couldn't keep pace with the demand. As a result, more than half of the 2.7 million service members who were sent to Iraq and Afghanistan were deployed more than once, increasing the stress caused by each transition. That also caused extended family separations, commonly resulting in high levels of anxiety among children and partners about the deployed person's safety, as well as the more mundane demands of adjusting daily routines during his or her absence (U.S. Department of Veterans Affairs, n.d.).

Those safety concerns were justified given what these military service members experienced. Compared with veterans who served prior to 2001, post-9/11 service members were more likely to have been deployed abroad (77% compared with 58% in the past), to have served in a combat zone (58% vs. 31%), and to report having had an emotionally traumatic or distressing experience (47% vs. 25%) (Parker, Igielnik, Barroso, & Cilluffo, 2019). They also had a more trouble returning home: In a Pew Research Center national survey of veterans, 21% of those who served in pre-9/11 wars said they had a somewhat or very difficult time readjusting to civilian life, compared with 47% of the post-9/11 veterans who said the transition was somewhat or very difficult (Parker et al., 2019).

Many who served returned with lasting physical or emotional wounds that took a toll on entire family systems. Close to one million veterans of the post-9/11 wars have a recognized disability, and many more grapple with undiagnosed emotional scars. Veterans have higher rates than the general population of mental illness, suicide, drug and alcohol dependence, un- or underemployment, and homelessness (Hautzinger, Howell, Scandlyn, Wool, & Zogas, n.d.). Their emotional problems and difficulties transitioning back to civilian life also can have direct effects on their partners and children in the form of higher rates of divorce and child abuse and neglect (Hautzinger et al., n.d.).

Of course, many veterans take great pride in their service and not all of the children with a parent who served in these wars suffered such negative consequences, but having a parent, partner, or other family member deploy to a war zone certainly added another layer of stress and anxiety for the minority of American families with this direct exposure to the wars in Iraq and Afghanistan in the years after 9/11. For example, Lester et al. (2016) assessed children's social and emotional adjustment, parent behavioral health, family adjustment, parental sensitivity, and marital instability among 680 military families with children under 10 years old. At the time (2012) the caregivers were surveyed, 71% of the families had experienced two or more deployments by the military parent, sometimes causing separations of more than a year from their young children.

Lester et al. (2016) found several patterns among the military families they surveyed. On the positive side, higher levels of parental sensitivity were correlated with significantly lower levels of all forms of child anxiety and problems except for separation anxiety. Also, deployment history was not significantly associated with alcohol use or parental sensitivity for the primary caregiving parent (meaning the one remaining at home with the children while the service member was deployed). However:

- More deployment exposure was significantly associated with higher levels of marital instability, as well as worse outcomes on all measures of family adjustment, including communication, problem-solving, affective involvement, and general functioning.
- Civilian caregiving parents in the military families reported higher levels of depression and post-traumatic stress, which the authors attributed to "exposure to a range of stressors common during high operational tempo, including awareness of a spouse's dangerous duties, increased caregiving burdens (for children and, in some cases, returning service members), and physical injuries or losses in the larger military community [which] may serve to activate an underlying history of prior traumatic exposure" (p. 947).
- Higher levels of caregiver depression were correlated with significantly higher rates of general anxiety, separation anxiety, and total anxiety among children ages 3 to 5 and with emotional problems, conduct problems, peer problems, and total difficulties among the 6- to 10-year-olds.

Once again, this shows us that parents have a tremendous influence on their children's well-being. When parents struggled more with caregiving in a military context, their children struggled as well. In contrast, when parents were able to remain sensitive to their children's needs, the kids had lower levels of problems and anxiety. Of course, understanding this phenomenon risks causing even *more* stress for parents who might feel that they're harming their children if they fail to fully manage their own emotions during difficult experiences like a disaster or family deployment—or during the less acute but no less intense stress of financial troubles.

The Great Recession

In Chapter 9, I return to how the lingering effects of the Great Recession and other economic forces (now compounded by the financial impact of the Covid-19 pandemic) are shaping Generation Disaster's expectations for their careers and futures, but for now let's focus on how this financial catastrophe impacted their parents while the group was young and how the resulting stress may have trickled down to the children. The direct effects of military service on families were limited to the relatively small percentage of Americans who had a member choose to enlist. However, vastly more of Generation Disaster's families faced extreme economic threats due to the recession and housing market crisis that peaked around 2008. Unemployment doubled to a high of 10% during this period, and nearly 10 million American families lost their homes to foreclosure when they couldn't afford to pay often overinflated mortgages that exceeded the real value of their property. Part of the blame for that overleveraging should be attributed to banks' and mortgage brokers' irresponsible lending practices, though of course those who took out unsustainable loans also were responsible for their choices—a painful lesson their children seem committed to avoid now that they're adults, as we'll see in that future chapter.

It will surprise exactly no one that economic struggles are associated with a variety of negative mental health reactions, including depression, anxiety, substance abuse, and in extreme cases, suicide (Frasquilho et al., 2016). It's equally unsurprising (but no less upsetting) that the consequences of any economic downturn are disproportionately felt by those who can least afford any losses, like those already at the lower end of the socioeconomic spectrum, people with less education, younger adults, and members of racial and ethnic minority groups (Engemann & Wall, 2010). For people with little to lose, it can feel impossible to bounce back from any financial setback, while those with more of a cushion may feel less anxious about their ability to weather a fiscal storm. This divide in recovery potential between haves and have-nots is another source of fuel for the growing wealth gap that feels so unfair to many emerging adults today—another point I expand in Chapter 9.

To try to understand the specific mental health consequences of the recession on the adults living through it, one study (Forbes & Krueger, 2019) tapped into records from the "Midlife in the United States" study. This ongoing longitudinal project has been periodically collecting data on adults since 1995, when the original 7,108 participants were ages 25 to 75. The researchers compared data collected in the 2003–2004 and 2012–2013 waves so they could assess mental health outcomes shortly before and after the low point of the recession in 2008. Fortunately for the authors' ability to use this study as a natural experiment, data about participants' financial resources had been collected during the earlier wave, and they were able to ask specifically about recession-related impacts in the later wave, including how many of the following effects the participants had experienced because of the economic crisis:

- **Financial impacts:** Declared bankruptcy; missed a credit card payment; missed other debt payments, car/student loans; increased credit card debt; sold possessions to make ends meet; cut back on spending; exhausted unemployment benefits

- **Job-related impacts:** Lost a job; started a new job but did not like it; took job below education/experience level; took on an additional job
- **Housing impacts:** Missed a mortgage or rent payment; was threatened with foreclosure or eviction; sold a home for less than it cost; lost a home to foreclosure; lost a home to something other than foreclosure; family/friends moved in to save money; moved in with family/friends to save money

Across the entire sample, Forbes and Krueger (2019) found that mental health outcomes, including depression, generalized anxiety, panic symptoms, problems related to alcohol use, and problems related to other substance use, remained stable or decreased slightly between the two waves. However, people who had experienced four or more recession impacts had the highest levels of mental health symptoms both before and after the recession. This suggests that those with preexisting mental health problems were also more vulnerable to suffering multiple impacts from the downturn.

Additionally, when the authors controlled for mental health symptoms before the recession, they found that for each impact a participant endorsed (meaning each item in the list above they said they had personally experienced), that person had 1.3 to 1.5 times higher odds of also reporting symptoms of panic, generalized anxiety, depression, or substance abuse at the later wave. For example, reports of the onset of new symptoms of depression between the pre- and postrecession interviews were 5.3% for those with no personal recession impacts, 6.1% for those with one impact, 8.2% for those with two or three forms of impacts, and 12.4% for those with four or more types. Results were very similar for the onset of symptoms of panic relative to recession impact, increasing from 4.1% and 5.4% for those with zero and one impacts, respectively, to 7.3% and 11.0% for those with two to three or four or more impacts respectively. The same pattern occurred for generalized anxiety, though at lower rates: 0.6%, 1.0%, 2.1%, and 4.0%, respectively.

As the authors (Forbes & Krueger, 2019) pointed out, their analysis revealed an important divide between group-level and experience-driven patterns. If they had only looked at the entire sample in the aggregate, they would have seen a general trend of stability of mental health functioning, with most reports of symptomology remaining very similar or even decreasing between the 2003–2004 and 2012–2013 waves. It was only because they drilled into the specifics of participants' direct problems resulting from the recession that they were able to see the linear pattern between multiple impacts and worse mental health outcomes. This again demonstrates how inequitably the consequences—emotional as well as financial—of the recession have been distributed, including among many of the families raising Generation Disaster.

In addition to adults' individual mental health reactions, stress from the Great Recession also likely impacted dynamics between parents in many families. Since we know that the family context creates the most important microsystem for children and adolescents, this could cause a ripple effect that also likely impacted kids at the time, if indirectly. In one creative study examining family communication dynamics around economic issues, Afifi et al. (2015) identified common forms of stress many parents experienced during the recession and as they struggled to recover, including fear of job loss, fear of losing their home, concerns about being able to retire as planned, worries about paying for healthcare and their children's education, and concerns about simply paying bills or putting food on the table. In addition to these specific worries, the authors noted the more general stress and anxiety created by a sense of economic uncertainty, which they defined as people's inability to predict their family's economic future. That uncertainty, like the dread about climate change I examine in Chapter 7, can be particularly hard to deal with because it's so nebulous: How can a person figure out how to manage anxiety about a problem whose future impact isn't really clear?

Afifi et al. (2015) specifically studied the effect of economic uncertainty on parents' communication skills and how those skills in turn impacted family members' mental health and stress reactions. They assessed 82 married couples and one of each couple's adolescent children, collecting data in Southern California between October 2011 and June 2013 when the effects of the Great Recession were still being strongly felt by many Americans. Indeed, one quarter of the participating adults were unemployed, and another quarter were underemployed; 15 of the families had experienced a recession-related home foreclosure or short sale, and five had filed for bankruptcy.

The researchers collected saliva samples from all participants to assess the presence of the hormone cortisol as a biological marker of stress levels for parents and child. The adolescents were asked how much each parent talked to them about their financial worries, and everyone answered questions about their general mental health. The adults completed surveys about perceived economic uncertainty concerning their expected financial situation 1 year in the future; their communal coping style (meaning how much the two parents felt they collaborated with each other in dealing with their economic situation); and other subjects, including interparental conflict, perceived community support, and corumination, which was described as an excessive focus on discussing problems together. The couples also completed a discussion task where they were "asked to talk with each other for as long as they could, up to 20 minutes, about their uncertainties regarding their family's finances, or things they were unsure about regarding their family's financial future, that made them stressed and that tended to produce conflict between the two of them" (Afifi et al., 2015, p. 275). This discussion occurred in private but was videotaped for later analysis of their communal coping as they discussed their economic situation, such as how often the parents used "I" versus "we" language in describing their concerns.

That analysis found that the wives were generally more likely to want to discuss economic uncertainty than the husbands were—a dynamic that often elicited frustration among wives, who thought their husbands were avoiding the topic. On the other hand, high levels of corumination, reflecting a persistent negative focus on the family's situation, were associated with higher levels of cortisol post-discussion for the women, indicating a heightened stress response to the discussion. Interestingly, both the husbands and the wives classified as having high economic uncertainty, who could be expected to be more stressed than those with fewer concerns about the future, demonstrated little change in cortisol before and after the discussion. The authors suggested that perhaps these groups were already dealing with chronic pressure that had shut down the release of stress hormones that would normally occur in response to a threat like a difficult conversation, so their blunted response reflected a kind of physiological exhaustion rather than an actual lack of stress. In fact, the only group that experienced a significant spike in cortisol during the discussion was wives with lower economic uncertainty—perhaps, the authors suggested, because "these wives felt secure about their finances going into the conversation, and they discovered information during the conversation, either through information about their finances or the way it was communicated, which made them stressed" (Afifi et al., 2015, p. 295).

Finally, Afifi et al. (2015) found that higher economic uncertainty and corumination were correlated with negative mental health responses for the parents, but the adolescents' cortisol levels and mental health scores were not associated with the amount the parents discussed financial worries with the child. The authors credited this to the parents' efforts to shield children from their own distress, even while they discussed their concerns (sometimes to the point of harmful rumination) with each other. Overall, the researchers found that the parents in this study tended to support each other in coping with their economic concerns and in protecting their children's sense of security.

A final point about the impact of the recession on families: Afifi et al. (2015) found generally low levels of interparental conflict between the wives and husbands they observed despite their economic stressors, but of course not every parent was so fortunate to have a partner supporting them emotionally, and possibly financially, through this time. That study only included heterosexual couples who had been married for long enough to raise an adolescent together (an average of 16.6 years), suggesting a high level of commitment and stability. These findings can't be generalized to single parents, couples with more conflict-filled relationships, or other caregivers who might have had to deal with the effects of the recession outside of the reasonably secure base of a cooperative partnership. Single parents were in an especially fragile position relative to households with two working partners during the recession (and in general) since a layoff for the sole breadwinner felt catastrophic. It's hard to imagine that parents in that position could have successfully buffered children from the consequences of the recession, no matter how hard they might have tried.

Indeed, one study (Brooks-Gunn, Schneider, & Waldfogel, 2013) drew on data from the longitudinal Fragile Families and Child Wellbeing Survey, which has tracked some 5,000 socioeconomically disadvantaged families, many led by single parents, in 20 large U.S. cities. Each family had a child born between 1998 and 2001, and they have been assessed over time when that child was just born and then when he or she was approximately 1, 3, 5, and 9 years old. The 9-year wave assessment was conducted between May 2007 and February 2010, so it essentially bracketed the worst period of the Great Recession. The authors found that a large decline in consumer confidence from the previous wave, defined as the parent's "confidence about the national economy and personal finances," was associated with worse parenting behavior. Specifically, they found an increased frequency of spanking—which the authors noted was particularly troubling as that is a punishment that tends to decrease as a child gets older, so it typically would be used less by a parent (if it was ever used at all) by the time a child is around age 9. They also pointed out that while spanking is not generally legally considered child abuse, past research has suggested that parental use of physical discipline increases the likelihood of an escalation to abuse, and being seen spanking may result in a witness calling Child Protective Services, creating the potential for family separation. Thus, the self-reported increase in the practice among parents struggling with the impact of the Great Recession is a particularly troubling indicator of the tangible ways caregiver stress about financial problems can impact child treatment, with potential long-term consequences for everyone in the family.

School Shootings: The Parental Perspective

Chapter 4 delves into the early impact of the threat of school shootings on today's emerging adults, so here I focus on how the phenomenon influenced the parents' generation while their children were young. Most of those parents likely became aware of the threat of attacks in school settings after two students opened fire at their high school in Littleton, Colorado, in 1999. The perpetrators killed 12 students and one teacher and wounded 21 more people before killing themselves; several homemade bombs they hoped to detonate failed to explode.

At the time of the Columbine attack, the oldest members of Generation Disaster were about 10 years old, and the youngest were a couple of years away from being born. This means that the majority of the cohort were young children at the time, so they may have been shielded from much of the news coverage (at least I hope they were). However, it also means that most of their parents processed the news *as parents*, who no doubt imagined the horror of having their own kids exposed to a similar experience at school while they were separated and unable to protect them. That understandable horror was relatively fresh when the 9/11 attacks occurred two and a half years later, and of course the Columbine attack has been followed by an escalating series of school rampage shootings perpetrated by adolescents and adults (Katsiyannis, Whitford, & Ennis, 2018), which makes the threat impossible to forget for either kids or their parents.

In the next chapter, I elaborate on how Columbine created the template for media coverage of subsequent shootings, resulting in distorted perceptions of their frequency for children and parents alike—though every single additional attack is one more too many. For now, I'll just say that the event attracted an extraordinary amount of media attention, and it generated countless public debates about related (if marginally, in some cases) topics, including gun control, mental illness and psychotropic medications, bullying in schools, the influence of video games and heavy metal music, the responsibility of parents for their children's actions, and all of the other issues that resurface every time there's another copycat event. And since the Columbine perpetrators were just 17 and 18 years old at the time they targeted their own classmates, the event fueled a lot of the kind of "What's wrong with kids today?" speculation among older adults that is explored throughout the book.

The event also inspired numerous documentaries and mass market books as well as academic studies, with psychology journals publishing analyses with titles like, "A Case of Collective Responsibility: Who Else Was to Blame for the Columbine High School Shootings?" (Lickel, Schmader, & Hamilton, 2003); "The Columbine Shootings and the Discourse of Fear" (Altheide, 2009); and "Separation and Socialization: A Feminist Analysis of the School Shootings at Columbine" (Mai & Alpert, 2000). Overall, it established a seemingly unshakable hold on the public imagination, attracting more media coverage and occupying a more prominent place in popular culture than any single mass shooting event before or after.

Columbine also birthed a new era of school security measures, including the broad implementation of lockdown drills, where teachers and students typically practice hiding and remaining silent in order to avoid attracting the attention of an active shooter. Other common post-Columbine security measures in schools include locked doors to control access, metal detectors to prevent students from bringing in weapons, school "resource officers" (also known as security guards, who sometimes carry firearms), and cameras to monitor activity in hallways and around entrances. I won't dismiss these measures as pure security theater because, like airport security practices, it's impossible to know how many potential attacks they have successfully deterred. However, the continuing series of school shootings subsequent to their implementation clearly proves that they're not 100% effective. Attacks keep happening in colleges, high schools, middle schools, and even in elementary schools as in the horrific case of the attack in Newtown, Connecticut, that resulted in the murder of 20 six-year-olds and six educators. And parents' fears about safety can't even be limited to the time their children are in school as perpetrators have also targeted concerts, movie theaters, and other public venues where young people are likely to gather.

How were parents supposed to handle their awareness of the risk of mass shootings while their children were in school, especially when that awareness concerned a phenomenon that felt new and shocking to a group who weren't generally conscious of this threat during their own childhoods? And how were those parents supposed to feel about their young children participating in lockdown drills that were sometimes conducted in ways intended to make them fear their lives were really in danger? This is a real divide between Generation Disaster and their parents (and all older people who finished school before these practices became widespread) regarding what's now perceived as a standard childhood experience, though one with clear negative ramifications that I return to in the next chapter.

In fact, when I've asked current emerging adults about their perceptions of the lockdown drills they participated in during primary and secondary school, in retrospect they often describe them as routine. That is not to say that they weren't afraid at the time of the drill, or that they don't remain actively afraid of being targeted by a school shooter in general. They were, and they do. But in early 2020 I asked my class of college seniors to write about their perceptions of lockdown drills and other security measures during their K–12 years, and the vast majority described them as just another part of school life, like this woman:

> In my school I feel that these drills weren't taken seriously by staff or students. It was almost fun to huddle as a class in the corner. Which is scary because in the case of a real emergency the right precautions would probably be ignored because we didn't take drills seriously.

Others wrote about just following the drill instructions unquestioningly because they didn't understand the significance, like this woman:

> I thought it was part of school life because they never really told us what the lockdown drills were for. I remember being in elementary school and just practicing a lockdown because we were told to. I guess as little kids we don't know what to expect and we just believe that it is part of school.

Now, these same students also expressed feeling great sadness whenever they heard about school shootings, as well as chronic concern that they might become involved in an attack in school or elsewhere. The same woman who wrote about drills almost feeling fun also wrote that:

> The attacks at schools are always extremely scary to hear about/think about. I always am just imagining what I would do in a situation like that. I always worry about my younger siblings experiencing something like that at school. . . . I am extremely conscious on a daily basis of attacks in school and in public. I find that certain places that are busy (concerts, airports, trains) are where I worry most because there are so many people in these places.

So it's not that members of this generation are oblivious to the threat of school shootings—far from it, as we'll see throughout the next two chapters—but they accepted the inclusion of lockdown drills as normal because they'd never known anything else. In contrast, one middle-aged parent I surveyed said she thought she was more aware of safety concerns and other stressors around her than members of previous generations had been. Asked why, she wrote:

> Because we are forever getting notifications of new doors at school that lock to prevent intruders, new kinds of drills (not just the fire drills of our youth), and all the stupid WARNINGS that people pass around on Facebook et al.
> —**Female, born 1961, parent of two emerging adults**

This comment reflects two key points that likely contributed to Generation Disaster's parents' anxiety about school shootings and other threats to their children's safety and well-being when they were young. First, many parents and children appear to have a distorted sense of the actual likelihood of these events due to constant reminders in the media—compounded for the adults by regular communications from school administrators who were no doubt trying to reassure parents that they were doing everything possible to protect students in their care, but who inadvertently also kept reminding parents of the threat, further fueling their anxiety. I wonder if members of Generation Disaster will actually find news about security measures at their future children's schools less unsettling than their parents did because it's the norm for them, rather than a reminder of how things have become less safe than in the past (Connell, 2018).

Second, the commenter's mention of Facebook alludes to the last post-9/11-era stressor I explore in detail in this chapter: the unprecedented intrusion of technology into parenting. That includes the constant stream of social media reminders of peril, as well as parents' new expectation of being constantly connected to children even when they're physically apart.

Parenting in the Digital Age

Parenting in the digital age is a topic worthy of extensive discussion, and indeed, the Internet offers well over a million resources, including popular books, magazine articles, blog posts, and policy reviews. For example, searching the term "digital parenting book" brought me to a list of dozens of options, including a handy Amazon "frequently bought together" package of books consisting of *Raising Humans in a Digital World: Helping Kids Build a Healthy Relationship With Technology* (Graber, 2019); *Screenwise: Helping Kids Thrive (and Survive) in Their Digital World* (Heitner, 2016); and *The Art of Screen Time: How Your Family Can Balance Digital Media and Real Life* (Kamenetz, 2018). Evidently many parents are looking for guidance on how to manage this new part of life, as these technologies have evolved so rapidly that adults haven't necessarily figured out how to incorporate them appropriately into their parenting practices, with developmental consequences that aren't entirely clear.

There's somewhat less formal academic research on the subject, perhaps because it's such a rapidly moving target that traditional scholarly research and publishing practices just can't keep up with the cultural shifts. I won't attempt a comprehensive analysis of the pros and cons of tech-mediated parenting here, or an analysis of the impact of social media on well-being at any age. That's another important topic, but one that's outside the scope of this chapter. Instead, I'll focus on what I see as the key developmental aspect that has changed dramatically in the post-9/11 era due to technology: security-minded parents' varying comfort with children's movement toward individuation.

This is one of the essential developmental tasks as children mature into adulthood. They need to establish their own identity and autonomy, becoming independent from—but ideally still connected to—parents in appropriate forms. It's a dynamic process that requires constant adjustment by both parties as young people gradually take on more control and responsibility for their lives. Their parents, in turn, cede more and more power over their maturing children, while continuing to provide emotional and practical support as needed (Padilla-Walker & Nelson, 2019). See Koepke and Denissen (2012) for a detailed review of different theoretical perspectives on how this individuation process occurs, but in general it involves an evolving balance of separateness, attachment, and autonomy between parent and child—a kind of loosening of the reins by the older generation, with a parallel increase in taking the lead over various aspects of their own lives by the younger people.

For recent generations who grew up in the century or so after attending at least primary school became the norm in the United States, but before cell phones were common, I posit that this process occurred largely organically as maturing children spent increasingly more time away from parents—first at school and with peers, and then when they entered the workforce and/or started families in their late teens or early 20s. Their environment naturally expanded from the family-centered microsystem of early childhood to a combination of interacting systems that didn't necessarily involve parents at all, and when young people were in those parent-free environments, they could be fully out of touch for hours at a time. Of course, they might return to the home base of family at the end of the day to catch up with parents and receive guidance (wanted or not), but once kids started school, they had long stretches of time without any parental contact. As a result, by the time they reached adolescence or early adulthood, the typical young person didn't have much choice but to individuate from parents to at least some degree, including learning to negotiate conflicts and complex social interactions at school or with peers on their own.

That's still the norm for many children, but for some members of Generation Disaster and those coming after them, the cleanly defined separation from parents while they were at school or otherwise physically apart has become blurred by the introduction of the mobile phone. While previously children and parents grew accustomed to being out of touch for long periods of time, suddenly the once unavoidable contact gap became optional. Parents could choose to provide their kids with a phone in order to maintain a channel of communication throughout the day, and children accepted that "electronic tether" (Hofer, 2008) in exchange for all of the other social benefits provided by having a phone (Coyne, Padilla-Walker, & Howard, 2013).

I'm absolutely not criticizing parents for wanting this ability to feel connected to their children at any age, especially given likely fears about school shootings and other threats discussed above. To be sure, smartphones have many positive effects that can give parents a sense of protecting their kids when they aren't physically together, and the ability to check in regularly throughout the day allows both sides to maintain a sense of closeness and involvement in each other's lives. However, it appears that the introduction of this digital tether actually sparked a kind of natural experiment that has upended norms established by the previous generations who had clear boundaries between times of family togetherness and separation, and it's worth questioning how that constant connectedness has impacted the younger generation's ability to individuate fully as they move into emerging adulthood.

This has led to disparagement of both children and parents in the popular media, including absurd charges that current emerging adults have globally failed to acquire the independence needed to succeed in life. Take the headline and beginning of this (badly written and outrageously exaggerated) newspaper article:

We've raised Generation Hopeless: Millennials who lack basic life and workplace skills. And it's a big issue.

Millennials are totally useless when it comes to basic life and work skills and we'll all pay for it, experts have warned. Forget lazy, self-centered or cocky—the truth about most Millennials is they're absolutely hopeless when it comes to basic life and workplace skills, experts say. Research shows young adults are comfortable putting themselves "out there" online, but all that time glued to screens has raised a generation incapable of small talk, critical thinking and problem-solving. And that's not to mention their staggering inability to cook, draft a personal budget, or change a tire. (Molloy, 2017)

The search that led me to that article helpfully suggested other terms that people also used, including

- Skills Millennials lack
- Hopeless Millennial
- Millennials flaws
- Millennial skill set

- Millennials lack of respect
- Millennials consumerism

In Chapter 5, I expand on how a lot of young people seem to have internalized these kinds of negative stereotypes about their entire generation. But their parents don't necessarily fare much better in public opinion, exemplified by a Pew Research Center poll, "Majority of Americans Say Parents Are Doing Too Much for Their Young Adult Children" (Barroso, Parker, & Fry, 2019). This national survey of just under 1,000 respondents found that overall, 55% of those polled said parents were doing too much for their children, 10% thought it was too little, and 34% thought the amount was about right. But that varied by respondent age: 65% of those aged 65 or older thought parents were doing too much, versus just 31% of respondents ages 18 to 29—the emerging adults themselves. Among this younger group, 51% thought parents provided about the right amount of support to their emerging adult children, while 18% thought they provided too little.

This survey also found an interesting divide between how parents of emerging adults viewed the amount of support they provided to their children relative to how much other parents did: "While 61% of adults who have children ages 18 to 29 say parents are doing too much for their young adult children these days, only 28% say *they themselves* do too much for their young adult children. Most of these parents (63%) say they do about the right amount for their young adult children, while only 8% say they do too little" (Barroso et al., 2019). There was a similar disconnection between the amount of emotional support parents believed they provided versus the amount young adults actually felt they received: "Half of young adults ages 18 to 29 say they rely on their parents a lot or some for emotional support, while 77% of parents report that their children rely on them at least somewhat for this type of support." So, parents of emerging adults appear to be overestimating the amount of emotional support their own children need from them, while simultaneously judging other parents for doing too much for their young adults!

I don't want to overgeneralize from this one poll, but the public belief that emerging adults remain overly dependent for practical and emotional support seems to reflect a kind of perception that some members of Generation Disaster have failed to complete the process of individuation from their parents. However, it's unclear whether that's a legitimate problem or simply a misperception based on older adults misinterpreting increased frequency of communication, thanks to the ease of today's technologies, between contemporary parents of emerging adults and their children as unhealthy overreliance.

Additionally, returning to the analogy above, the continuing level of dependence in some families appears to be driven primarily by parents' resistance to loosening the reins, as much as or more than by any alleged failure by the maturing children to take the lead. In some cases, this could reflect an extension of so-called helicopter parenting into the cohort's emerging adulthood. Padilla-Walker and Nelson (2012) described this fairly rare phenomenon as parents "doing for their children what they developmentally can and should be doing for themselves." They liken it to overprotective or oversolicitous parenting of younger children. These parents are motivated by a desire to shield children from distress, but their "intrusive and unnecessary micromanagement of a child's independent activities . . . has repeatedly been linked with maladaptive outcomes (e.g., anxiety-related problems, social withdrawal/ shyness, peer difficulties) in young children from ages 2 to 5" (p. 1178).

There appear to be similar connections between overly controlling parenting and negative outcomes in emerging adulthood—a time partly defined by the need to establish autonomy. Indeed, after surveying 438 college students and at least one of their parents about parenting behaviors and child outcomes, Padilla-Walker and Nelson (2012) found that "children of helicopter parents appeared to see their parents in terms of a relationship high in guidance, involvement, and emotional support but likewise acknowledged a lack of autonomy being granted them by their parents. . . . That is, helicopter parenting appears to be inappropriately intrusive and managing, but done out of strong parental concern for the well-being and success of the child" (p. 1188). They concluded that, unlike parenting that uses psychological or behavioral control to shape child behavior, this oversolicitous style of parenting may not be actively destructive, but it is generally not conducive to growth and autonomy for emerging adults (Nelson, Padilla-Walker, & Nielson, 2015; Padilla-Walker, Son, & Nelson, 2019).

While there are dozens of published studies on various outcomes resulting from helicopter parenting or other overly intrusive ways of interacting with children, I couldn't find any scholarly examinations of parents' *motivations* for taking this approach. I wonder how much of this style of parenting and reluctance to foster autonomy among a minority of caregivers is due to concerns about child safety in the post-Columbine and post-9/11 world, relative to how much should be attributed to the electronic tether that has allowed parents to retain an expectation of constant contact with their kids long past the age when that was the norm for most previous generations of Americans. The two influences are so temporally intertwined that we'll never know how these parents would have acted if they'd had the elevated security concerns but didn't have the technology to remain in contact throughout the school day or vice versa.

Given this simultaneity, it seems reasonable to think that the fear and the technology reinforced each other, with the reassuring ping of an arriving text from a safe child providing the same kind of emotional reward for parents that their children seek through likes and other affirmations on their social media accounts. If so, it's a natural next step to suggest that the need for that reward became equally habit-forming for parents, which would explain why some—though clearly not the majority—have been unable to give it up even after their children left the home and theoretically entered adulthood. In an extreme example, one *Washington Post* article described parents using apps on their children's phones to track their location at all times, and it quoted children who received irate emails or calls from parents who were furious when they turned the tracking app off without permission (Ohlheiser, 2019). That may seem reasonable for the parent of a middle schooler who is just starting to move through the world without direct parental supervision, but many of the children in question were college students.

To be sure, this level of ongoing technology-based tracking is not the norm. Vaterlaus, Beckert, and Bird (2015) studied the extent to which parents intervened in college student children's technology use and found that just 24% of parents mediated cell phone use and only 11% mediated Internet use in any way. For those parents who did have any form of involvement, it generally involved measures like monitoring overall use because they paid the bills; very few reported the use of blockers that prevented kids from accessing certain websites or other invasive behavioral measures. Both children and parents most commonly cited trust as a reason for the lack of intervention—a seemingly healthy and developmentally appropriate arrangement by the time a child reached emerging adulthood.

However, not all parents achieve this level of trust, likely for a variety of psychological reasons that have yet to be fully explored empirically. One young woman quoted in the *Post* article (Ohlheiser, 2019) described her parents' insistence that she keep a tracking app on at all times as a condition of paying her college tuition and expenses, which would seem to reflect the kind of authoritarian behavioral control Padilla-Walker and Nelson (2012) differentiated from well-intentioned, if overzealous, helicopter parenting. On the other hand, one mother who was quoted described herself as a former "stalker" who needed to wean herself off of constantly monitoring her daughter's whereabouts after she left for college. This particular mother eventually broke her surveillance habit, though she acknowledged still using the tracker when her daughter was traveling so she could be sure she arrived safely.

It's easy for critics to claim that this kind of constant connectedness via text, tracking app, and other technology-mediated interactions has led to compromised independence for Generation Disaster as they move through emerging adulthood. According to a 2019 Pew study, fully 99% of Americans between the ages of 18 and 49 own a cell phone, as do 95% of those ages 50 to 64 and 91% of those 65 and older (though rates of smartphone usage are lower in the older age ranges, 79% and 53%, respectively). The ubiquitous presence of the technology means emerging adults have the ability to keep seeking instant advice and interventions from parents any time they want to, relieving them of the forced need to individuate sooner than earlier generations who didn't have access to parents throughout the school day or workday. In turn, many parents maintain far more frequent contact with adult children than was the norm in the past—which may be another kind of societal change, but it is not necessarily a bad shift if it's mutually desired by both parties and comes from a desire to be close rather than a desire to monitor or control the emerging adult's behavior in a developmentally inappropriate way.

In fact, some of my students have told me that they like being able to keep in touch this way while they're away at college—and in a reversal of expected roles, some even said they enjoyed being able to track their parents' movements. One of my recent seniors told me she liked being able to see that her mother had arrived safely at work each day, and in return she had no objection to her parents monitoring her own movements while she was away at school. However, others perceive the tracking as invasive, describing it as unhealthy, controlling, and even abusive. Clearly, the problem isn't the technology itself, but how families use it—especially how they succeed or fail at adapting use to accommodate children's need for evolving boundaries (Peer, 2017).

And that's not even getting into parents' perceptions of the impact of technology and social media on young people's well-being, as reflected in these concerned comments about their children's use by parents I surveyed:

Relentless supervision, largely but not solely electronic, from schools, parents, the general public, etc.

—Female, born 1961, parent of two emerging adults

[They're] capable and committed to social change, but also anxious and shaped by constant access to social media in ways that are harmful.

—Male, born 1970, parent of one emerging adult

Too dependent on their electronics. Can't communicate face to face as well, life more focused on appearances, personal branding.

—Female, unspecified birth year, parent of one emerging adult

It's brand new territory for both generations to navigate, with some parents refusing to loosen their hold on the reins even as their children go off to college, begin their careers, or otherwise pursue the tasks of emerging adulthood. Indeed, in some cases it appears to be the parents who are impeding their children's individuation process because they themselves are experiencing a kind of separation anxiety, not the usual other way around as might be assumed. But who can really blame these parents for wanting to stay close to their kids, having raised them in an era of anxiety and now trying to launch them into a world with an uncertain future due to climate change, the pandemic, and other threats?

* * *

Overall, the period when their parents were raising Generation Disaster has not been an easy time to be a full-fledged adult, especially one in the increasingly precarious middle class or below. The various studies I've cited throughout this chapter all reinforce the basic premise that children and adolescents take their cues from parents' reactions to upsetting news, even if the family is not directly impacted by a particular disaster or other event. Consciously or not, caregivers set the emotional tone of the microsystem that is the child's main environment. Unfortunately, that phenomenon puts even more pressure on adults who are aware of it: Not only must they handle their own stress, but also they need to do so in a way that's sensitive to and protective of their children's response to their own reactions.

If they can manage that, it means caregivers can buffer kids from the worst effects of news about disasters and other threatening information. They can potentially serve as a kind of emotional shock absorber for their children—but that means fully absorbing the blows themselves, which is never easy and not always possible. We can't expect caregivers to manage this perfectly, especially in the face of repeated or chronic threats like those many in the United States have experienced over the past two decades. As a result, many of the parents I surveyed recognized the impact of stress on themselves and on their children (and this was before the pandemic entered the mix for everyone):

> It's so much harder than I think our parents thought it would be. Facing down the end of life as we know it is hard to live with. I'd've liked to have been thinking about grandchildren in 10 years; instead I'm thinking about trying to get a house for my kids so they have a place to grow food.
>
> —Female, born 1962, parent of two emerging adults

[They're] tough, a little sad, very willing to make noise when they need to. They live with diminished possibility but a heightened sense of justice.

—**Female, born 1975, parent of two emerging adults**

They are smart, motivated, and involved. They don't trust my generation, for good reason. They are very stressed. They work much harder than my generation did. The stakes for failure or breaking the law are way out of proportion, and they know it. I wish they could move to a country where things are better.

—**Female, unspecified birth year, parent of two emerging adults**

I find this generation very smart and very cynical. There's an undercurrent of despair hidden by nonchalance, and most frustratingly, a resigned acceptance that leads to some not taking opportunities that present themselves.

—**Female, born 1972, parent of one emerging adult**

Parents of today's emerging adults didn't have it easy when their kids were young, and some of their stress undoubtedly rubbed off on their children, contributing to the challenges members of Generation Disaster are facing today. Still, many of the parents I surveyed expressed great pride in their children, and optimism about what the generation is capable of:

My generation believed we would change the world for the better, and we did, but not enough. Our vision was limited. I'm convinced our children will excel where we fell short. . . . I love them! Their energy, creativity and open minds make them irresistible.

—**Female, unspecified birth year, parent of two emerging adults**

[They're] compassionate, innovative, open-minded, adventurous, hard-working, determined, forward-looking.

—**Female, born 1955, parent of two emerging adults**

As hard as it is, I'm amazed at how much more aware of the world my son's generation is. These kids/young adults give me hope.

—**Female, born 1972, parent of one emerging adult**

Then there's this detailed comment from a mother who outlines both optimism and concerns for her children's future:

Housing prices are insane. Competition academically and for jobs is crazy. Most of the people I know with top jobs, doing very well and functioning very competently, would never have gotten a foot in the door if they had to apply now. Not to mention the "gig economy," the huge income disparity, and the cretins in public office. My kids have it much rougher than we did. . . . Every kid I know works at least two jobs. Smart phones and working from home and global connectivity mean you're never off the clock. They are afraid to have kids. They are afraid to get married. Everything is constantly in flux, and it takes a great deal of concentration and balance to stay on your feet, but it makes it very hard to relax. They are amazing, as a group. Not just my own kids. They got the shitty end of the stick, but they are powering through.

—**Female, born 1959, parent of four emerging adults**

We'll explore how the cohort is indeed powering through these multiple challenges throughout the rest of the book, but first, in the last chapter in this section on formative experiences, I examine the impact of the threat of school shootings on Generation Disaster during their youth. While awareness of that threat was a disturbing new experience for their parents, for the younger group it was a central part of their daily lives, with distinct developmental consequences that continue to influence them now that they're emerging adults.

References

Afifi, T., Davis, S., Merrill, A. F., Coveleski, S., Denes, A., & Afifi, W. (2015). In the wake of the Great Recession: Economic uncertainty, communication, and biological stress responses in families. *Human Communication Research, 41*(2), 268–302.

Altheide, D. L. (2009). The Columbine shootings and the discourse of fear. *American Behavioral Scientist, 52*(10), 1354–1370.

Barroso, A., Parker, K., & Fry, R. (2019). Majority of Americans say parents are doing too much for their young adult children. Pew Research Center. Downloaded from https://www.pewsocialtrends.org/2019/10/23/majority-of-americans-say-parents-are-doing-too-much-for-their-young-adult-children/

Brooks-Gunn, J., Schneider, W., & Waldfogel, J. (2013). The Great Recession and the risk for child maltreatment. *Child Abuse & Neglect, 37*(10), 721–729.

Carpenter, A. L., Elkins, R. M., Kerns, C., Chou, T., Green, J. G., & Comer, J. S. (2017). Event-related household discussions following the Boston Marathon bombing and associated posttraumatic stress among area youth. *Journal of Clinical Child and Adolescent Psychology, 46&6*(3), 331–342.

Connell, N. M. (2018). Fear of crime at school: Understanding student perceptions of safety as function of historical context. *Youth Violence and Juvenile Justice, 16*(2), 124–136.

Conway, A., McDonough, S. C., MacKenzie, M. J., Follett, C., & Sameroff, A. (2013). Stress-related changes in toddlers and their mothers following the attack of September 11. *American Journal of Orthopsychiatry, 83*(4), 536–544.

Coyne, S. M., Padilla-Walker, L. M., Howard, E. (2013). Emerging in a digital world: A decade review of media use, effects, and gratifications in emerging adulthood. *Emerging Adulthood, 1*, 125–137.

Department of Defense. (2017). Profile of the military community: 2017 demographics. Downloaded from https://download.militaryonesource.mil/12038/MOS/Reports/2017-demographics-report.pdf

Engemann, K., & Wall, H. J. (2010). The effects of recessions across demographic groups. *Federal Reserve Bank of St. Louis Review, 92*, 1–26.

Forbes, M. K., & Krueger, R. F. (2019). The Great Recession and mental health in the United States. *Clinical Psychological Science, 7*(5), 900–913.

Frasquilho, D., Matos, M. G., Salonna, F., Guerreiro, D., Storti, C. C., Gaspar, T., & Caldas-de-Almeida, J. M. (2016). Mental health outcomes in times of economic recession: A systematic literature review. *BMC Public Health, 16*, 115. Downloaded from https://www.ncbi.nlm.nih.gov/pmc/articles/PMC4741013/

Garfin, D. R., Poulin, M. J., Blum, S., & Silver, R. C. (2018). Aftermath of terror: A nation-wide longitudinal study of posttraumatic stress and worry across the decade following the September 11, 2001 terrorist attacks. *Journal of Traumatic Stress, 31*(1), 146–156.

Graber, D. (2019). *Raising humans in a digital world: Helping kids build a healthy relationship with technology*. AMACOM.

Halpern, J., & Vermeulen, K. (2017). *Disaster mental health interventions: Core principles and practices*. Routledge.

Hautzinger, S., Howell, A., Scandlyn, J., Wool, Z. H., & Zogas, A. (n.d.). Costs of war: U.S. veterans and military families. Watson Institute of International and Public Affairs. Downloaded from https://watson.brown.edu/costsofwar/costs/human/veterans

Heitner, D. (2016). *Screenwise: Helping kids thrive (and survive) in their digital world*. Routledge.

Hendricks, C., & Bornstein, M. H. (2007). Ecological analysis of early adolescents' stress responses to 9/11 in the Washington, DC, area. *Applied Development Science, 11*(2), 71–88.

Hofer, B. (2008). The electronic tether: Parental regulation, self-regulation, and the role of technology in college transitions. *Journal of The First-Year Experience & Students in Transition, 2*, 9–24.

Kamenetz, A. (2018). *The art of screen time: How your family can balance digital media and real life*. Public Affairs.

Katsiyannis, A., Whitford, D. K., & Ennis, R. P. (2018). Historical examination of United States intentional mass school shootings in the 20th and 21st centuries: Implications for students, schools, and society. *Journal of Child and Family Studies, 27*, 2562–2573.

Koepke, S., & Denissen, J. J. A. (2012). Dynamics of identity development and separation–individuation in parent–child relationships during adolescence and emerging adulthood—A conceptual integration. *Developmental Review, 32*(1), 67–88.

Lester, P., Aralis, H., Sinclair, M., Kiff, C., Lee, K., Mustillo, S., & Wadsworth, S. M. (2016). The impact of deployment on parental, family and child adjustment in military families. *Child Psychiatry and Human Development, 47*, 938–949.

Lickel, B., Schmader, T., & Hamilton, D. L. (2003). A case of collective responsibility: Who else was to blame for the Columbine High School shootings? *Personality and Social Psychology Bulletin, 29*(2), 194–204.

Mai, R. Y., & Alpert, J. L. (2000). Separation and socialization: A feminist analysis of the school shootings at Columbine. *Journal for the Psychoanalysis of Culture & Society, 5*(2), 264–275.

Molloy, S. (2017). We've raised Generation Hopeless: millennials who lack basic life and workplace skills. And it's a big issue. *News.com.au*. Downloaded from https://www.news.com.au/finance/business/weve-raised-generation-hopeless-millennials-who-lack-basic-life-and-workplace-skills-and-its-a-big-issue/news-story/f3256c05c19c356002103eb50e50cee1

Mowder, B. A., Guttman, M., Rubinson, F., & Sossin, K. M. (2006). Parents, children, and trauma: Parent role perceptions and behaviors related to the 9/11 tragedy. *Journal of Child and Family Studies, 15*(6), 733–743.

Nelson, L. J., Padilla-Walker, L. M., & Nielson, M. (2015). Is hovering smothering or loving? An examination of parental warmth as a moderator of relations between helicopter parenting and emerging adults' indices of adjustment. *Emerging Adulthood, 3*, 282–285.

Ohlheiser, A. (2019). "Don't leave campus": Parents are now using tracking apps to watch their kids at college. *Washington Post.* Downloaded from https://www.washingtonpost.com/technology/2019/10/22/dont-leave-campus-parents-are-now-using-tracking-apps-watch-their-kids-college/

Padilla-Walker, L. M., & Nelson, L. J. (2012). Black hawk down? Establishing helicopter parenting as a distinct construct from other forms of parental control during emerging adulthood. *Journal of Adolescence, 35*(5), 1177–1190.

Padilla-Walker, L. M., & Nelson, L. J. (2019). Parenting emerging adults. In M. Bornstein (Ed.), *Handbook of parenting* (3rd ed., pp. 168–190). Erlbaum.

Padilla-Walker, L. M., Son, D., & Nelson, L. J. (2019). Profiles of helicopter parenting, parental warmth, and psychological control during emerging adulthood. *Emerging Adulthood, 9*(2), 132–144.

Parker, K., Igielnik, R., Barroso, A., & Cilluffo, A. (2021). The American veteran experience and the post-9/11 generation. *Pew Research Center.* Downloaded from https://www.pewsocialtrends.org/2019/09/10/the-american-veteran-experience-and-the-post-9-11-generation/

Peer, J. (2017). Parent-emerging adult relationships in the digital age: A family systems theoretical perspective. In M. F. Wright (Ed.), *Identity, Sexuality, and Relationships among Emerging Adults in the Digital Age* (pp. 112–127). IGI Global.

Pew Research Center. (2019). *Mobile fact sheet.* Downloaded from https://www.pewresearch.org/internet/fact-sheet/mobile/

Pfefferbaum, B., Noffsinger, M. A., Wind, L. H., & Allen, J. R. (2014). Children's coping in the context of disasters and terrorism. *Journal of Loss and Trauma, 19*(1), 78–97.

Schlenger, W. E., Caddell, J. M., Ebert, L., Jordan, B. K., Rourke, K. M., Wilson, D., … Kulka, R. A. (2002). Psychological reactions to terrorist attacks: Findings from the national study of Americans' reactions to September 11. *JAMA, 288*, 581–588.

Schuster, M. A., Stein, B. D., Jaycox, L., Collins, R. L., Marshall, G. N., Elliott, M. N., … Berry, S. H. (2001). A national survey of stress reactions after the September 11, 2001 terrorist attacks. *New England Journal of Medicine, 345*, 1507–1512.

Sprague, C. M., Kia-Keating, M., Felix, E., Afifi, T., Reyes, G., & Afifi, W. (2016). Youth psychosocial adjustment following wildfire: The role of family resilience, emotional support, and concrete support. *Child Youth Care Forum, 44*, 433–450.

Summers, F. (2017). Fear and its vicissitudes. *International Forum of Psychoanalysis, 26*(3), 186–192.

Tumulty, K., & Novak, V. (2003). Goodbye, soccer mom. Hello, security mom. *Time Magazine.* Downloaded from http://content.time.com/time/magazine/article/0,9171,454487,00.html

Vaterlaus, J. M., Beckert, T. E., & Bird, C. V. (2015). "At a certain age it's not appropriate to monitor one's child": Perceptions of parental mediation of emerging adult interactive technology use. *Emerging Adulthood, 3*(5), 353–358.

U.S. Bureau of the Census. (1989). *Current population reports, series P-23, No. 163: Changes in American family life.* Washington, DC: U.S. Government Printing Office.

U.S. Department of Veterans Affairs. (n.d.). How deployment stress affects families. National Center for PTSD. Downloaded from https://www.ptsd.va.gov/family/effect_deployment_stress.asp

Wilson, A. C., Lengua, L. J., Meltzoff, A. N., & Smith, K. A. (2010). Parenting and temperament prior to September 11, 2001, and parenting specific to 9/11 as predictors of children's posttraumatic stress symptoms following 9/11. *Journal of Clinical Child and Adolescent Psychology, 39*(4), 445–459.

4

Lockdown Drills in Kindergarten

The Threat (Perceived and Actual) of School Shootings

> We live in a world of constant anxiety. Things like terrorist attacks
> and school shootings are extremely real, and extremely possible to
> happen to us. Especially when it comes to school shootings, "it won't
> ever happen to me" no longer is realistic. Statistically speaking, we
> are very likely to experience such a thing. I hear kids talk about how
> when they are bored in class sometimes they think about what they
> would do if a school shooter came into the building. I don't think that
> is something my parents ever thought about. And I think it really has
> an effect on our mental health.
>
> **—College student's response to a 2015 survey about**
> **perceived safety**

This chapter examines the primary childhood experience that really sets
Generation Disaster apart from previous cohorts: their early awareness of the
threat of school shootings and other types of mass gun violence. As this is the
final chapter in this section on formative experiences for the group, I focus
here on what they were subjected to by the media, educators, and presumably
well-intentioned adults throughout their childhood and adolescence; the next
section will move into how these influences have shaped the cohort now that
they've become emerging adults.

A couple of general points about this subject: First, note that when I describe specific attacks, I follow the growing media practice of not identifying
any perpetrators by name, as that risks glorifying these criminals and fueling
copycat acts by those seeking attention. I also don't address the psychology or
motivations of those perpetrators, but there are numerous books dedicated
to the topic if readers are interested in that aspect, including Jonathan Fast's

Generation Disaster. Karla Vermeulen, Oxford University Press. © Oxford University Press 2021.
DOI: 10.1093/oso/9780190061630.003.0004

Ceremonial Violence: A Psychological Explanation of School Shootings (2008) and Peter Langman's *Why Kids Kill: Inside the Minds of School Shooters* (2009).

Second, my main focus is on the general population of American students for whom this threat remains frightening but hypothetical, *not* those who have actually experienced a school-based shooting. Those events are undeniably horrifying and traumatic for all impacted, including school staff members, first responders, and community members, as well as for the students themselves. Everyone involved in any incident of gun violence or other targeted attack needs to receive appropriate mental health support, immediately and throughout the recovery process (Novotney, 2018). That need is generally recognized now, and most schools have response plans in place should an incident occur—though those short-term, crisis-focused plans are not always sufficient to address the long-term consequences for survivors, which are often underestimated. Professional mental health organizations, including the American Psychological Association, the National Center for PTSD, and the National Child Traumatic Stress Network, all provide extensive resources for those impacted and for the professionals trying to help them, so interested readers can visit their websites for information on planning the mental health response to a shooting.

Instead, the focus here is primarily on the effect of students' simple *awareness of the threat of mass violence in school*, which started to rise nationally after the Columbine High School attack in 1999, when the oldest members of Generation Disaster were 10 years old and the youngest were not yet born. It may surprise some readers to learn that Columbine was far from the first school-based shooting in the United States. As far back as 1853, a student shot his teacher at a Louisville, Kentucky, school, and I described the 1989 Stockton, California, elementary school attack in Chapter 2. Throughout the twentieth century, there were 22 mass shootings in American schools, and the pace has clearly escalated since then (Katsiyannis, Whitford, & Ennis, 2018).

However, Columbine seemed to capture public attention in an unprecedented way, in part because the perpetrators were students themselves who targeted their own classmates. They also documented their plans and intentions, creating a disturbing model for subsequent school shooters, who often emulate aspects of the Columbine killers' actions. That mass murder also inspired a kind of template for how the media covers these events (Schildkraut & Muschert, 2014), inadvertently fueling exaggerated perceptions about the frequency of mass shootings—like the belief that "statistically speaking, we are very likely to experience such a thing" that a survey participant expressed in the comment that opened this chapter. In fact, the lifetime odds of being killed in a mass shooting in the United States is 1 in 11,125, while the likelihood of dying in a motor vehicle accident is 1 in 108 (Mosher & Gould, 2018).

That misperception about risk is further compounded by this generation's experience of lockdowns and active shooter drills in school, starting for many in kindergarten or even earlier. These drills, and other school-based security measures like armed guards and metal detectors at school entrances, send a repeated message to students that they're in constant peril (Connell, 2018). It's no wonder that this combination of media exposure and personal experience of threat reminders results in anxiety among young people who believe they're highly likely to experience a school shooting. They're not, of course (thankfully), but that doesn't reduce the impact of that chronic perception of being in danger. As a result, vastly more students feel affected by the *threat* of school-based gun violence than ever actually experience it, but that fear is harmful in and of itself. And from early childhood on, that fear has been a part of Generation Disaster's lives at every level from micro- to macrosystem, in a way that's unique to this generation. But before we get into the psychological impact of these threat perceptions, let's examine the facts about gun violence in the United States.

Mass Shootings by the Numbers

As with all disasters, statistics about shootings' prevalence and impact depend on how you define an event. (Note that this same measurement problem applies to all mass shootings, not just those that occur in school settings.) A major source of confusion in both general media and academic analyses of gun attacks is that there isn't even a generally accepted definition of what qualifies an event as a "mass shooting."

Many researchers adopt the Federal Bureau of Investigation's (FBI's) definition of a "mass murderer" as someone who kills four or more people in a single incident, not including him- or herself, applying that same number of deaths to define a mass shooting. However, that four-fatality criterion would not recognize events where multiple people are shot and wounded but fewer than four are killed, which would clearly undercount attacks that still impose a significant human impact (Smart, 2018). In an all too timely example, on the day I started writing this chapter I woke up to news accounts of a shooting the previous evening at a California food festival that killed three people, including an 8-year-old boy and a 13-year-old girl. The perpetrator also wounded 12 more people with an assault-style rifle before fatally shooting himself (Ronayne, 2019), and he terrified the hundreds of people present who recognized that their lives were in danger. Yet if it were measured by applying the adapted FBI standard for fatalities, this event would not qualify as a mass shooting.

This lack of definitional clarity makes it difficult to track trends in mass shooting incidence over time as there's disagreement about which events to include at all in the records. That problem is compounded by how relatively rare these events actually are, so one particularly large attack can skew data trends. For example, 2017 is often cited as the deadliest year on record for mass shootings, with four times as many deaths and injuries than the average of the 8 years prior (Everytown for Gun Safety, 2018). However, most of that spike was due to a single major incident, the Las Vegas music festival attack, where the heavily armed perpetrator killed 58 people and shot and injured another 413.

That point is in no way meant to downplay the significance of the Las Vegas event or any other attack, which often leave many survivors with life-altering physical and emotional wounds in addition to the lives lost. (Unbelievably, three survivors of the Las Vegas attack were also present at the 2019 California food festival shooting, and another Las Vegas attack survivor was killed along with 11 other victims in 2018 in a mass shooting at a bar in Thousand Oaks, CA.) I mention this point only to demonstrate that year-to-year comparisons can easily be skewed to advance an agenda. Gun control advocates can point to the general increase in mass shootings over time and the high toll in 2017 to support more stringent policies, while those opposed could cite a decrease in shooting deaths from 2017 to 2018 as evidence that the number of victims has already declined without changing laws. Both would be accurate, if incomplete, interpretations of the data.

Another debate in tracking these events is whether the perpetrator's motivation should be considered. Should statistics distinguish between a shooter who fires indiscriminately into a crowd or classroom from one who targets particular people in a domestic dispute, revenge killing, or gang conflict? The former are sometimes referred to as "rampage shootings," and they're generally what the term *school shooting* evokes for most of us—Columbine, Virginia Tech, Marjory Stoneman Douglas High School, Sandy Hook. In reality, these rampage attacks are the *least* frequent form of school shooting, but they're also by far the most visible due to the broader media coverage they always elicit, unlike the smaller scale, more frequent incidents that usually receive much less attention.

Demonstrating the disparity between these types of shootings, the Naval Postgraduate School's Center for Homeland Defense and Security (Riedman & O'Neill, 2019) conducted a careful analysis of all gun incidents in kindergarten through grade 12 schools (so these data don't include events on college campuses) from 1970 to the present. They included all times a firearm was wielded or discharged on school property, not just events where someone was actually shot. They found that the number of incidents per year fluctuated widely. Events numbered in the teens during 20 of the 48 years monitored, including years as recent as 2010, 2011, and 2012. However, the numbers did reach a high of 97 incidents in 2018, the year that also set the record for school shooting fatalities with 56 deaths. That included the 17 dead at Marjory Stoneman Douglas High School in Parkland, Florida and 10 dead at Santa Fe High School in Benton, Texas. The remaining grim total for that year consisted of the non-mass variety of fatal shootings—murders that came in ones and twos and rarely attracted much media coverage outside of the immediate areas where they occurred.

That 2018 fatality count is inarguably 56 school-based shooting deaths too many. However, to put it in context, the Gun Violence Archive counted 14,769 deaths and 28,236 injuries nationwide during the same year due to gun violence. Among those killed or injured, 668 victims were age 11 or younger, and 2,851 were ages 12 to 17. Most of those deaths received little public notice because they were connected to domestic disputes, neighborhood violence, or gang activity—and because they disproportionately affected people of color (Cox & Rich, 2018). Accidents and suicides are also common types of gun-related fatalities. In fact, it may surprise readers to learn that in 2017, despite the occurrence of the Las Vegas attack, the vast majority of gun deaths in the U.S. were not due to mass shootings or even individual assaults, but suicides (The Trace, 2018). Nearly 60% of the 39,773 gun fatalities that year were self-inflicted, while 346—less than 1%—were due to mass shooting incidents (Gun Violence Archive, 2019).

So while far too many people are being killed by guns in the United States every year, only a fraction of those deaths occur in school-based shootings, and fewer still result from the kind of active shooter rampage scenario we all imagine when we think about school shootings. Yet that atypical scenario is what many schools focus on, with elaborate security measures like lockdown drills, which may cause more harm than good for students' sense of safety and emotional well-being (Rich & Cox, 2018). Before examining those direct effects on young people, let's look at the role of media in inadvertently fueling misperceptions about mass shootings.

Mainstream Media Coverage and Threat Misperceptions

Why do we remember those school rampage attacks so vividly, and put such intensive resources into preparing for them, when they really make up a tiny fraction of the shooting deaths and injuries inflicted on American youth each year? It's primarily because they've been publicized and reinforced in our minds by extensive media coverage, which, while understandable, distorts our risk perceptions. That media coverage is also a factor in inspiring contagion or copycat attacks (Dahmen, 2018), creating a kind of toxic feedback loop that inadvertently exacerbates the problem.

Because these events are so horrific when they do occur—and I'll say it again, any incident is one too many—they receive disproportionate media attention relative to more common forms of gun violence like domestic crimes and suicides, which means that they carve disproportionate traces into our memories. It's a form of "availability heuristic" (Tversky & Kahneman, 1973), a mental shortcut that becomes self-reinforcing: Because reports of school shootings are so gripping and we pay so much attention to them, we assume the fact that we remember news about these events so vividly means they happen more frequently than they really do.

It's not surprising that the public is hungry for information about these shocking events, which journalists are very willing to provide. As Schildkraut and Muschert (2014) put it in an analysis of media coverage of the Columbine and Sandy Hook shootings:

> Mass murders, and in particular those that involve children in schools, generate high levels of media coverage, as audiences have a desire to learn the facts of the events, and, in a more sustained way, to understand the social implications and deeper meaning of such events. The ensuing discussions often reflect ongoing value conflicts within society, and indeed the discourse (and at times discord) heard following school massacres seem to reflect the deeply latent social value conflicts frequently at tension below the surface of social life. (p. 24)

Thus, the public seeks out media coverage after shootings and other distressing events not only to learn *what* happened, but also to try to understand *why* it happened. We have a deep need to make meaning out of incomprehensible actions, so we turn to journalists and pundits for analysis as well as factual reporting. In other words, we generate the demand, which media outlets respond to by generating an ongoing supply of articles and stories. To retain audience share in today's hypercompetitive market, media professionals often maintain a focus on an event long past the point where there is any actual new information to report. This is described as "frame changing" (Schildkraut & Muschert, 2014), the journalistic process of reframing coverage to focus on different angles of a story in order to maintain audience interest.

For example, *New York Times* coverage of the Sandy Hook shooting in Newtown, Connecticut, which resulted in the deaths of 20 first graders and six educators (as well as the perpetrator and his mother), focused at different points in the first 30 days after the 2012 event on the perpetrator, the victims, the community impact, the national impact, and possible gun control policy effects. There was only 1 day during that first month that the *Times* did not include at least one feature article on the aftermath of the shooting (Schildkraut & Muschert, 2014). The event was similarly omnipresent on television and online, across partisan lines. For example, a search of the *Fox News* archive finds an average of six items per day that mentioned the shooting during the month after it occurred, including opinion pieces, poll results, and policy analyses as well as news updates. That kind of ongoing coverage keeps these events present in our awareness long after they occur or there's any real news to report about them, further fueling the availability heuristic.

Again, this reflects a symbiotic relationship in which each party gets what it wants—information for the public and revenues for the media outlets. But what is the psychological cost of these constant reminders of tragedy, especially for young people who may identify closely with accounts of school shootings and who don't have the broader life experience to place their actual frequency in context?

There doesn't appear to be much empirical research quantifying specific effects of media exposure to school shootings on children at different developmental stages, and there are certainly no randomized controlled trials as it wouldn't be ethical to intentionally expose children to potentially traumatic media (even if it's fictionalized) for the sake of research. However, general consensus in the field of disaster mental health is that media exposure to disasters of all kinds should be limited as much as possible, especially for younger kids (Halpern & Vermeulen, 2017). For example, there are many anecdotal accounts of young children viewing repeated television images of the World Trade Center buildings collapsing on 9/11 and believing the event was happening anew each time, and increased television viewing about the attack was associated with more trauma symptoms for children at the time (Pfefferbaum et al., 2003). One thing parents often don't realize is that even if children are too young to really understand what they're seeing on television, they may still pick up on the emotions of the reporters delivering the stories. They also definitely notice how their caregivers are reacting to dreadful news and may mirror adults' distress or anxiety, as was found in many of the studies discussed in the previous chapter, so caregivers should be sure to limit media exposure about shootings and other disasters—ideally for themselves as well as their children.

It's also important to consider the role caregivers can play in contextual-izing media coverage of shootings and other disasters, which was demon-strated in a study conducted after the Boston Marathon bombing (Carpenter et al., 2017). The authors examined associations between attack-related household discussions and child post-traumatic stress symptoms among 460 Boston area youth, ages 4 to 19 (with a mean age of 11.8 years), following the bombing. Caregivers completed surveys 2 to 6 months after the event. They were asked to describe immediate household conversations about the attack and subsequent search for the perpetrators; child exposure to poten-tially traumatic attack-related experiences; and child post-traumatic stress symptoms.

Carpenter et al. (2017) found lower rates of child stress among those who learned about the event from caregivers rather than the media or peers. Stress was also lower among those whose caregivers discussed their own feelings about the search with their child and who expressed confidence in their safety. This contrasted with higher stress among children whose caregivers expressed concerns about safety and those whose caregivers did not discuss the event at all or asked others to avoid mentioning it in front of the child. This last point suggests that avoiding discussions with children and adolescents about a dis-aster out of the belief it will protect them from distress not only is fruitless, but also may actually be counterproductive. Instead, caregivers may need to push themselves to hold what might be difficult conversations with children who need parental support in order to process disturbing news and place it in the context of their limited life experience. This is consistent with the theme that ran throughout the previous chapter on parenting: Caregivers can play a powerful role in buffering children from stress, not only by limiting what they're exposed to directly or via media, but also by helping to contextualize upsetting news that might otherwise lead children to develop exaggerated risk perceptions.

The Dangers of Unfiltered Social Media

While older children may be less reliant on caregivers to interpret events depicted in mainstream media, adolescents and emerging adults face a dif-ferent risk when it comes to news about shootings and other disasters: Their immersion in social media means they're likely to receive a flood of unveri-fied information during and after any event, exposing them to questionable facts, misinformation, rumors, and possibly upsetting images. This can create a kind of echo chamber effect that both feeds and feeds on user anxiety as frightened people pass along information without knowing its veracity, usually not out of any malevolent intent but simply because they're so hungry for any information at all.

In situations where there is an actual ongoing threat, that user-generated noise can drown out the signal of official information that is eventually disseminated by emergency managers or school administrators once the facts have been verified. For instance, in one study of university students who experienced a campus lockdown following an active shooter event, many turned to Twitter and other forms of social media because of what they perceived to be an absence of adequate official information about what was going on. These platforms proliferated conflicting advice and rumors (e.g., that there were multiple shooters rather than just one) that significantly increased student distress (Jones, Thompson, Schetter, & Silver, 2017).

Even more pernicious, social media now allows perpetrators to publicize their motives and even to broadcast their actions live, fueling copycat attacks that strive to top previous death tolls. I won't glorify that intentionally evil choice by giving it any more attention here, but I will address the unintended consequences that can occur when the ones doing the live posting and streaming are not the perpetrators, but the victims of an attack, sharing their traumatic experience as it occurs. For a vivid example, an article published the day after the Marjory Stoneman Douglas shooting in Parkland, Florida, describes the high school students filming and posting the terrifying events while these events were still unfolding:

> Milan [Parodie, age 15] said her brother, Roman, was sheltered in a classroom during the attack. "Someone knocked on the door and asked to be let in, and they locked the door and stayed quiet," she said.
>
> Roman sent Milan a video of a person shot dead inside a classroom.
>
> Throughout the school, students recorded the shooting on their phones and uploaded the harrowing footage to social media for the world to see. In one video, the deafening blasts of rifle fire nearly drown out shouts of "Holy shit! Oh my God!" The video pans to a laptop with bullet holes punched through its screen.
>
> In another video, students are seen crouched and sheltering in the back of a classroom when a SWAT team enters, guns pointing directly at them. The students raise shaking hands in the air as bright police flashlights shine into their eyes. "Put your phones away! Put your phones away!" an officer orders (LaPorta & Lorenz, 2018).

That lockdown lasted for 3½ until the surviving students knew they were safe, and during that time some who were trapped inside the school were exchanging rumors via text and Twitter, as well as watching live news coverage on their phones, including viewing helicopter television shots of the exterior of the building they were trapped inside (Cullen, 2019). Overall, it's difficult to imagine a more media-saturated event than the Parkland attack—including, on the positive side, the survivors' masterful use of social and mainstream media to advance their gun advocacy efforts in the days and months afterward. (For a detailed account of their inspiring activism, read Dave Cullen's 2019 book, *Parkland*.)

I understand these young people's impulse to document and share what they were experiencing: It's second nature for their generation to use social media on their phones to feel connected to others, and I can't imagine circumstances when that sense of connection would feel more crucial than during an ongoing attack. However, I suspect few of those students were considering the potential impact on the people *receiving* their terrified messages and images. I don't intend that as a criticism at all, but we do need to recognize the vicarious trauma that can be caused by exposure to troubling information about school shootings and other types of violence among those without direct experience of the event, spreading the emotional impact beyond the original survivors.

In fact, as much as the extended and sometimes sensationalized mainstream media coverage of school shootings can be psychologically problematic, it may be even more devastating for adolescents and young adults (and for older adults as well) to be exposed to unvetted peer-to-peer social media posts about unfolding events, especially those including photos or videos. They don't always get credit for it, but most professional journalists and editors are very conscientious about selecting which images to use to illustrate a news item. They carefully consider who is likely to see a photograph or video and how to balance an image's storytelling impact with its risk of disturbing or upsetting viewers—or of inspiring imitators who fantasize about seeing their own picture on the news (Dahmen, 2018).

"Citizen journalists" seldom work as conscientiously. Instead, they unthinkingly push out raw and often graphic pictures and videos through social media platforms, and that risks causing vicarious trauma for viewers who may be unwittingly exposed to images they can never unsee. It's also possible that friends and family members of victims may see these terrible images or read posts naming those who have been killed, perhaps before official death notifications are made. There's no good way to learn about a loved one's death, but stumbling on the news through social media seems highly likely to compound the trauma, while exposure to actual images can implant horrific visions of what a friend or relative suffered through.

Again, I certainly don't think the survivors who post these eyewitness accounts of school shootings and other tragedies have any malicious intent. (The same does not apply, obviously, to the disturbing trend of perpetrators streaming their attacks.) One could even argue that the public *should* be exposed to the full terror and brutality of these events from the perspective of the victims in order to motivate more effective preventative actions. However, the potential for vicarious traumatization of a group far beyond the actual survivors is undeniably magnified by social media in a way that was never even conceivable at the time of the Columbine massacre. It may be a secondary and unintended consequence of gun violence's impact, but it's another facet of this multipart stressor for Generation Disaster, their parents, and everyone else.

Lockdown Drills: Classroom Security Theater or Necessary Ill?

The final aspect of school shootings I address in this chapter is another way in which some children may be harmed, not intentionally by perpetrators, but inadvertently by the adults who are trying to protect them: by being required to participate in lockdown drills and other highly visible school-based security measures. Through these practices, the terrible but very rare risk of school rampage shootings is transformed into an actual, sometimes distressing experience that impacts most U.S. students.

During typical school lockdown drills, students and teachers practice hiding silently in darkened classrooms, closets, bathrooms, or other relatively secure areas, with the goal of avoiding detection by a perpetrator looking for targets. These drills became a standard part of many K through 12 schools' emergency preparedness activities after the Columbine shooting. By the 2015–2016 school year, 95% of U.S. public schools practiced lockdown procedures (Diliberti, Jackson, & Kemp, 2017). Now, as I wrote in the previous chapter, many of my students recall them as being a fairly routine part of their elementary, middle, and high school experiences, especially when they were aware they were participating in a practice session. However, not all children come through drills unscathed.

Because realism is considered an important part of practicing responses, children (and often teachers) may not be informed whether a lockdown is a practice drill or the response to an actual threat, which means they may genuinely believe their lives are in danger. That is highly unlikely in fact, but it's not an implausible fear because as we've seen, they've learned from prior media accounts of school shootings that kids like them can die in these events. In particularly security-conscious school districts, drills are sometimes elaborately staged, with gun-wielding actors firing blanks, spilling fake blood, and setting off fake explosives. It's big business for companies selling security consulting services and products (Raymond, 2018), but there's growing acknowledgment that taking the practice to this extreme traumatizes many children and adolescents—not to mention their teachers, who have also been exposed to physical injuries during intense drill practices, like sustaining hearing loss from having blank guns fired near them or bruises from being shot with paintballs.

Like the impact of media exposure about school shootings, this is another area where there is limited empirical research in the academic literature, likely due to ethical problems with conducting randomized experiments. In fact, searching the PsycINFO database found only a handful of articles that mentioned school lockdowns, and all of them focused on assessing the practice's effectiveness, not its emotional impact. (That short list of results included one article chillingly titled, "Training Kindergarten Students Lockdown Drill Procedures Using Behavioral Skills Training"; Dickson and Vargo, 2017.)

To date, much of the published criticism of these practices comes from popular media, including excellent reporting in 2018 in the *Washington Post* by journalists Steve Rich and John Woodrow Cox. Among their troubling findings:

- The total number of lockdowns in the 2017–2018 school year exceeded 6,200. That included lockdowns in response to a real threat or false alarm as well as planned drills.
- More than 4.1 million U.S. students experienced at least one lockdown. Many of them were very young: More than 1 million elementary school-age children experienced a lockdown in 2017–2018, including at least 220,000 in kindergarten or prekindergarten.
- Terrified locked down students have had panic attacks, soiled themselves from fear, written wills in their class notebooks, and texted parents farewell messages.

It's not a stretch to suggest that in some cases, these lockdown experiences are actually causing childhood trauma, which can be associated with diverse negative outcomes, including academic and social problems, depression, anxiety, poor sleep, and substance abuse.

Cox and Rich (2018) also pointed out the limited effectiveness of on-campus police as a deterrent to school shootings, noting that "resource officers or security guards were present during four of the five worst rampages (which left the highest number of people dead or injured): Columbine and Marjory Stoneman Douglas, Marshall County High in Kentucky [in 2018] and Santana High in California in 2001." In one case, the journalists wrote, awareness that his middle school had armed security guards present led an aspiring shooter to target his community's unguarded elementary school instead—hardly the intention of the safety plans. It's also believed that the perpetrator of the Marjory Stoneman Douglas shooting, a former student, used his familiarity with the school's active shooter procedure to increase his death toll (Daly, 2018).

Clearly the current approach to school security is not completely successful at preventing rampage attacks, but it is psychologically harming some students who are forced to go through sometimes terrifying drills with questionable benefits or to see armed security guards in their hallways as a regular reminder of the threat of violence.

* * *

I am not immune to fears about school shootings. I work on an open campus where a perpetrator could easily bring a weapon into any building, and I consider it my responsibility to prepare for how I could best protect my students should something happen. At the start of every semester, I analyze each new classroom I'm assigned to. What floor is it on, and do the windows open wide enough to allow escape? Where is it positioned in the hallway relative to exits? Does the door to the classroom open in or out, and how could I barricade it if necessary? Is there an area students could move to so they wouldn't be visible through the door or windows? Is the furniture fixed to the floor or could it be moved to block the door or throw at an intruder? I also try to learn about my new students' backgrounds, and I make a mental note of those who would be most useful to call on for support in an emergency (one of many reasons I love having military veterans in my classes).

It's as much a part of my start-of-semester to-do list as updating the syllabus—but I would never choose to alarm my students by putting them through a simulated attack. They're conscious enough of the risk, having been raised from kindergarten to be aware of it, and I'm sure many are doing the same kind of threat assessment and mental rehearsal as I am. Their daily lives are stressful enough without me adding yet another reminder that they can't quite consider themselves safe in any setting.

Of course, the real problem isn't the drills or the media coverage. The problem is the actual shootings, however rare, that make these security measures seem necessary. I'm not claiming that lockdown drills in primary and secondary school aren't needed, but the way they're often handled now seems counterproductive. It would be easy to accuse the school administrators who implement these practices of doing more harm than good in an effort to demonstrate to parents that they're doing everything possible to protect children, like the reactive airport security theater measures described in the second chapter. But I don't believe that's the case. A better comparison comes from a security expert quoted by Rich and Cox (2018), who likened lockdowns to car airbags: "They save drivers' lives in car crashes, but the devices might also break noses and crack teeth. . . . Full-scale lockdowns should be employed only when absolutely necessary."

As a result, administrators and parents need to recognize that the same procedures that are meant to help school community members be and feel safe—and to help parents trust that their children are safe while they're at school—instead appear to be contributing to a culture of fear and anxiety that may shape children's development in multiple realms. Many participants in my national survey cited school shootings and lockdowns during their early school years as a reason they think they're more aware of safety concerns and other stressors than members of previous generations were. For example,

We now live in a world full of terrorist attacks and school shootings.

—Female, born 1997

I believe I am more aware than previous generations specifically because of the surge in school shootings. We had many drills, practice lockdowns, and actual scares when I was in school.

—Female, born 2000

Increase in media prevalence—with the pervasiveness of social media, we are always surrounded by the news and constantly receiving updates through our phones regarding what is happening in our local news as well as the world. Also, there has been an increase in mass shootings in recent years, especially school shootings, and I have had to prepare for those both physically (e.g., active shooter drills) and emotionally (e.g., planning out in my mind what I would do in any given disaster situation).

—Female, born 1994

And simply,

> I'm part of the school shooting generation.
>
> —Male, born 1999

Perhaps rather than focusing primarily on security practices that inadvertently distort threat perceptions, parents and educators might do more to teach today's children and adolescents how to analyze risk so they better understand how unlikely it is they'll ever actually experience a mass shooting. Obviously, we can't promise them that they'll never be exposed to a shooting or terrorist attack, any more than we can claim that they'll be spared the impact of climate change, a global pandemic, and other dangers that exist in the world they live in. But perhaps the next cohort of young people could be raised in an environment that focuses less on reminding them constantly that they're unsafe. It seems that our failure to do that during Generation Disaster's formative years has contributed to their heightened security concerns now that they're emerging adults, resulting in mental health consequences for many like anxiety and depression. That is the focus of the next chapter, as we move into the book's section on the group's current functioning as they cope with key aspects of emerging adulthood, and we explore how the various formative influences discussed so far have shaped them into an often stressed, yet remarkably resilient, generation.

References

Carpenter, A. L., Elkins, R. M., Kerns, C., Chou, T., Green, J. G., & Comer, J. S. (2017). Event-related household discussions following the Boston Marathon bombing and associated posttraumatic stress among area youth. *Journal of Clinical Child and Adolescent Psychology, 46*(3), 331–342.

Connell, N. M. (2018). Fear of crime at school: Understanding student perceptions of safety as function of historical context. *Youth Violence and Juvenile Justice, 16*(2), 124–136.

Cox, J. W., & Rich, S. (2018, March 21). Scarred by school shootings. *Washington Post.* Downloaded from https://www.washingtonpost.com/graphics/2018/local/us-school-shootings-history/?utm_term=.939051ea5c79

Cullen, D. (2019). *Parkland.* New York: HarperCollins.

Dahmen, N. S. (2018). Visually reporting mass shootings: U.S. newpaper photographic coverage of three mass school shootings. *American Behavioral Scientist, 62*(2), 163–180.

Daly, M. (2018, February 15). Florida shooter made sick use of school's active-shooter drill. *The Daily Beast.* Downloaded from https://www.thedailybeast.com/florida-shooter-made-sick-use-of-schools-active-shooter-drill

Dickson, M. J., & Vargo, K. K. (2017). Training kindergarten students lockdown drill procedures using behavioral skills training. *Journal of Applied Behavior Analysis, 50*(2), 407–412.

Diliberti, M., Jackson, M., & Kemp, J. (2017). Crime, violence, discipline, and safety in U. S. public schools: Findings from the School Survey on Crime and Safety: 2015–16. Washington, DC: U.S. Department of Education, National Center for Education Statistics. Downloaded from http://nces.ed.gov/pubsearch

Everytown for Gun Safety. (2018). Mass shootings in the United States: 2009–2017. Downloaded from https://everytownresearch.org/reports/mass-shootings-analysis/

Fast, J. (2008). *Ceremonial violence: A psychological explanation of school shootings*. New York: Overlook Press.

Gun Violence Archive. (2019). 2017 Gun violence summary ledger. Downloaded from https://www.gunviolencearchive.org/past-tolls

Halpern, J., & Vermeulen, K. (2017). *Disaster mental health interventions: Core principles and practices*. Abingdon-on-Thames, UK: Routledge.

Jones, N. M., Thompson, R. R., Schetter, C. D., & Silver, R. C. (2017). Distress and rumor exposure on social media during a campus lockdown. *Proceedings of the National Academy of Sciences of the United States of America, 114*(44), 11663–11668.

Katsiyannis, A., Whitford, D. K., & Ennis, R. P. (2018). Historical examination of United States intentional mass school shootings in the 20th and 21st centuries: Implications for students, schools, and society. *Journal of Child and Family Studies, 27*, 2562–2573.

Langman, P. (2009). *Why kids kill: Inside the minds of school shooters*. New York: Palgrave Macmillan.

LaPorta, J., & Lorenz, T. (2018, February 15). Students' videos capture shooting horror inside Florida high school. *The Daily Beast*. Downloaded from https://www.thedailybeast.com/parkland-florida-school-shooting-stoneman-douglas-high

Liao, Y., Shonkoff, E. T., Barnett, E., Wen, C. K. F., Miller, K. A., & Eddy, J. M. (2015). Brief report: Examining children's disruptive behavior in the wake of trauma—A two-piece growth curve model before and after a school shooting. *Journal of Adolescence, 44*, 219–223.

Mosher, D., & Gould, S. (2018, October 29). The odds that a gun will kill the average American may surprise you. *Business Insider*. Downloaded from https://www.businessinsider.com/us-gun-death-murder-risk-statistics-2018-3

Novotney, A. (2018). What happens to the survivors: Long-term outcomes for survivors of mass shootings are improved with the help of community connections and continuing access to mental health support. *APA Monitor, 49*(8), 36. Downloaded from https://www.apa.org/monitor/2018/09/survivors

Pfefferbaum, B., Seale, T. W., Brandt, E. N., Jr., Pfefferbaum, R. L., Doughty, D. E., & Rainwater, S. M. (2003). Media exposure in children one hundred miles from a terrorist bombing. *Annals of Clinical Psychiatry, 15*, 1–8.

Raymond, A. K. (2018, September 12). How active shooter drills became a big (and possibly traumatizing) business. *Medium*. Downloaded from https://medium.com/s/youthnow/the-response-to-school-shootings-may-be-a-misfire-active-shooter-drills-teachers-students-6acb56418062

Rich, S., & Cox, J. W. (2018, December 26). What if someone was shooting? *Washington Post*. Downloaded from https://www.washingtonpost.com/graphics/2018/local/school-lockdowns-in-america/?utm_term=.f9661f871e23

Riedman, D., & O'Neill, D. (2019). CHDS—K-12 School Shooting Database. Center for Homeland Defense and Security. Downloaded from https://www.chds.us/ssdb.

Ronayne, K. (2019, July 29). Gunman kills 2 kids, 1 other in California festival attack. *SFGate*. Downloaded from https://www.sfgate.com/news/crime/article/Shooting-reported-at-site-of-California-garlic-14192010.php

Schildkraut, J., & Muschert, G. W. (2014). Media salience and the framing of mass murder in schools: A comparison of the Columbine and Sandy Hook massacres. *Criminology & Penology, 18*, 23–43.

Smart, R. (2018, March 18). Mass shootings: Definitions and trends. RAND Gun Policy in America. Downloaded from https://www.rand.org/research/gun-policy/analysis/essays/mass-shootings.html

The Trace. (2018, December 25). 13 Statistics that tell the story of gun violence in 2018. Downloaded from https://www.thetrace.org/2018/12/gun-violence-facts-statistics-2018/

Tversky, A., & Kahneman, D. (1973). Availability: A heuristic for judging frequency and probability. *Cognitive Psychology, 5,* 207–232.

SECTION 2

GENERATION DISASTER IN EMERGING ADULTHOOD

The Current Impact of Cumulative Early Stressors

The second section explores the current impact of those cumulative stressors as the group moves through the period of emerging adulthood, with chapters that examine their perceptions about personal safety, their attitudes toward politicians and other authorities, their concerns about climate change, and their very mixed emotions about the value of a college education.

5

Unsafe at Any Time

The world feels less safe. I felt invincible before [9/11] and I didn't after.

—**Female, born 1992**

I've grown up in the 21st century, where disasters happen every 20 minutes.

—**Male, born 2000**

If one of your earliest memories is of a massive disaster or a lockdown drill, how do you learn to feel secure and believe that the world is a safe place— and should that be the goal as a person takes on adult roles and responsibilities? As we begin this section on Generation Disaster's beliefs and behaviors as they move through emerging adulthood, this chapter examines the group's perceptions of safety, risk, fairness, and other consequences of their early environment. How do these concerns relate to the high rates of anxiety and depression reported by this generation? Are these risk perceptions actually more realistic than those held by previous American cohorts, who perhaps had an inflated sense of personal immunity to disaster and loss? And can we even make valid comparisons to previous generations given all of the dramatic societal changes of the past few decades?

In particular, this chapter explores the psychological consequences of Generation Disaster's risk perceptions and whether their often cautious worldview is a flaw to be overcome (as those who label them as coddled "snowflakes" tend to suggest) or an adaptive response to a genuinely more dangerous world.

Let's start with some disturbing statistics about mental health among today's emerging adults, drawn from a national survey by the federal Substance Abuse and Mental Health Services Administration (SAMHSA) in 2018 about drug use and mental health in 2017. Note that SAMHSA categorizes the young adult age range as including 18- to 25-year-olds, so these statistics don't

Generation Disaster. Karla Vermeulen, Oxford University Press. © Oxford University Press 2021.
DOI: 10.1093/oso/9780190061630.003.0005

include the oldest slice of our usual 18- to 29-year-old emerging adult range. The survey asked whether a respondent experienced various conditions at least once during the past year. Among the findings, these 18- to 25-year-olds reported the following rates of mental health problems:

- **Any mental illness**, defined by SAMHSA as "any mental, behavioral, or emotional disorder in the past year that met DSM-IV criteria (excluding developmental disorders and substance use disorders": 25.8%
- **Serious mental illness**, defined as "any mental, behavioral, or emotional disorder that substantially interfered with or limited one or more major life activities": 7.5%
- **Major depressive episode**, defined as "a period of 2 weeks or longer in that period when they experienced a depressed mood or loss of interest or pleasure in daily activities, and they had at least some additional symptoms, such as problems with sleep, eating, energy, concentration, or self-worth": 13.1%
- **Major depressive episode involving major impairment**, defined as depression that "caused severe problems with their ability to manage at home, manage well at work, have relationships with others, or have a social life": 8.5%

This means that in 2017, some 8.8 million Americans between 18 and 25 were dealing with some form of mental illness. On top of that, 3.4 million young adults had an alcohol use disorder, and 2.5 million had an illicit drug use disorder, which includes the misuse of prescription medications like painkillers or stimulants as well as dependence on, or abuse of, illegal drugs like heroin. During that year, 5.1 million 18- to 25-year-olds, or about 15% of all young adults, received some form of mental health services, yet only half of those who had experienced a major depressive episode in the past year received treatment, defined as talking to a professional or using prescription depression medication. That's a *lot* of young people grappling with mental health issues and substance abuse disorders, many without professional assistance.

In addition to diagnosed mental health disorders, many people of all ages experience high levels of concern and anxiety that may be subclinical but cause suffering nonetheless. For example, each year the American Psychiatric Association (APA) conducts a national survey about anxiety and other mental health issues. Among their 2019 results, participants aged 18 to 34 (so in this case the range used extends slightly beyond the traditional upper age limit for emerging adulthood) reported being somewhat or extremely anxious about daily concerns at the following rates:

- The impact of politics on my daily life: 52%
- My relationships with family, friends, and coworkers: 63%
- My health: 67%
- Keeping myself or my family safe: 68%
- Paying my bills or expenses: 74%

That means only one quarter to one half of the young adult respondents said they were rarely or never anxious about any of these particular life stressors. Anxiety is the norm for the group, not the exception.

Even more troubling, suicide is the second most common cause of death for Americans aged 20 to 34, especially for men, following deaths due to accidents (Heron, 2019). According to the Centers for Disease Control and Prevention, suicide rates for all races and ages have increased drastically over the past two decades, growing by 53% for women (though from a small base, increasing from 4 suicides per 100,000 population in 1999 to 6.1 per 100,000 in 2017) and increasing by a smaller percentage but at greater numbers overall for men, growing by 25% (from 17.8 to 22.4 per 100,000 population). The increase was much higher for those aged 15 to 24, growing by 35% for young men and a startling 93% for young women, though young men's overall rates still greatly exceeded young women's at 22.7 male suicides and 5.8 female suicides per 100,000 population aged 15 to 24 in 2017 (Curtin & Hedegaard, 2019).

This generation also grew up during the rise and height of the opioid epidemic, and many have experienced the effects of substance abuse on friends and family even if they've avoided becoming addicted themselves. Out of my thousand-person national sample, just over half (53.4%) said they knew someone who had an active drug and/or alcohol addiction. Even more shocking, 37.3% of the sample said they knew someone who had died of an overdose, including an acquaintance ($n = 112$), close friend ($n = 63$), extended family member ($n = 80$), immediate family member ($n = 46$), or partner/spouse ($n = 3$). Sixty-eight respondents had experienced deaths in two or more of those relationships, and two said they had lost people in all five categories to overdose.

These rates of anxiety, depression, substance abuse, suicide, and other problems among emerging adults are striking, but are they exceptional or do they simply reflect the stress of life these days for everyone? To judge, we need to compare mental health functioning among today's emerging adults to two sets of people. First, we need to examine this cohort relative to older age groups' current mental health functioning in order to see if these levels are specific to young adults or if they're shared by everyone living in in the present environment. In other words, are these young people suffering differently from everyone else in our complicated modern world? Second, we need to compare these levels with earlier cohorts at the time of their own emerging adulthood to see if this is a typical developmental effect that occurs regardless of contemporaneous stressors. In other words, is the 18- to 29-year-old period just a uniquely stressful time of life, regardless of when it occurs in history?

Current Mental Health by Cohort Group

The first comparison is relatively simple as the major national surveys generally collect data across age groups, so we can directly compare current cross sections.

Looking at the APA survey cited above, here are 2019 reports about the frequency of being somewhat or extremely anxious about the same issues for members of Generation X, defined by APA as those aged 38 to 53:

- The impact of politics on my daily life: 44%
- My relationships with family, friends, and coworkers: 49%
- My health: 64%
- Keeping myself or my family safe: 72%
- Paying my bills or expenses: 70%

And here are 2019 rates for Baby Boomers, aged 54 to 72:

- The impact of politics on my daily life: 51%
- My relationships with family, friends, and coworkers: 39%
- My health: 61%
- Keeping myself or my family safe: 59%
- Paying my bills or expenses: 56%

Compare those percentages to the 18- to 34-year-olds' responses (in the listed order, 52%, 63%, 67%, 68%, and 74%) and you'll see a general downward trend in anxiety about most topics across age groups, but even among the Boomers more than half still said they were somewhat or extremely anxious about all of the topics except for relationships. Even pre-pandemic, it appears we're living a time of high anxiety for all age groups, which undermines claims that today's emerging adults are exceptionally fragile.

One difference the APA survey did find was in the *stability* of anxiety: When asked "In general, are you more or less anxious than you were at this time last year?" the Baby Boomers reported far lower levels of change, with 23% saying they were more anxious, 17% less anxious, and 58% reporting no change. In contrast, 37% of the 18- to 34-year-olds said they were more anxious than a year ago, 31% were less anxious, and 29% were at about the same level. Both groups did report more increase than decrease in overall anxiety, but there was significantly less change for the older participants, perhaps reflecting less reactivity to external circumstances later in life. This makes sense given the fluctuations and exploration that are recognized as a defining characteristic of emerging adulthood: While these changes are often ultimately positive, they can also be stressful while they're occurring, so the younger group's responses may have been more variable depending on each individual's satisfaction with their current situation at the time they responded to the survey.

We can also compare the prevalence of depression and other types of mental illness across age groups. Remember, according to SAMHSA (2018), 13.1% of 18- to 25-year-old survey respondents reported having at least one major depressive episode (MDE) in 2017, and for 8.5% that involved major impairment. Those rates were significantly lower among older groups: Among those aged 26 to 49, an MDE was reported by 7.7%, and 5.0% involved major impairment. Those 50 or older had even lower rates, 4.7% overall and 2.8% with major impairment. (Disturbingly, major depression was even more prevalent among some youth aged 12 to 17, who reported rates even worse than the 18- to 25-year-olds: 13.3% MDE prevalence and 9.4% with major impairment.) The same decreasing pattern occurred for other types of mental illness, with 2017 rates for 18- to 25-year olds, 26- to 49-year olds, and 50 or older reported as 25.8%, 22.2%, and 13.8%, respectively, for any mental illness, and 7.5%, 5.6%, and 2.7%, respectively, for serious mental illness (SAMHSA, 2018). This downward trend also occurred for alcohol use disorder and illicit drug use disorder, with rates peaking among people aged 18 to 25 and then declining by age group.

All of these cross-sectional data clearly demonstrate that rates of mental health challenges vary by age group, and while they tend to decrease over time, these issues are still somewhat prevalent among middle-aged and older adults. Comparison number one: Accomplished: Current emerging adults *are* more distressed than older adults at this time, though it's not like turning 30 magically wipes away these problems for those in middle or late adulthood.

Emerging Adult Stress Then and Now

The second needed comparison, contrasting current and historic cohorts of 18- to 29-year-olds, is a lot trickier in several important ways. First, methodologically it's more difficult because, lacking a time machine to go back and collect precise data on earlier generations, we have to rely on historical data.

That means today's developmental psychologists are limited by how previous researchers chose to tackle the topic and how accessible that archival data may be. We can't alter the earlier studies to match our current focus, so we're often left comparing current apples to historic oranges, or to older apples that are missing major chunks because the earlier researcher didn't ask about something we're now interested in. And, of course, some of those topics of interest are entirely new, like the impact of climate change or social media on emotional well-being, so no comparison could ever be possible. Similarly, some past stressors, like concerns about getting drafted or contracting polio, are no longer salient, so comparisons to today's issues may miss the psychological significance of these threats for earlier cohorts.

Let's also remember that the entire concept of emerging adulthood as a distinct developmental stage is quite recent, dating back only to 2000 when Jeffrey Arnett began publishing his research on what it means for young people to make the transition to adulthood from adolescence—itself a fairly new concept dating only to the early twentieth century (Hall, 1907). As Arnett wrote in a history of the development of the field of emerging adulthood:

> People used to go directly from adolescence to a more or less settled young adulthood by their early 20s. Now there was adolescence, then this new life stage, and then a more settled young adulthood, beginning in the late 20s or early 30s. I decided to call the new life stage "emerging adulthood" to reflect the widespread feeling among people in this age period that they were still in the process of becoming adults, on their way to adulthood but not there yet. (Arnett, 2014, p. 157)

(Indeed, I went through this stage before it received a name, and if pressured to label my status as I moved through my 20s, I'd have gone with something like "maybe, kinda, occasionally, sometimes, mostly, pretty much adulthood." Arnett's term is better.)

The fact that this is such a newly identified life stage—and one that resulted from major societal changes like young people spending more time in school before beginning careers and delaying marriage and starting a family until much later than historic norms—also makes comparisons over time difficult. For example, say we want to look at stress associated with work today and in the past. Now that the majority of Americans attend college, most people aren't seriously trying to launch a career until they graduate at around age 23. (Though, of course, not everyone does proceed from high school through college today, with employment and economic ramifications that are discussed in detail in Chapters 8 and 9.)

Should we compare today's typical 23-year-old with a 23-year-old from a few decades ago when attending college was not the norm? That historic person might have started working at age 18 when they finished high school (if they even got that far in school), so by 23 they were already 5 years into their career. Our modern subject theoretically has the advantage of advanced education as they pursue a first post-school job, but that might be offset by the burden of student loans that limit their flexibility in choosing a career path. Our historic subject had no student loans to worry about, but they were far more likely to already have a mortgage and children than today's 23-year-old, who might not take on those traditional adulthood responsibilities until years in the future, if ever. Their lives are so different at the same age; does it make sense to even try to compare them?

In an effort to standardize comparisons, some researchers use measures that have been around for decades, like the Narcissistic Personality Inventory (NPI), which has been in use since the 1960s. By tracking scores on the NPI over time, some researchers (i.e., Twenge, 2006) posit a problematic increase in narcissism in today's emerging adults. However, as critics, including Arnett himself, pointed out, some items on the NPI do not tap into what most would consider true narcissism but instead "seem well within the range of normal personality and may even be considered to reflect desirable traits, such as 'I am assertive' and 'I like to take responsibility for making decisions'" (Arnett, 2013, p. 6).

While continuing use of the NPI does allow for direct comparisons over time, that benefit is offset by the way the measure treats these common and benign traits as pathological, and it fails to consider how their meaning has changed over time. When researchers don't disaggregate these items in their analyses and they fail to recognize social shifts like evolving gender roles that should influence interpretation of results, their conclusions about how modern 18- to 29-year-olds compare with earlier groups should be treated with suspicion. (See Arnett, Trzesniewski, & Donnellan, 2013, and Trzesniewski & Donnellan, 2010, for much more on this issue.)

Compounding the challenges inherent in all efforts to compare age groups across time, there's a secondary methodological concern that characterizes even a lot of the current research on emerging adults, which I mentioned briefly in the Introduction chapter. Rather than reflecting the full range of backgrounds across the entire age group, research participants tend to be heavily skewed toward the population that's conveniently available to the academics conducting the studies: college students. That's limiting enough today when almost 70% of high school graduates continue on to higher education (Bureau of Labor Statistics, 2019), as at the very least it means the research is largely ignoring the 30% of emerging adults who don't attend college. And, since that segment of the population is often at the lower end of the socioeconomic scale, they may experience more stressors in multiple aspects of life, especially during economic downturns when employment options are limited. Failing to include them in the research means we're missing highly relevant perspectives, especially when it comes to topics like life stress and mental health functioning.

Also, since college students are generally in their late teens to early 20s, studies relying on them generally omit the experiences of those in the older half of emerging adulthood who may be considering or undertaking major developmental tasks, like settling into a committed career path and starting a family. This point is why the accepted definition of the entire stage was expanded from Arnett's original conception of ages 18 to 25 to the current range of 18 to 29, though much of the research still skews toward the younger side given that reliance on college samples. To be clear, I'm not suggesting that college students don't have important perspectives on many psychological facets of emerging adulthood, but they only represent one piece of the generational picture, so only studying that segment limits our understanding of many important contemporary issues.

Beyond that, the historic overreliance on student samples also severely impairs our ability to make fair comparisons with earlier studies from, for example, the 1950s when attending college was limited to a privileged few—and those few were mostly male, predominantly White, and largely unburdened by the stress of student loans (National Center for Education Statistics, 1993, 2019). Returning to our example above about the 23-year-old now and then, is it any more valid to compare today's typical recent college graduate, trying to launch a career while stressed out by student debt, in a tight job market where their degree no longer provides much competitive advantage, with their relatively elite college-educated 1950s counterpart? That earlier person's experiences likely were not representative of the entire population of their contemporaries who had fewer resources, less education, and one could imagine, more life stressors, yet those are the voices that are seen as speaking for their generation because they're the ones whose voices were most often captured in the research of the time.

This is the crux of why it's so difficult to draw any solid conclusions about whether the mental health and stress levels of today's emerging adults differ meaningfully from those of earlier groups at the same age. First, the timing of taking on traditional adult responsibilities has changed so dramatically that, arguably, age-matched groups across eras really shouldn't be viewed as going through the same developmental period, so we're back to apples and oranges.

Second, if we only have data from the most privileged portion of an earlier cohort, we can't fully understand what the entire age group faced at that time. As a result, even if we compare today's vastly more diverse college students (while still ignoring the 30% who don't pursue higher education) to earlier groups of college students, we risk underestimating the historic levels of stress and mental health issues that might have been present across the entire 18- to 29-year-old population at the time.

Then if we compare today's data on undeniably high levels of stress to an underestimated historic level, we're likely to end up with a distorted, inaccurate perception of how much more troubled emerging adults are now than people the same ages might have been in the past. As a result of this combination of difficulties, while we can have confidence in our understanding of Generation Disaster's mental health relative to older Millennials, Gen Xers, and Baby Boomers at this moment, that second comparison to earlier groups at the same age or developmental stage is frustratingly inconclusive, and anyone who claims otherwise isn't basing their accusations on sound methodology.

"Kids Today" Versus "OK Boomer"

This leads us to the final major problem that plagues cohort comparisons across time, which can be described as the "kids today" issue. I suspect this phenomenon will be immediately familiar to readers of any age: the tendency, typically without much basis in fact, of older generations to disparage younger ones, especially those just moving into adulthood. This is not a new phenomenon, and you can find plenty of popular media articles, books, and lists of quotations of older adults criticizing the young across history. (As a teacher, I'm partial to Aristotle's dig about fourth century B.C. youths, "They think they know everything, and are always quite sure about it.")

Usually these criticisms focus on the various ways in which the upcoming generation is allegedly weaker, softer, has it easier, or is generally inferior to the ones making the accusations. Each group experiences this derision from their elders, and so far each has survived it. However, the tone of the current criticism seems to have taken a crueler turn than in the past, and it appears to be fueling overt hostility between Generation Disaster and the Baby Boomers who they blame—fairly or not—for many of the problems they've inherited, like climate change and the limited job market. There will be much more on this dynamic throughout future chapters.

I won't get into older adults' psychological motivations for this drive to undermine those who will ultimately replace them (well, beyond that very obvious psychological motivation), but it is important to understand its impact on emerging adults. To explore this, as part of my thousand-person national survey of 18- to 29-year-olds, I asked participants to write in a response to the prompt, "Using one word, describe how others most commonly describe your generation," and then to rate how accurate they thought that description was.

The results are, frankly, depressing to read. The most common descriptions that participants volunteered were lazy ($n = 185$), entitled ($n = 72$), stupid ($n = 29$), selfish ($n = 23$), dumb ($n = 19$), crazy ($n = 14$), lost ($n = 14$), ignorant ($n = 12$), spoiled ($n = 12$), bad ($n = 11$), sensitive ($n = 10$), snowflake ($n = 9$), annoying ($n = 7$), fucked ($n = 7$), careless ($n = 6$), horrible ($n = 6$), doomed ($n = 5$), weak ($n = 5$), and weird ($n = 5$). Other responses included (among others) addicted, apathetic, easily offended, easily misinformed, incompetent, irresponsible, naïve, offended, pathetic, soft, stressed, struggling, useless, whiny, and worthless. (On the bright side, only three people wrote in narcissistic, so perhaps that particular misperception has finally been debunked.) Only about 1 in 10 descriptions was positive, including advanced, amazing, aware, connected, cool, creative, energetic, good, happy, independent, informed, innovative, moral, open minded, passionate, powerful, respectful, responsible, smart, and tech savvy.

As I mentioned in the Introduction, I remember feeling irritated when my hard-working 20-something Generation X peers and I were dismissed as "slackers," which directly parallels the "lazy" label that was most common in this survey. Perhaps that's a perennial complaint of the old about the young. However, I certainly don't remember being judged as crazy, stupid, ignorant, or horrible. Yet this is the message Generation Disaster is receiving about their character and value from older people, echoed regularly in popular and social media.

Even more disturbing, many of the generation's members appear to have accepted that message about their alleged flaws. Looking only at the 736 negative descriptions (after removing the positive entries and the nonjudgmental ones, like "90s" and "technology"), participants were equally likely to say the critical perception about their generation was somewhat or very accurate (40%, $n = 295$) as they were to say it was somewhat or strongly inaccurate (41%, $n = 302$), with the remaining 19% ($n = 139$) being neutral about accuracy.

They were more likely to reject the two most common and most clichéd entries, lazy (66% inaccurate, 20% accurate, 14% neutral) and entitled (74% inaccurate, 18% accurate, 8% neutral), but they were more accepting of many of the most negative labels. For example, 48% thought "stupid" was accurate compared with 45% inaccurate and 7% neutral, and 48% also agreed that "selfish" was accurate compared with 35% inaccurate and 17% neutral. Remember, these are descriptions the participants provided themselves about how others perceive their generation. They were perfectly free to reject the negative labels, yet fewer than half did, suggesting that they've internalized these dismissive and hostile characterizations as true.

I also asked participants to describe their own cohort with the prompt "Using one word, describe how YOU perceive your generation." The descriptions these 18- to 29-year-olds provided about their own generation varied widely, but many were not much more positive than the perceptions they reported others had about them. For example, here are the self-descriptions provided by the 23 participants who said others viewed them as selfish:

- Passive
- Hyperaware
- Passionate
- Technology addicted
- Smart (two entries)
- Stressed
- Hopeful
- Future
- Annoying
- Dimwitted
- Confused
- Self-absorbed
- Unmotivated
- Social
- Overwhelmed
- Different
- Oblivious
- Resourceful

Three in this group also entered "selfish" as their own perception of their generation as well as that expressed by others, demonstrating full agreement with the external message they've received.

The remaining responses to this prompt present a wildly divergent generational self-image across the thousand participants. "Lazy" again led the list as the response of 33 participants. The other descriptions that were entered by five or more people make for a kind of roller coaster of self-assessments: good

($n = 24$), stupid ($n = 24$), innovative ($n = 22$), smart ($n = 18$), hard-working ($n = 17$), entitled ($n = 16$), dumb ($n = 15$), sensitive ($n = 12$), aware ($n = 11$), fun ($n = 11$), technological ($n = 11$), active ($n = 9$), annoying ($n = 9$), change ($n = 9$), lost ($n = 9$), confused ($n = 8$), cool ($n = 8$), determined ($n = 8$), great ($n = 8$), progressive ($n = 8$), creative ($n = 7$), bad ($n = 7$), awesome ($n = 7$), fucked ($n = 7$), future ($n = 7$), hopeful ($n = 7$), sad ($n = 7$), scared ($n = 7$), crazy ($n = 6$), informed ($n = 6$), intelligent ($n = 6$), motivated ($n = 6$), stressed ($n = 6$), amazing ($n = 5$), disadvantaged ($n = 5$), overwhelmed ($n = 5$), passionate ($n = 5$), and struggling ($n = 5$). Less frequent responses included ambitious, angry, anxious, blameless, blind, broke, caring, compassionate, concerned, desperate, different, disillusioned, evolved, exhausted, frustrated, gig economy, hopeless, idealistic, liberal, misunderstood, open-minded, over-extended, persevering, poor, powerful, questioning, resilient, screwed, skeptical, strong, tired, trying, undervalued, and unlucky. And, exceeding the one-word limit, one woman described her generation as "literally just trying to survive."

It's difficult to know how to interpret these data, but between the roughly half of the participants who found others' negative descriptions of their generation to be accurate and the provision of so many negative labels themselves, it appears that many people surveyed have accepted the disparaging external messages about their cohort's value and potential. That sense of self-judgment also surfaced in some survey participants' responses to an open-ended question about their generation's challenges relative to older groups. To be sure, some rejected the negative labels or turned responsibility back to older groups. For example:

We work hard and are held back by previous generations' selfishness and bias.

—Female, born 1990

We are not lazy—we live in a scary and hard time.

—Male, born 2000

Our challenges are often either ignored or dismissed. I think we face similar things as the previous generations but their struggles are looked at through a lens of hard work and perseverance while ours are looked at through the idea that we are lazy and entitled due to technological advancements, thus "having it easier" than past generations. While I think we definitely have more opportunities than previous generations, the path to achieve those opportunities is more difficult and comes with more obstacles.

—Female, born 1990

However, many others endorsed the critical descriptions of their character:

> My generation was told they were special and never told no. A majority of them are selfish and lazy. But those that do work hard cannot get jobs or advance.
>
> —Female, born 1995

> We are more lazy and ignorant than prior generations in general, and therefore less likely to be hired for certain jobs. . . . Generally a group of coddled snowflakes.
>
> —Male, born 1990

> I'm ashamed of how unfeeling and selfish my generation is.
>
> —Female, born 1995

> My generation has been coddled, spoiled, and undisciplined by their parents. They have grown up feeling entitled, and that has led to laziness, and not being able to handle situations that are stressful. The majority of my generation have mental health issues because it's cool to have anxiety, depression, and whatnot, instead of dealing with issues as grown-ass adults.
>
> —Male, born 1998

Let's build on that last comment to recap this chapter so far.

1. Today's emerging adults are indeed demonstrably more anxious, depressed, and addicted than current older groups, though members of Generation X and Baby Boomers also grapple with these problems, if at lower rates. (I also would challenge the description of mental health issues as being perceived as "cool" in any way, though they are clearly far less stigmatized among this group than in previous generations.)
2. Due to limited historical data and changing societal norms, it's difficult to be clear about whether these rates reflect an increase in distress over previous cohorts moving through the same stage or if this is a developmental rite of passage that all groups go through as they move into adulthood.
3. That makes it difficult to either refute or confirm older people's claims about kids today being lazier and more entitled, narcissistic, stupid, and so on than they were in their youth.
4. Regardless of the questionable veracity of those claims, many current emerging adults appear to have internalized the hostile and diminishing messages about their alleged frailty, possibly (though I can't demonstrate this with my correlational data) further fueling their anxiety, depression, and substance abuse.

Above all, there seems to be a major empathy gap between today's emerging adults and the older generation they blame for many of their problems, as summarized bluntly by one female survey participant, born in 1994: "We're misunderstood . . . and Baby Boomers are the absolute worst." We'll return to the political and societal ramifications of this divide in the next chapter.

Still, as problematic as this dynamic is, it's highly unlikely that these harsh judgments by older people would be sufficient on their own to cause the high rates of mental health issues and general hopelessness that many in the younger group experience. Instead, I believe these dismissive evaluations are just another source adding to the generation's cumulative stress, compounding the litany of other challenges this group has faced since childhood that were described in the first section of the book: 9/11, school shootings and lockdown drills, media exposure to (and sometimes personal experience of) disasters, the economic recession, climate change, and so on—with constant reminders of all of these threats via social media creating distorted risk perceptions. How could members of Generation Disaster *not* be stressed and vulnerable to internalizing criticism in this destabilizing environment?

"Pockmarked by Disaster"

Let's examine how all of these factors are impacting Generation Disaster's functioning as emerging adults according to my national survey, beginning with their perceptions of 9/11's lingering effects.

Here are a few quotes about the attacks' direct impact:

> I think [9/11] has influenced everyone who was alive at the time. You don't feel safe and invincible. You know no one is completely safe.
>
> **—Male, born 1990**

> [9/11] has made us be raised in an environment full of fear. Security changed everywhere because of it. It also made us live with adults full of hate, calling every brown person a terrorist.
>
> **—Female, born 1997**

> I think it's hard to say that [9/11] hasn't influenced nearly every American. At the time, I was 9 or so, so I didn't understand the magnitude of the situation, but now I realize I saw one of the greatest American tragedies happen within minutes of it happening. I saw how it affected my family and other adults at the time, and eventually realized how big it was, especially as I grew up.
>
> **—Male, born 1992**

Then there is this eloquent description of the attacks' societal and personal impact, written by a trans man who was born in 1994:

> The terrorist attacks on 9/11 personally affected how I would see the world around me as a child. It's really difficult to describe what it felt like to come home after school and watch news coverage that surrounded 9/11. When I think about how it affected me I think about the news coverage that talked about this sound of bodies falling as people jumped from the upper floors of the Twin Towers. It gave me a sense of mortality as a child that I didn't expect to have at that age, made me keenly aware that sometimes people choose to end their own lives. I wonder sometimes if I hadn't gone through the experience of 9/11 as a child if I would have as many of the anxiety issues that I do now. I don't feel like my parents were prepared to deal with the questions that I had in the wake of the disaster and I don't feel like I was given any support for what I had been through. I know that a lot of generations are pockmarked by disaster and they deal with their own version of this—there's the Apollo disaster, there was the JFK assassination, but this was on such a grander scale. It's terrifying to me—I hate it, I hate thinking about it. I don't know how to explain to people that this thing affected every aspect of my young perception. The 9/11 disaster plunged us into a decade of war, put us through another presidency which was defined by the war, and led us into a new era of propaganda. I think I'm more aware of the safety concerns and the stressors around me because I've dealt with a lot of them in my lifetime. I'm sure that they may have existed in the past but I don't think that we were necessarily as aware of them. There are a lot of things like medical concerns [and] climate change concerns that we just didn't have the full scope of during previous generations and now that they are close to reaching critical mass it's my generation and the generation that follows that's going to have to deal with them.

How does this kind of childhood exposure to catastrophe—even when it was experienced through media and not directly—shape perceptions of the world during emerging adulthood? Of course the impact will be different for each individual depending on variables like their personality characteristics and how well their parents were able to help them process the upsetting information, but here are some group-level findings from my national survey concerning fears about future disasters:

- Of the participants, 29.5% said they were very or extremely concerned that they will be affected by a natural disaster like a tornado, hurricane, or flood; 48.1% were somewhat concerned; and 22.4% were not at all concerned.
- There were 35.6% who said they were very or extremely concerned that they or their community will be affected by a human-caused disaster

(terrorist attack, mass shooting, etc.); 44.6% were somewhat concerned; and 19.8% were not at all concerned.

- There were 45.7% who said they were very or extremely concerned that they or their community will be affected by climate change; 35.3% were somewhat concerned; and 19% were not at all concerned.

So overall only about one in five respondents were not at all concerned about these different threats, suggesting that this is a population with a moderate-to-high level of stress about future disasters.

I also asked "Do you think you're more aware of safety concerns and other stressors around you than members of previous generations were? If yes, why?" Again, I don't have equivalent historical data about earlier group's concerns to compare with these responses, so this finding is limited to Generation Disaster's *perceptions* about relative awareness over time; there's no evidence that there has been an actual change. Overall, 37.3% said they believe they're more aware of safety concerns, and those with a college education were significantly more likely to feel this concern than those whose highest education level was high school.

The majority of the responses to the "why?" follow-up prompt focused on the role of media in increasing awareness—and usually not in a positive way, like these comments:

The media throws it in our face and now we believe that the world is more dangerous.

—Female, born 1992

Yes, because I have a screen in my hand that keeps me constantly aware of all of the worst daily events. It was easier in previous generations to ignore world events.

—Male, born 1991

With access to the Internet, and having been raised throughout this mess, I feel hyperconnected and hypersensitive to what the world holds. I am also more likely to doubt and double check information from any source, regardless of perceived credibility.

—Male, born 1995

That's all consistent with the media impact described in Chapter 4: When events like school shootings and other disasters do occur, the media exposure they receive feeds that availability heuristic and distorts risk assessments.

Those commenters seemed aware of the potential for these distorted perceptions, but other participants attributed their heightened security concerns to beliefs that the world is indeed unsafe:

I'm always on my toes, I can't speak for others.

—Male, born 1993

With the particularly high rates of mass shootings in America, anyone and everyone is a potential target or can be caught in the cross hairs.

—Female, born 1994

I study situations and mentally simulate how to handle them.

—Male, born 1993

I believe I am more aware than previous generations specifically because of the surge in school shootings. We had many drills, practice lockdowns, and actual scares when I was in school.

—Female, born 2000

I always think of everything that can ever happen at any time.

—Male, born 2000

Asked whether they have made changes to their day-to-day life or overall life as a result of their concerns about safety, about one quarter (23.7%) of participants said they had. Write-in answers about those changes ran the gamut from increasing yoga and prayer to cope with stress to buying a gun. Many mentioned therapy and antianxiety medication. Some discussed disaster-specific preparations like creating a go bag or emergency kit, and several said they avoided crowded events that could be terrorist targets.

There was no statistical difference by gender in whether people said they had made life changes in response to safety concerns, but reflecting the reality of being a young female today, more women's than men's write-in responses focused on avoiding interpersonal violence like being the target of a sexual assault. Some specifically addressed the additional danger they perceived as a result of their gender, like this woman, born in 1990:

I'm careful about locking my door immediately in my car or home. I make sure I'm not followed, since as a woman, I'm more of a target. [I] try to do more mindfulness practice to feel better about the things I can't do anything about.

Another woman, born in 1992, took a wide-ranging approach to reducing threat:

> Read books, attended self-defense classes, got anxiety meds, went to therapy, took boxing, avoided situations that felt unsafe (shopping at night, walking home alone at night, parking next to vans at night, etc.).

I then asked participants how strongly they agreed with a series of statements meant to tap into their perceptions about security, justice, and the general fairness of life. (The original scale included five options: strongly agree, agree, neither agree nor disagree, disagree, and strongly disagree. For simplicity, I've combined the two levels of agreement and disagreement.) Here's what they said:

- **Disasters are "acts of God" and there's nothing we can do to prepare for them.**
  22.0% agree; 29.3% neither agree nor disagree; 48.7% disagree
- **Disasters and accidents can happen to anyone.**
  80.6% agree; 15.1% neither agree nor disagree; 4.3% disagree
- **I believe individuals should be responsible for their own safety and preparedness.**
  48.6% agree; 36.7% neither agree nor disagree; 14.7% disagree
- **People should help each other out in times of need.**
  80.8% agree; 14.9% neither agree nor disagree; 4.3% disagree
- **I'm frequently concerned about something bad happening to me or the people I love.**
  58.0% agree; 25.2% neither agree nor disagree; 16.8% disagree
- **I believe the world is generally safe.**
  25.7% agree; 31.2% neither agree nor disagree; 43.1% disagree
- **I believe the world is generally fair.**
  22.5% agree; 29.0% neither agree nor disagree; 48.5% disagree
- **I believe people usually get what they deserve.**
  33.1% agree; 32.8% neither agree nor disagree; 34.1% disagree

I want to be careful about imposing my own values on any interpretation of these findings, though it does warm my heart that fewer than 1 in 20 participants didn't think people should help each other out in times of need. But even if we're not comparing these beliefs to other cohorts, the responses do suggest a fairly low expectation of security among members of Generation Disaster.

Let's focus on the last three items, which can be considered measures of worldview. The final item in particular reflects what's sometimes referred to as "belief in a just world" or the "just world hypothesis." It's the assumption that life is rational and equitable, so if something negative happens to a person, it's likely an appropriate consequence for something they did. This is sometimes considered a delusion, as bad things undeniably do indeed happen to good people on a regular basis—but that's not a comfortable truth to acknowledge, so we often ignore or deny it.

"Just world" beliefs can also be a form of victim blaming. The thought process, conscious or not, is that if someone experienced a disaster or tragedy, they must have done something to bring it on themselves. That may explain why there was somewhat higher agreement with the statement "I believe people usually get what they deserve" than the statements that the world is generally safe or fair, as it's also a defense mechanism: If I don't do anything to deserve punishment, we tell ourselves, nothing bad will happen to me, even if the world isn't particularly safe or fair. And given the remarkably low rates of agreement about safety and fairness, this group appears to be functioning with few protective delusions about the world being a just place.

I also asked participants to report how frequently they experienced a variety of negative emotions, asking "Based on your awareness of safety concerns and/or stressors have you ever felt a feeling of . . . ." Responses for the entire sample were as follows:

- **Uneasiness:**
  8.8% never; 17.0% rarely; 39.8% occasionally; 25.2% often; 9.2% always
- **Fear:**
  7.2% never; 22.7% rarely; 39.1% occasionally; 22.0% often; 9.0% always
- **Vigilance:**
  14.6% never; 26.1% rarely; 36.3% occasionally; 14.3% often; 8.7% always
- **Anger:**
  8.4% never; 22.1% rarely; 40.7% occasionally; 20.7% often; 8.1% always
- **Helplessness:**
  11.3% never; 22.7% rarely; 34.8% occasionally; 22.1% often; 9.1% always
- **Sadness:**
  6.1% never; 15.8% rarely; 40.8% occasionally; 25.3% often; 12.0% always
- **Anxiety:**
  7.1% never; 12.9% rarely; 32.6% occasionally; 28.6% often; 18.8% always

Those strike me as very high levels of all of the different forms of distress, particularly sadness and anxiety. And rates were even more extreme (all statistically significant at the $p < .05$ level or higher) for some groups:

- Women reported significantly worse levels than men for all emotions except for anger, which was about equal, and vigilance, which was statistically lower among women than men.
- Those with only a high school education reported significantly higher frequency of all emotions except for vigilance, which was about equal to those with more education.
- Those with a lower household socioeconomic status had significantly more frequent rates of sadness, anxiety, uneasiness, anger, and helplessness.
- Democrats reported a higher frequency of all negative emotions than other party affiliations, while Republicans had significantly lower rates of sadness, anxiety, uneasiness, fear, and helplessness than other parties.
- Participants who reported having experienced at least one disaster in the past reported significantly higher rates for every single emotion.

All of these correlations (apart from perhaps the political affiliation difference) support established trends: Women tend to express higher rates of mental health distress than men in general, as do groups that can be considered vulnerable because they typically face more life stressors and often have access to fewer resources, including those with lower education or socioeconomic status. So, while these patterns are not surprising, they do remind us that suffering is not distributed equally, just as access to opportunity varies between populations, as we'll see in future chapters. But even for those in the more fortunate or privileged groups, these emerging adults' rates of various negative emotions and general perceptions about the world are troubling.

Snowflakes or Realists?

What does all of this say about Generation Disaster's current functioning, and how should they be judged for their attitudes and struggles?

Tackling the second question first, I'll take this opportunity to respectfully request that my fellow Gen Xers and the esteemed Baby Boomers try to knock off the judging for a while and see if that helps at least mitigate some of the stress this group is under. Remember, in the not too distant future they're going to be paying for our Social Security benefits and running our nursing homes, so it behooves us to start making peace now.

Joking aside (though that was actually a serious request), all of the previously published literature reviewed here, supplemented by my own research, paints a picture of a generation whose members grew up in a destabilized post-9/11 environment, who never got to feel like school was a safe place where they could just focus on learning, whose families took a financial hit during the Great Recession, and who aren't even sure they have a future at all due to climate change and other disasters (now including a global pandemic). Should we really be surprised that they report such high rates of anxiety, depression, and other mental health problems? Or could we reframe those responses not as an indication of generational weakness, but as a realistic response to the messed up world they're inheriting from us? None of us older people can say for sure that we would have coped any better if this had been our environment during childhood and emerging adulthood. Perhaps instead of perpetuating the tired custom of criticizing the rising generation, we can work on understanding the world from their perspective.

And let's not overlook the fact that many emerging adults are flourishing— protesting various forms of social injustice, mobilizing to address climate change, voting at unprecedented levels, starting innovative businesses, and so on. We shouldn't keep minimizing their challenges, but let's also acknowledge their resilience. I'll leave it to a few of them to wrap up this chapter, before moving on to a deeper look at their attitudes toward authorities.

We have the opportunity to make big changes in our society before it is too late. . . . My generation is the catalyst for change.

—Female, born 2000

We are smart. We are strong. We have the most potential. We will only grow.

—Male, born 1995

We are the generation of a new turning. We were raised in a time of crisis (9/11, dot-com bubble, 2008 housing bubble) and we weren't given a fair chance at adult life like previous generations. We have a positive outlook on life even though times might be personally hard for us. We're never taken seriously and that's a sad realization as an adult. . . . I think my generation is capable of great things, the world just needs to give us a chance.

—Female, born 1990

References

American Psychiatric Association. (2019). APA public opinion poll—annual meeting 2019. Downloaded from https://www.psychiatry.org/newsroom/apa-public-opinion-poll-annual-meeting-2019

Arnett, J. J. (2000). Emerging adulthood: A theory of development from the late teens through the twenties. *American Psychologist, 55,* 469–480.

Arnett, J. J. (2013). The evidence for Generation We and against Generation Me. *Emerging Adulthood, 1*(1), 5–10.

Arnett, J. J. (2014). Presidential address: The emergence of emerging adulthood: A personal history. *Emerging Adulthood, 2*(3), 155–162.

Arnett, J. J., Trzesniewski, K. H., & Donnellan, M. B. (2013). The dangers of generational myth-making: Rejoinder to Twenge. *Emerging Adulthood, 1*(1), 5–10.

Bureau of Labor Statistics. (2019). College enrollment and work activity of recent high school and college graduates summary. Downloaded from https://www.bls.gov/news.release/hsgec.nr0.htm

Curtin, S. C., & Hedegaard, H. (2019). Suicide rates for females and males by race and ethnicity: United States, 1999 and 2017. National Center for Health Statistics. Downloaded from https://www.cdc.gov/nchs/data/hestat/suicide/rates_1999_2017.pdf

Hall, G. S. (1907). *Adolescence: Its psychology and its relations to physiology, anthropology, sociology, sex, crime, religion and education.* New York: Appleton.

Heron, M. (2019). Deaths: Leading causes for 2017. *National Vital Statistics Reports, 68*(6). Downloaded from https://www.cdc.gov/nchs/data/nvsr/nvsr68/nvsr68_06-508.pdf

National Center for Education Statistics (NCES). (1993). *120 years of American education: A statistical portrait.* Downloaded from https://nces.ed.gov/pubs93/93442.pdf

National Center for Education Statistics (NCES). (2019). Price of attending an undergraduate institution. Downloaded from https://nces.ed.gov/programs/coe/indicator_coj.asp

Substance Abuse and Mental Health Services Administration (SAMHSA). (2018). *Key substance use and mental health indicators in the United States: Results from the 2017 National Survey on Drug Use and Health* (HHS publication no. SMA 18-5068, NSDUH Series H-53). Rockville, MD: Center for Behavioral Health Statistics and Quality, Substance Abuse and Mental Health Services Administration. Retrieved from https://www. samhsa.gov/data/

Trzesniewski, K. H., & Donnellan, M. B. (2010). Rethinking "Generation Me": A study of cohort effects from 1976–2006. *Perspectives in Psychological Science, 5,* 58–75.

Twenge, J. M. (2006). *Generation Me: Why today's young Americans are more confident, assertive, entitled—and more miserable than ever before.* New York: Free Press.

6

Mistrusting Authorities in an Unstable World

A big part of the challenges of younger generations is having to deal with the greed and mistakes of the previous generations not thinking or caring about the future.

—Female, born 1999

I feel my generation has more challenges created by previous generations as they don't think about how their decisions would impact future generations.

—Male, born 1990

We have no future and no hope. We are the end of history.

—Male, born 1999

Having grown up in a post-9/11, wartime climate when many young people felt lied to or misrepresented by politicians and other authorities, how do members of Generation Disaster now engage with the system? What are the effects of growing up while perceiving that authorities can't be trusted to keep the world safe at the most basic level, let alone be expected to look out for young people's best interests? What are the resulting perceptions of justice, security, and the intentions of those in power? And how have the several most recent presidential elections and ensuing political divisiveness—compounded by concern about authorities' management of the pandemic response—affected the group?

The previous chapter examined societal judgments about Generation Disaster, including how older adults have consistently misinterpreted their heightened stress levels as signs of weakness rather than an arguably rational response to constant duress. Now let's flip the focus and look at how this cohort

Generation Disaster. Karla Vermeulen, Oxford University Press. © Oxford University Press 2021.
DOI: 10.1093/oso/9780190061630.003.0006

views the consequences of their elders' performance as authorities and what they hope to do differently as they move into adulthood and tap into their potential societal and political power. As we'll see, some emerging adults have been motivated to take action, participating in social and political protests, campaigning energetically for their candidates, and in some cases, initiating political careers of their own. Others have disconnected, expressing apathy or outright disgust about the political process. What will this mean for the near future of politics and civic engagement, and for the more extended future of American leadership as this generation eventually takes over—whether or not that's welcomed by their elders?

First, for historic context, it seems relevant to provide some brief background on the national tradition of youth challenging the establishment. We'll stay focused on this tradition in the United States, though many parallel movements have occurred globally, sometimes in step with and sometimes at a different pace than the American version of this societal evolution.

Questioning Authority: A U.S. Tradition

In many ways, this generation's dissatisfaction with those in power is a return to or an increase in intensity over the past, not a new phenomenon. Ever since the first settlers came to North America seeking religious and political freedom, the United States has functioned as a nation where each generation coming into power seeks to change, and hopes to improve, the ways their predecessors ran things. However, let's fully acknowledge that this assumption by each upcoming generation that they know better than their elders reflects individualistic values that emphasize personal desires and accomplishments over those of the community. This attitude differs from people in more collectivist cultures who tend to put more trust in older generations to look out for the shared good of the group. That includes some traditions among the Indigenous Peoples, whose collectivist customs have been marginalized, if not outright steamrolled, by the centuries of newcomers to the United States who intentionally displaced indigenous groups in terms of both geography and power.

Let's also remain mindful that the freedom to seek or exercise political power was historically limited to White men until at least the twentieth century, and discrepancies in opportunities clearly continue today in practice if not by law. American women didn't gain the nationwide right to vote until 1920, though under some circumstances they were able to run for office before then (National Constitution Center, 2016). Enslaved people certainly didn't have that power prior to emancipation at the end of the Civil War. After Black citizens were legally freed, ongoing racial oppression and discrimination continued to limit their access to fundamental rights like quality education and fair employment opportunities. Even when they had equal rights according to the law, entrenched racism largely prevented Black people from running for office or winning positions of authority in proportion to their share of the population. The resulting underrepresentation in politics has perpetuated the group's unequal access to resources and opportunities. (And let's not forget the continuing dominance of White men in the private sector: As of Summer 2020, chief executive officers of the Fortune 500 companies included just three African Americans, all male, and 30 women—or 0.6% and 6%, respectively, of total representation leading these top companies.)

Resistance to systemic racial inequality sparked the first of several major cultural shifts in the United States between the 1950s and 1980s that were largely, though not exclusively, led by young activists. (Note that these time frames refer to peak activity for each movement. None had a distinct starting point, and the fight to attain full equality for each population continues today.) First, during the 1950s and 1960s, participants in the civil rights movement used primarily nonviolent protest methods to advocate for an end to segregation and discrimination against African Americans. While these efforts did succeed in fostering the passage of major equal rights legislation in the mid-1960s, the new laws did not magically erase the lasting effects of decades of discrimination and entrenched racism (Carson, 2019). The complex history of the early civil rights movement is worthy of multiple books, such as Henry Louis Gates Jr.'s *And Still I Rise* (Gates & Burke, 2015) and *The African Americans: Many Rivers to Cross* (Gates & Yacovone, 2016).

Around the early to mid-1960s, that wave of African American–driven resistance, which many non-Blacks supported and participated in, was joined by a broader political and cultural "youth movement" as the population wave of Baby Boomers, born between 1946 and 1964, reached adolescence and early adulthood. Of course not all of them rebelled, but some began to challenge the status quo in highly visible ways. They protested the Vietnam War, openly used drugs and had sex outside of marriage, gathered at folk and rock festivals, and generally rejected many of the more conservative values of their predecessors (Savage, 2015). "Don't trust anyone over 30" became a catchphrase for the generation (*Berkeley Daily Planet*, 2000).

This did not go unnoticed—often with some alarm—by the older portion of the population, but the younger cohort's sheer numbers meant their voices and actions could not just be ignored. *Time* magazine even named the entire generation of men and women aged 25 and under as the collective "Man of the

Year" for 1966, with a prescient description of the Baby Boomers' impending influence:

> In the closing third of the 20th century, that generation looms larger than all the exponential promises of science or technology: It will soon be the majority in charge. In the U.S., citizens of 25 and under in 1966 nearly outnumbered their elders: by 1970, there will be 100 million Americans in that age bracket. . . . If the statistics imply change, the credentials of the younger generation guarantee it. Never have the young been so assertive or so articulate, so well educated or so worldly. Predictably, they are a highly independent breed and—to adult eyes—their independence has made them highly unpredictable. This is not just a new generation, but a new kind of generation. (*Time,* 1967)

Yes, readers, this was a time when the young Baby Boomers were seen as worldly, unpredictable, and a bit threatening to their elders—a twist on the usual "kids today" trope discussed in the previous chapter. I'll leave it to other authors to consider how this early sense of power may have shaped the Boomers' characters in lasting ways, but the sheer demographic force of this population wave has given the group disproportionate influence over U.S. society during each stage of their lives.

The next major cultural shift that occurred around this time, in part as an extension of the youth movement, was the women's liberation, or women's rights, movement that was most visible during the late 1960s and 1970s. Sometimes referred to as the "second wave" of feminism, to contrast it with the suffrage movement's pursuit of the vote and other legal rights in the early twentieth century, this era's women wanted broader parity with men in areas like personal freedom and professional and educational opportunities (Burkett, n.d.). Women also started drawing attention to issues like rape and domestic violence that had previously been denied or concealed as private matters. The political pressure applied by these activists led to many achievements, like legislation preventing discrimination on the basis of sex in employment and higher education, and the movement earned its own *Time* magazine Man of the Year recognition in 1975 when the award went to "American Women." (Yet it still took until 1999 for the magazine to rename the award to "Person of the Year.")

The final major social shift that started to become prominent around this time was the gay rights movement. This is another extremely complex history, with societal treatment of the LGBTQ (lesbian, gay, bisexual, transgender, queer/questioning) community varying widely by time and place, but same-sex relationships in the United States had typically been stigmatized at best and criminalized at worst. Advocacy groups started to form around the mid-twentieth century, but it wasn't until a 1969 police raid on a gay bar, the Stonewall Inn in New York City, triggered a riot that the community started protesting their treatment en masse. Gay rights groups proliferated through the 1970s and 1980s, with some fighting against discrimination and for equal rights and some more focused on combating the spread of HIV/AIDS after it started devastating the community in the 1980s (Levy, n.d.).

Each of these social movements, led largely though certainly not entirely by young people, began to accomplish progress toward equality for the underrepresented or oppressed group. For example, the LGBTQ population in the United States has secured many landmark rights, including the right to same-sex marriage in all states, and when I wrote the first draft of this chapter there was an openly gay candidate running in the Democratic primary for U.S. president. Trans and non-gender-conforming people are increasingly visible and vocal. It's no longer a big deal when actors and musicians come out publicly, and stigma is even decreasing (if more slowly) among professional athletes.

However, despite many gains, there is still more work to be done for each of these groups to achieve full equality. Many LGBTQ young people continue to experience bullying and harassment based on their sexual orientation or gender identity (Gower, Valdez, & Watson, 2019), and not everyone feels comfortable being open about their sexuality. Disparities between men and women still exist in important areas like average income, relative time spent on child care and housework, and political representation, and the rise of the #MeToo movement shows how prevalent sexual harassment and assault remain today. Similarly, for people of color, the struggle for true equality—and simply for humane treatment by police—continues. Activism around this particular issue has been energized in recent years by the #BlackLivesMatter movement, which has surged as outraged people of all backgrounds protested the deaths of numerous Black citizens at the hands of law enforcement officers, gathering to demand change even amid the pandemic.

While the work isn't done, great progress has undeniably been made toward the goal of equality in each of these areas over the past several decades, and that would not have occurred if it weren't for the activism—sometimes at the cost of experiencing violence or arrest or risking family relationships—of previous groups of (mostly) young people who were willing to confront those in power in order to effect change. That tradition continues today, and as we'll see later in the chapter, Generation Disaster's activists are particularly adept at mobilizing technology and social media as powerful tools for protest, giving their voices far broader reach than most earlier advocates were able to achieve with their bullhorns and mimeograph machines. They're building on the earlier foundations and trying to finish the work of those who started each fight decades ago—perhaps without even realizing that those earlier activists were, in fact, often the very same Baby Boomers who they now blame for the state of the world, like the survey participant quoted in the last chapter who described Boomers as "the absolute worst."

Which brings us to one of the confounding patterns in this tradition of youth uprising against authority: Since each new generation historically learns the power of protest through personal experience during adolescence and emerging adulthood, the older ones should be pleased to see the youngest cohort follow in their footsteps to rise up together and mobilize the next needed social movement, right? Not exactly. In fact, the trend across generations has been that once each group is middle aged or older, they become a lot less receptive to the value of the next cohort's youthful passion and determination to change the world. Suddenly the former agents of change are now perceived as the gatekeepers blocking further progress, and that does not sit well with the next lineup of aspiring revolutionaries. One of my students who read an early draft of this chapter captured the contrariness of this phenomenon well:

> Across history in the United States, it had always been the youth who took a stand against authority figures to fight causes they found unjust. For this reason, I found it interesting that older generations seem to feel that Generation Disaster is trying to undermine the hard work they had done in their youth by fighting for causes that are important to them. In actuality, the inclination to fight for change is directly attributable to the example set by older generations as they'd fought for women's rights, racial equality, and LGBTQ issues among other causes. Generation Disaster has learned from their history textbooks that it is essential to stand up and say something when something doesn't sit well. The emerging adults today are merely following in the footsteps of those that came and fought before. So, I think to be met with such disgust from the older generations we are trying to emulate is only producing a dissonant sensation that leads to increases in anxiety in our generation over how to confront the obstacles we currently face.

A similar frustration was expressed a lot more bluntly by two of the youngest participants in my national survey:

> We are more "liberal" and accepting than previous generations and more open to the idea that the way the system does things isn't necessarily the correct one. We want change and we want it now.
>
> —Female, born 2001

We are fighting and trying to change but no one is listening.

—Female, born 2000

So the spirit and energy to protest are there, at least among some contemporary emerging adults, but what exactly are members of Generation Disaster fighting to change?

Today's Generational Conflict

It would be easy to dismiss the tendency of each cohort of emerging adults to criticize older groups as reflecting simple resentment of the increased stability and power that tends to come with age, but I argue that this is the corollary or flip side of the "kids today" phenomenon discussed in the previous chapter: Each established group criticizes the upcoming generation because they perceive the younger ones as unappreciative of what they themselves fought for, and they fear that the young people are trying to change or undermine their accomplishments. In turn, the emerging adults are upset because their elders seem to be clinging to the values or practices of their own youth and standing in the way of their generation, who feel it's now their turn to update the world. This conflict seems to be particularly strong between current emerging adults and Baby Boomers, but is it justified?

Of course, that's a subjective matter that's likely to be perceived differently by those on each side of the generational divide, and when it comes to political issues, it's also likely to be influenced by whether or not one supports the party (typically led by older people) currently in power. However, when it comes to shaping attitudes about other groups, perceptions usually carry more weight than facts. Take this detailed description of her cohort's challenges that was written by a woman who was born in 1991, placing her at the oldest end of Generation Disaster:

I can't remember not being at war. Politicians use vague, ongoing "wars" to further their own agendas and as excuses to ignore major, imminent problems (like climate change and the embarrassing healthcare situation) and to defund programs that matter. . . . The previous generation squandered this nation's wealth, entered into wars we couldn't afford and had no business being involved in, all to support the greed of the uber-wealthy and powerful. What's more is that generation is still alive and hanging on to power, so my generation is ruled by the outdated thinking of people born in the '30s and '40s. They are legislating on issues they do not understand and which do not affect them, so they make choices based on greed, lobbying, and fear-mongering. Company loyalty is a thing of the past, as well. Most of the time, the only way to get a raise is to quit one job and get hired at a higher pay at another job. Entry-level jobs require years of experience and advanced education. But be careful to not have too much education or experience, or you won't be hired out of fear that your qualifications will be a threat to those in charge. Technology has steadily had many impacts on job opportunities, but the biggest one is making job applications available to anyone. Job applicants no longer compete with other applicants from their area. Instead, they compete with people from all over the country. Since my generation can't afford to buy houses or put down roots of any kind, we can and do just up and move across the country if we manage to get work. . . . We'd be better off if the previous generation weren't in power. There really should be an age cap for politicians. My life shouldn't be governed by people who were born before NATO was founded. I'm afraid the damage is done, though. I think Gen Z will be able to do some good, but Gen Y (Millennials) are pretty much browbeaten and worn down. We can't get ahead, and no one will listen to us.

Let's unpack this statement to see how true each critical element is in terms of the role of older groups in creating Generation Disaster's perceived problems. I return to the employment market issues in Chapter 9, as that's clearly a major source of stress for many in this group and it merits detailed exploration.

Commenter's point 1. Politicians funded wars at the cost of addressing problems like climate change and healthcare: This brings us back to the ripple effects of 9/11 on this generation, even if they had no direct connection to the attacks or to the post-9/11 wars in Iraq and Afghanistan. I discussed the human toll of these wars in Chapter 2, so now let's focus on their economic costs. The Watson Institute of International & Public Affairs at Brown University (2019), which tracks all war-related spending, provides a breakdown, including Department of Defense and State Department spending on military operations; interest on the additional funds the government borrowed to support that spending; medical and disability care for veterans of the post-9/11 wars; and Homeland Security spending on terrorism prevention and response. Their total estimate of these costs for the period from 2001 through 2020: $5.4 trillion dollars.

In addition to those past expenditures, the nation also faces the ongoing future cost of caring for the 4.1 million veterans of these wars throughout their lives. Because of improvements in protective equipment and emergency medical treatment, many of these veterans survived serious injuries that would previously have been fatal, including limb amputations and traumatic brain injuries. While their survival is, of course, a very good thing, it also means that their ongoing healthcare needs are more complex and expensive than for most veterans of previous wars. Between the extreme costs for the worst wounded and the obligation to pay for the general healthcare services that all veterans are entitled to, the Watson Institute projects the cost of care for survivors of these wars at more than $1 trillion between 2020 and 2059.

This means that the total economic cost the U.S. government faces of the post-9/11 wars is around $6.4 trillion. For context, that's about 50% more than total 2019 federal expenditures—all of the money the federal government spent on everything—of $4.4 trillion. That enormous expense was clearly a factor in the federal budget flipping from a surplus of $236 billion in 2000 to a deficit of $413 billion in 2004 at the height of both wars, as the government borrowed funds to support war-related expenses. However, those costs did not have nearly as major an impact on the federal budget as the housing and stock market crashes of 2008 that were described in Chapters 2 and 3, causing the deficit to soar to $1.29 trillion in 2010 as the government bailed out major corporations to prevent their total collapse.

That record post-recession deficit was gradually reduced throughout the Obama administration to a low of $442 billion in 2015, but it subsequently spiked again during the Trump administration. Early in 2020, it was projected to hit $1 trillion for the year—and then the global pandemic hit, shutting down businesses and necessitating unexpected emergency expenditures like stimulus payments and vastly increased unemployment benefit expenses to keep the economy going. That resulted in an estimated deficit for 2020 of $3.3 trillion (Congressional Budget Office, 2020). Before the pandemic's economic blow was felt, part of the deficit increase was due to rising costs for Social Security and Medicare as the population wave of Baby Boomers become eligible for these benefits, providing yet more fuel for younger people's resentment of the Boomers, and part of it was due to major tax cuts that benefited corporations and wealthy people, potentially fueling adults of all ages' resentment about the growing wealth gap. (More on that is presented in Chapter 9.)

So, we can't *entirely* blame the nation's fiscal problems on war-related expenses, but they were a significant factor in shifting the federal economy from a pre-9/11 surplus to a post-9/11 deficit. Still, the Obama administration managed to get the Patient Protection and Affordable Care Act (also known as Obamacare), which increased access to health insurance and constrained healthcare costs, passed in 2010 while the federal budget deficit was at its previous peak. This demonstrates that, contrary to the commenter's claim, differences in spending on healthcare and climate change reduction are more a matter of the ruling administration's political values than the direct result of the costs of the wars. However, the commenter is correct that the post-9/11 wars certainly placed a lasting financial burden on the country in addition to their terrible human costs, and that may have prevented the government from spending money on services that might have benefitted emerging adults, like subsidized healthcare or college tuition support.

Commenter's point 2. There "should be an age cap for politicians": That's a matter of opinion which I leave to readers to debate, but it raises an odd disconnection between many emerging adults' stated attitudes toward older politicians and their actual voting behaviors, which contributed to the outcomes of the 2016 and 2020 presidential elections. In 2016, younger Democratic voters, especially those under 30, largely preferred the oldest candidate in the party's primary race. Among primary voters ages 18 to 29, Bernie Sanders (born in 1941, so he was 75 during the run up to the 2016 primary) received 71.6% of their votes, but that wasn't enough to counter the higher popularity of Hillary Clinton (born in 1947, so she was 69 at the time) with the much larger population of older voters. When they handed her the party nomination by a 12-percentage point gap (55% to Sanders' 43%), many formerly engaged young people appeared to lose interest in the race. Fewer than half of all eligible voters in the 18- to 29-year-old group voted in the actual presidential election, with 46.1% turning out. That was slightly above the 2012 election's 45% turnout when Barack Obama was reelected, but way down from the 51.1% in 2008 when he was originally voted into office at age 47 (File, 2017).

Ironically, this kind of apathy-induced decision not to vote appears to have played a role in driving the outcome nationally, demonstrating that choosing inaction is itself a form of action when it comes to politics. Post-election polls found that more Democratic-leaning registered voters than Republican-leaning ones did not participate in the general election, which probably contributed to Clinton's loss in key states—especially as younger Democratic-leaning voters who stayed home were disproportionately Hispanic and Black, groups who presumably would have been more likely to vote for Clinton than Trump (Enten, 2017). And even though younger voters were less enthusiastic about Donald Trump in the Republican primary relative to the alternatives, they did turn out to vote along party lines at the same rate as in the 2012 election, with 37% of 18- to 29-year-olds' votes going to the Republican candidate in both years. In contrast, this age group's support for the Democratic candidate dropped from 60% in 2012 to 55% in 2016, bumping support for third-party candidates up to 8%, mostly at Clinton's expense (Tufts Center for Information & Research on Civic Learning and Engagement, 2016). As a result, Trump captured enough electoral votes to overturn Clinton's majority in the popular vote. While not quite as old as Sanders, he was born in 1946, making him the oldest person ever to be elected U.S. president at that time, at age 70.

And despite the survey participant's comment about age caps for politicians, it's worth noting that the Sanders love remained strong among younger Democrats even as he aged another 4 years, and they expressed little interest in the 2020 primary candidates closer to their own age. (As Trump was essentially unopposed by any other Republican in the 2020 primary, there's no parallel to report on that party's side.) As I started writing this chapter, while there were still some 20-plus contenders for the Democratic presidential candidate, a Quinnipiac poll asked who participants would vote for if the Democratic primary were held that day. Among those aged 18 to 34, Sanders, age 78 at the time, was favored by 52%, followed by 17% for Elizabeth Warren (age 70) and 11% for Joe Biden (age 77). Voters' enthusiasm for the younger candidates who were then in the race was drastically lower: 7% favored Andrew Yang, age 44; 3% picked Tulsi Gabbard, age 38; 2% preferred Pete Buttigieg, age 37; and 1% liked Julian Castro, age 45. As candidate after candidate dropped out due to low support, the Democratic primary race again came down to Sanders versus another old-school politician, Joe Biden, and once again the youth vote for Sanders wasn't enough to outnumber older voters' preference for his opponent.

While younger voters did turn out at much higher rates for the 2020 general election—perhaps having learned a lesson about the cost of opting out in 2016—their choice at that point was between two septuagenarian White men. Much of Biden's victory came down to younger voters, especially those of color, in key swing states, while Trump captured 36% of this age group's votes (Tufts Center for Information & Research on Civic Learning and Engagement, 2020). Biden took office in January 2021 at age 78, making him the oldest president in U.S. history. So while many emerging adults express disdain for Baby Boomers and other older politicians they view as not understanding their concerns, they still played a key role in electing one as president in 2020, despite having had numerous younger options to choose from earlier in the Democratic primary race.

Commenter's point 3. The older generation is holding on to power, "legislating on issues they do not understand and which do not affect them": Which brings us to that woman's final criticism about the groups in power not making way for younger, more diverse voices. It's a point that was echoed by these other national survey respondents:

Hard to get our opinions to make [an] impact due to politicians staying in office for extended amounts of time, i.e., generations before could get elected at younger ages and are still in office, whereas younger people now have a hard time breaking into the system.

—Male, born 1998

Old White men ruining the country for everyone else that isn't old, rich, and White.

—Male, born 1993

Lest you think that's just the view of disgruntled emerging adults reacting to their current lack of power, former President Barack Obama made a similar comment while discussing the need for more diversity among world leaders, especially more female representation, at an event in December 2019: "If you look at the world and look at the problems, it's usually old people, usually old men, not getting out of the way. . . . They cling to power, they are insecure, they have outdated ideas, and the energy and fresh vision and new approaches are squashed" (Chappell, 2019).

This point about older politicians dominating the field is arguably true at the highest levels of U.S. government. Looking at the incoming 117th Congress as of late 2020 (Manning, 2020), the average age of the 436 members of House of Representatives had increased from 49 in 1981 to 57.6 today. The average age of the 100 senators increased from 53 in 1981 to 62.9 today. This means that representatives in Congress are typically 20 years older than the average American (King, n.d.). Looking at those taking seats for the first time as an indicator of new voices ascending into power, the average age of newly elected representatives has actually decreased slightly over the past few years to just under 47.9. However, averages for newly elected senators have increased steadily, from 50.7 in the 114th Congress to 58.1 today. There are some younger people entering the field, though. The youngest current senator was born in 1979 and the oldest in 1933. The youngest representative in the 117th Congress was born in 1989 and the oldest in 1933—a 56-year age spread between newcomers and those holding on to power.

Once elected, the current average length of service is 8.6 years for representatives (equaling 4.3 House terms of 2 years) and 10.1 years for senators (equaling 1.7 Senate terms of 6 years) (Manning, 2020). However, some politicians hold on to their seats for much longer. As of 2020, Congress included 14 members who have served as representatives, senators, or a combination for 36 years or longer. All of them were White, and all but one was male.

Thanks in part to an influx of newly elected female and minority members (almost entirely in the House), the 117th Congress' gender and racial diversity is currently at a record high, but it's still nowhere near representative of national demographics: While 10.5% of current members are African American, which is not too far from the 13.4% share of total population, just 9.4% are Latinx and 24% of all members are female—both about half the national population rates of 18.3% and 50.8%, respectively.

So, yes, our commenters' points about political power being dominated by older people (primarily White male ones) is accurate, at least at the highest levels. However, cracks in that hegemony are starting to appear as younger, more diverse candidates start to enter the political pipeline. Many of these new representatives were motivated to get involved as a direct result of the 2016 presidential election. That event also appears to have sparked political and civic engagement among at least a portion of Generation Disaster, as evidenced by the spike in youth voting and advocacy around the 2020 presidential election (even amid the pandemic), as well as their growing participation in the social movements described above. Regardless of party affiliation, it seems positive that emerging adults are opting in to civic engagement more than in recent years—but let's back up and consider why this aspect of adulthood matters for any citizen of a democracy, and what it encompasses.

Civic Engagement Post-2016

Political activity traditionally includes actions like voting, volunteering for a political campaign, and running for office. Civic engagement can take broader forms of participation in democratic processes, including activities like signing petitions, attending protests, joining community organizations, volunteering, and simply paying attention to politics and civic events. Note that civic *disengagement* is also considered a form of participation as it reflects an individual's choice about how much to become involved: "It rather can be viewed as an expression and a position in itself when dealing with political and civic questions. . . . Disengagement comprises active antipolitical forms such as rejection of or disgust with politics, and passive apolitical forms like disinterest" (Lannegrand-Willems, Chevrier, Perchec, & Carrizales, 2018, p. 732).

Dating back to Aristotle, active civic and political engagement has generally been viewed as an essential element of full development for all citizens in democracies, and more recently it has been recognized as a marker of flourishing in emerging adulthood (e.g., Núñez & Flanagan, 2016; O'Connor et al., 2016). But in certain contexts this participation becomes more complicated than just registering to vote or signing a petition. As Hart and Van Goethem (2017) observed, at times citizens' moral values are at odds with existing political structures. When this occurs, ethical civic engagement may need to take the form of challenging or rejecting the status quo rather than supporting it, even to the extent of using violent protests to overthrow what are perceived as corrupt regimes like apartheid or immoral practices like police violence against unarmed people of color. That type of moral objection to discriminatory laws and practices clearly fueled the social movements of the 1960s through 1980s described above as well as the more recent #BlackLivesMatter and #MeToo movements. And, of course, the determination of what makes a regime corrupt or a practice immoral is in the eyes of the beholder; as we saw in the violent actions of Trump supporters rejecting the 2020 election outcome, one person's armed mob insurrection is another's necessary uprising for justice; one person's grounds for impeachment is another's witch hunt.

As these examples indicate, engagement does not occur in a vacuum, and societal circumstances are likely to inform each individual's choices about participation or disinterest. Returning to our Bronfenbrenner developmental psychology framework, Chryssochoou and Barrett (2017) pointed out that the context surrounding any analysis of civic engagement must be considered at the micro-, meso-, macro-, and chronosystem levels: "Talking about politics is neither ahistorical nor without location. It is important to ask ourselves about the kinds of political issues with which youth are involved at particular moments in time and in particular places. Time, place, and types of engagement are paramount" (p. 292).

Let's start with the time of engagement for today's emerging adults and then work inward to their attitudes and behaviors. To demonstrate why this matters, consider the political climate of recent years, which Generation Disaster experienced as adolescents or emerging adults and which may have shaped their interest in political engagement—or destroyed it. I conducted most of the research for this book during the Trump presidency, throughout a highly volatile period of political conflict and divisiveness—the worst I can recall in my five decades in America, regardless of one's party allegiance (and this was before the pandemic arrived!). A survey I conducted at the time of the inauguration in 2017 found extremely high levels of anxiety among my college student participants about the incoming administration, with many respondents saying they had lost friendships or even severed connections with family members due to their irreconcilable political differences. As I started writing this chapter, we were 3 years into the Trump administration, with months to go before Democrats would settle on one of numerous primary candidates. Those candidates were beginning to publicly undermine each other's qualifications in their bids to win the race, spreading intraparty dissent on top of interparty conflict between Democrats and Republicans. There was almost a year to go before the 2020 presidential election, which promised (and in fact turned out, beyond all expectations) to be highly contentious.

The impending election alone would have made the antagonistic political environment salient for anyone paying attention to the news, but another factor fanned the flames even higher during the exact period while I started writing and which I think is worth revisiting, even if its impact fades somewhat relative to the drama around the 2020 election and subsequent transfer of power. In 2019, the Democrat-led House pursued impeachment proceedings against the president, accusing him of obstructing justice and soliciting foreign interference in the upcoming election. Predictably, as representatives largely voted along party lines, Trump was ultimately acquitted by the Republican-led Senate, but only after weeks of hyperbolic media coverage and polarized testimony by various government officials and attorneys that, polls showed, did little to actually change anyone's mind on either side about his culpability. As one columnist for the generally liberal *New York Times* said about the two parties' wildly conflicting interpretations of the same facts presented in hearings leading up to the charges, it "feels like the truth itself is on trial" (Baker, 2019). As a result, the existing partisan divide grew even wider than before.

Shortly after the acquittal was announced, a progressive *Washington Post* columnist wrote that:

> Trump is unchastened, unchained, and unhinged. I fear for the future of our democracy with such a vindictive bully wielding the awesome powers of the presidency with less and less restraint. He is making an example of all those who have exposed his misconduct in the past to ensure that he can get away with even greater wrongdoing in the future. (Boot, 2020)

A few days later, a columnist for the conservative *Wall Street Journal* editorialized that:

> Voters chose Donald Trump as an antidote to the growing inflammation caused by the (OK, deep breath . . .) prosperity-crushing, speech-inhibiting, nanny state-building, carbon-obsessing, patriarchy-bashing, implicit bias-accusing, tokey-wokey, globalist, swamp-creature governing class—all perfectly embodied by the Democrats' 2016 nominee. . . . The president's success comes from his ability to shrug off critics. My son went to college in the early days of the social justice power grab. He recalls heated discussions in which someone would interrupt him to say, "Sorry, but you don't get a say—you have white privilege." My son would shoot right back: "Yeah, I don't believe in that," and resume his argument. That's what Mr.

Trump does. Rather than cower at the criticism he faces from the mobs, he probably smirks and thinks to himself, "Yeah, I don't believe in that" and tweets away.
(Kessler, 2020)

Even if we assume that these two columnists represent views to the extreme
end of each side of the political spectrum and don't necessarily reflect the
perspectives of more moderate citizens, how are people living in such polarizing times supposed to be able to reach across the partisan divide and simply
listen to each other's perspectives? And without that fundamental ability,
how are emerging adults supposed to imagine that they could actually effect
change through normal political processes, like voting for representatives
who will advance their values? It would be understandable if civic disengagement became the norm for this group out of frustration or disgust with the
way their elders are running the country, but that does not appear to be the
path most are choosing based on behaviors I'll elaborate on below. However,
for many citizens of all ages, their participation is coming at the cost of a lot
of emotional distress, which the contested 2020 election and subsequent sedi-
tion and riots is unlikely to reverse any time soon.

Another *New York Times* columnist (Goldberg, 2019) described the result of
the current political situation as "democracy grief" over what felt to some like
the destruction of core American principles and practices, analogous to the
existential despair many people report feeling about climate change. (Much
more on that is presented in the next chapter.) Goldberg quoted multiple
mental health professionals, who described high rates of politically driven
distress and depression among their patients. This is consistent with the 2019
American Psychiatric Association survey cited in the previous chapter where
respondents rated various stressors, with 52% of those ages 18 to 34, 44% of
38- to 53-year-olds, and 51% of 54- to 72-year-olds reporting being somewhat
or extremely anxious about the impact of politics on daily life. Across all age
groups, just one in five people or fewer reported never feeling anxious about
politics.

I was unable to find parallel studies about the impact of previous political
conflicts like the Watergate hearings on citizens' mental health to see if these
levels of anxiety differ from the past. (However, I did find one 1974 study
by Lupfer and Kenny examining children's and adolescents' attitudes about
President Nixon, which is worth citing purely because of its spectacular title,
"'Watergate Is Just a Bunch of Honky Jive': The Impact of Watergate on Black
and White Youths' View of the Presidency"). Certainly citizens living through
earlier social and political crises had the advantage of doing so before the
24/7 media barrage that now keeps blood pressure–elevating news present in

our awareness at all times, though the trade-off is that they didn't have the ability to use social media as a positive tool for engagement.

Clearly distress about today's political climate is not exclusive to any generation, but I think that older people gain some protective advantage from our previous experiences: We know that the current situation in the United States is not normal. We can remember that things have been different in the past, which allows us to hope they will be different again in the future. That perspective may be less available to younger adults who came of age during the ever-increasingly partisan and hostile post-9/11 era and who then lived through the exponentially more partisan and hostile Trump era (and then through a global pandemic, where even the simple act of wearing a face mask in public became a political statement). Given how entrenched these dynamics have become, there is little promise that life under the Biden administration and whatever comes next will magically soothe the anger and mistrust between parties, allowing us to reunite as citizens with common political goals, though I choose to hope that we'll eventually move toward that status for everyone's sake. The key point here is that, at least in terms of what they've personally experienced, today's state of affairs *is* the norm for Generation Disaster, which appears to be causing many to view politics with disgust as well as anxiety. That effect may be strongest for those who oppose the current administration, whatever that is at a given time, but the divisiveness also affects many young people whose party is in power but who can't approve of how their elders are running the show.

That distaste and mistrust was evident in a national study conducted in March 2019 (so these data were collected before the first impeachment hearings and the spread of the pandemic, and early in the start of the Democratic primary battle) by the Harvard Kennedy School Institute of Politics (IOP) that asked 3,022 18- to 29-year-old Americans about their political opinions, voting trends, and views on public service. Most participants reported high levels of dissatisfaction with politics and politicians from both parties. Some key IOP findings related to views about older generations (with any missing percentages reflecting some participants' refusal to answer a particular question):

Elected officials who are part of the Baby Boomer generation (age 55 to 73) care about people like me.
- Agree: 16%
- Neither agree nor disagree: 40%
- Disagree: 41%

Voters who are part of the Baby Boomer generation care about people like me.

- Agree: 18%
- Neither agree nor disagree: 41%
- Disagree: 39%

Those results essentially quantify the sense that emerged from the qualitative responses to my national survey quoted throughout this chapter that older generations in power don't represent young people's concerns. Additionally, many of the IOP survey responses demonstrated dismayingly little confidence among these emerging adults that civic engagement would have any impact at all:

People like me don't have any say about what the government does.

- Agree: 39%
- Neither agree nor disagree: 32%
- Disagree: 26%

Political involvement rarely has any tangible results.

- Agree: 26%
- Neither agree nor disagree: 43%
- Disagree: 28%

I don't believe my vote will make a real difference.

- Agree: 34%
- Neither agree nor disagree: 29%
- Disagree: 34%

Elected officials seem to be motivated by selfish reasons.

- Agree: 62%
- Neither agree nor disagree: 28%
- Disagree: 7%

All of this led to a generally gloomy assessment of the country's future among the IOP survey respondents. When they were prompted, "All in all, do you think that things in the nation are . . ." 48% selected "off on the wrong track," 30% said they were "not sure what direction the country is headed in," and just 20% said they thought the country was "generally headed in the right direction." Given these dire responses, it wouldn't be surprising if we saw high rates of disengagement from all forms of civic involvement among this generation, many of whom are clearly disgusted with the current state of politicians in the nation. And yet, 18- to 29-year-olds voted at record rates in both the 2018 midterms and the 2020 election. Those actions support the claims made by many participants in my national survey, conducted at around the same time as the IOP study, which at least partially belie my fears that the cohort might reject politics entirely.

To directly measure changes in engagement since the 2016 election, I asked my sample a series of questions about political interest and activity, starting with, "How interested in general are you in politics at this time?" There were no significant differences in interest by political party affiliation, though the 154 respondents with no affiliation were (unsurprisingly) less interested overall: 48% not very or not at all interested, 32% neutral, 19% somewhat or very interested. But reported interest was considerably higher across those affiliated with any party:

- Not at all or not very interested: 22%
- Neutral: 28%
- Somewhat or very interested: 50%

I then asked, "Since the 2016 presidential election have you paid more or less attention to politics?" Among the entire sample, 18.5% said they were paying less attention, 32.5% were about the same, and 49.0% were paying more attention. Members of the two main political parties reported paying significantly more attention, especially Democrats:

- Republicans: 16.5% less, 36.7% same, 46.8% more
- Democrats: 17.4% less, 21.2% same, 61.4% more

Slightly fewer Independents reported being more interested (16.6% less, 43.0% same, 40.4% more). Those with no party affiliation said 24.7% less, 44.2% same, and 31.4% more interested.

Finally, to see whether that interest had translated into action at a point about 18 months before the next presidential election, I asked, "What political activities have you participated in over the past year? Select all that apply." About one third ($n = 326$) reported no participation. The other activities, in order of frequency for the entire thousand-person sample and by major political affiliation, are presented in the list that follows. (For simplicity in reporting these results, I do not list the small number of members of third parties like

Green or Libertarian, so totals listed may slightly exceed the breakdown by affiliation.)

- **Voted in 2018 midterm elections**: 398 total, including 197 Democrats; 76 Republicans; 66 Independents; 31 no affiliation
- **Signed a petition**: 313 total, including 149 Democrats; 43 Republicans; 65 Independents; 33 no affiliation
- **Spread political news through social media**: 188 total, including 103 Democrats; 26 Republicans; 34 Independents; 15 no affiliation
- **Attended protests or rallies**: 94 total, including 50 Democrats; 8 Republicans; 14 Independents; 10 no affiliation
- **Participated in a march or a parade**: 91 total, including 58 Democrats; 10 Republicans; 10 Independents; 9 no affiliation
- **Donated money to an organization or movement**: 64 total, including 32 Democrats; 11 Republicans; 13 Independents; 7 no affiliation
- **Donated money to a political candidate or party**: 59 total, including 33 Democrats; 10 Republicans; 10 Independents; 3 no affiliation
- **Volunteered with or joined an organization or movement**: 50 total, including 19 Democrats; 7 Republicans; 16 Independents; 5 no affiliation
- **Volunteered with a political candidate or party**: 43 total, including 16 Democrats; 6 Republicans; 10 Independents; 4 no affiliation

Some of these activities, like attending protests or marches or volunteering with a movement or candidate, would be familiar to participants in the mid-twentieth century social movements—or even to the women leading the suffrage movement for the right to vote starting in the mid-nineteenth century. Other forms, like spreading political news through social media, are entirely modern. This form of social media–focused participation, sometimes referred to "hashtag activism," is often dismissed by older people who underestimate its power. It's true that this particular action may require less time and physical effort than some of the more traditional forms of civic engagement, but that shouldn't devalue its significance for those participating in it (Chryssochoou & Barrett, 2017).

As many researchers who study factors in civic engagement (e.g., Barrett & Zani, 2015) point out, in order to remain motivated to participate, citizens need to experience both a sense of self-efficacy (i.e., "I am capable of taking this action") and collective efficacy (i.e., "taking this action will actually lead to change"). It seems plausible that the quantified nature of social media and the instant feedback in the form of views, likes, retweets, and the like gives emerging adults a sense of efficacy that's harder to achieve from some of the more traditional forms of activity like attending a rally. It also allows them to reclaim and disseminate the narrative about issues of concern that they feel are not adequately covered by mainstream media sources or by the politicians in power (Koc-Michalska, Lilleker, & Vedel, 2016).

Tech-based activism also offers real potential influence in terms of getting out the vote, sharing information using multiple media formats (text, video, memes, etc.), or forcing authorities to address relevant issues. (For a fascinating account of how in-person and digital activism intersected powerfully, read Bonilla and Rosa's 2015 account of how the Ferguson, MO, protests were organized following the police shooting of an unarmed African American man in the early days of the #BlackLivesMatter movement.) However, social media also can expose users to misleading or outright false information, and the tendency for users to only interact with like-minded people can create a kind of echo chamber effect that fails to reach the precise "others" whose views they'd most want to change. That was certainly an issue during the highly polarized Trump administration and throughout the 2020 election and subsequent civil unrest.

Social media is an important new tool in the political toolbox, but it's far from a perfect medium for aspiring activists, and it's unlikely to wholly supplant more traditional forms of participation—a point that I think was demonstrated by the thousands of people who risked exposure to Covid-19 in order to gather for rallies and protests around various causes in 2020 and 2021, showing the essential power of coming together physically to show a united front that can't quite be replicated using technology. Still, the important point is that forms of civic engagement are evolving, and young people's adoption of these newer tools should be viewed as a smart adaptation, particularly as a way to reach other young people, rather than a lazy rejection of older forms of activism (Chryssochoou & Barrett, 2017).

The (Mostly) Good News

To summarize this chapter's main points, today's emerging adults are continuing a long American tradition of mistrusting and resenting those in positions of power, often because they believe they could do better if they were in charge. That hostility—which, as we saw in Chapter 5, is returned by many older adults in the form of dismissive judgments about Generation Disaster's essential character—seems to be simmering at a more intense level than has been the norm in the past few decades. But at this point in our national experience, it's not only young people who are feeling stress and anxiety about politics and the status quo, but also many middle-aged and older adults who are distressed by the divisive nature of our increasingly partisan system and what that means for the future of the country. As I've written before, it's an anxious time for everyone.

But here's the promising part: According to indicators like my national survey, the Harvard Institute of Politics (2019) survey, and the spike in voting by 18- to 29-year-olds in the 2018 and 2020 elections, the majority of emerging adults are not sitting by passively or intentionally disengaging from civic participation. They may not have complete faith that their votes will matter or their activism will change society, but that's not stopping them from trying. And they're doing so in creative ways that combine classic forms of activism with the new media tools that are their native language, allowing them to accomplish feats like rapidly coordinating simultaneous national protest marches about politics, gun control, and other concerns, with an efficiency that simply wasn't possible during twentieth century social movements. Many are using their energy and talents to support candidates they believe in as campaign volunteers or staff members, and some are even starting to run for office, inspired by role models like New York's Representative Alexandria Ocasio-Cortez, who took office in 2019 at the age of 29, making her the youngest woman ever to serve in the U.S. Congress.

Of course, there's some risk that Generation Disaster's refusal to sit down and let their elders continue to rule the country may backfire if emerging adults fail to achieve their goals in the post-Trump political world, and not surprisingly their efforts to seize what they perceive as their fair share of power seems to be antagonizing some of their elders who don't want to give it up. But to return to the *New York Times* columnist's description of democracy grief: "Left to fester, it can lead to apathy and withdrawal. Channeled properly, it can fuel an uprising" (Goldberg, 2019). I end with a few relatively optimistic quotes from my national survey to counter the pessimistic ones that opened this chapter:

I think we're pretty much driven and trying to stay informed of current events so that we can be more involved in the decision making process of our government and our future.

—Female, born 1990

I believe this generation can have the opportunity to select and/or join political leadership that better represents the will of the American people, young and old.

—Male, born 1996

There's a lot of political change going on as well as more awareness surrounding issues minorities face . . . . We are the future, not the older generations.

—Female, born 2000

We'll have to wait to see how this latest youth movement plays out in the unprecedentedly divisive current political arena, but it's clear that many members of Generation Disaster are anything but apathetic about taking charge of their own futures when it comes to civic engagement. Unfortunately, as we'll see in the next chapter, they face a more difficult road when it comes to building a sense of efficacy about tackling the impact of climate change on their lives.

References

American Psychiatric Association. (2019). APA public opinion poll—annual meeting 2019. https://www.psychiatry.org/newsroom/apa-public-opinion-poll-annual-meeting-2019

Baker, P. (2019, December 9). Lies, damned lies and Washington. *New York Times*. Downloaded from https://www.nytimes.com/2019/12/09/us/politics/lies-damned-lies-and-washington.html

Barrett, M., & Zani, B. (Eds.). (2015). *Political and civic engagement: Multidisciplinary perspectives*. Routledge/Taylor & Francis Group.

Berkeley Daily Planet. (2000). Don't trust anyone over 30, unless it's Jack Weinberg. Downloaded from https://www.berkeleydailyplanet.com/issue/2000-04-06/article/759

Bonilla, Y., & Rosa, J. (2015). #Ferguson: Digital protest, hashtag ethnography, and the racial politics of social media in the United States. *American Ethnologist, 42*(1), 4–17.

Boot, M. (2020). Trump's "Friday night massacre" is just the beginning. I fear what's to come. *Washington Post*. Downloaded from https://www.washingtonpost.com/opinions/2020/02/08/trumps-friday-night-massacre-is-just-beginning-i-fear-whats-come/

Burkett, E. (n.d.). Women's rights movement. *Encyclopedia Britannica*. Downloaded from https://www.britannica.com/event/womens-movement

Carson, C. (2019). American civil rights movement. *Encyclopedia Britannica*. Downloaded from https://www.britannica.com/event/American-civil-rights-movement/Montgomery-bus-boycott-to-the-Voting-Rights-Act

Chappell, B. (2019). Barack Obama says women could solve many of world's problems—which men have caused. National Public Radio. Download from https://www.npr.org/2019/12/16/788549518/obama-links-many-of-world-s-problems-to-old-men-not-getting-out-of-the-way

Chryssochoou, X., & Barrett, M. (2017). Civic and political engagement in youth: Findings and prospects. *Zeitschrift für Psychologie, 2017 Special Issue: Political and Civic Engagement in Youth, 225*(4), 291–301.

Congressional Budget Office. (2020). Monthly budget review for July 2020. Downloaded from https://www.cbo.gov/publication/56020

Enten, H. (2017). Registered voters who stayed home probably cost Clinton the election. FiveThirtyEight. Downloaded from https://fivethirtyeight.com/features/registered-voters-who-stayed-home-probably-cost-clinton-the-election/

File, T. (2017). Voting in America: A look at the 2016 presidential election. U.S. Census Bureau. Downloaded from https://www.census.gov/newsroom/blogs/random-samplings/2017/05/voting_in_america.html

Gates, H. L., Jr., & Burke, K. M. (2015). *And still I rise: Black America since MLK*. Ecco.

Gates, H. L., Jr., & Yacovone, D. (2016). *The African Americans: Many rivers to cross*. Smiley Books.

Goldberg, M. (2019). Democracy grief is real. *New York Times*. Downloaded from https://www.nytimes.com/2019/12/13/opinion/sunday/trump-democracy.html

Gower, A. L., Valdez, C. A. B., & Watson, R. J. (2019). First- and second-hand experiences of enacted stigma among LGBTQ youth. *Journal of School Nursing*. Downloaded from https://doi.org/10.1177/1059840519863094

Hart, D., & van Goethem, A. (2017). The role of civic and political participation in successful early adulthood. In L. M. Padilla-Walker & L. J. Nelson (Eds.), *Flourishing in emerging adulthood: Positive development during the third decade of life* (pp. 139–166). New York: Oxford University Press.

Harvard Kennedy School Institute of Politics. (2019). Spring 2019 poll. Downloaded from https://iop.harvard.edu/youth-poll/spring-2019-poll

Kessler, A. (2020). President Donald J. MacGuffin: His wild persona is a device that baits enemies and clears space for his agenda. *Wall Street Journal*. Downloaded from https://www.wsj.com/articles/president-donald-j-macguffin-11581278117

King, K. (n.d.). The 115th Congress is among the oldest in history. Quorum. Downloaded from https://www.quorum.us/data-driven-insights/the-115th-congress-is-among-the-oldest-in-history/175/

Koc-Michalska, K., Lilleker, D. G., & Vedel, T. (2016). Civic political engagement and social change in the new digital age. *New Media & Society, 18*(9), 1807–1816.

Lannegrand-Willems, L., Chevrier, B., Perchec, C., & Carrizales, A. (2018). How is civic engagement related to personal identity and social identity in late adolescents and emerging adults? A person-oriented approach. *Journal of Youth and Adolescence, 47*(4), 731–748.

Levy, M. (n.d.). Gay rights movement. *Encyclopedia Britannica*. Downloaded from https://www.britannica.com/topic/gay-rights-movement

Lupfer, M., & Kenny, C. (1974). "Watergate is just a bunch of honky jive": The impact of Watergate on Black and White youths' view of the presidency. *Personality and Social Psychology Bulletin, 1*(1), 163–165.

Manning, J. E. (2020). Membership of the 116th Congress: A profile. Congressional Research Service. Downloaded from https://fas.org/sgp/crs/misc/R45583.pdf

National Constitution Center. (2016). The history of women in politics. Downloaded from https://constitutioncenter.org/blog/the-history-of-women-in-politics

Núñez, J., & Flanagan, C. (2016). Political beliefs and civic engagement in emerging adulthood. In A. J. Arnett (Ed.), *The Oxford handbook of emerging adulthood* (pp. 481–496). New York: Oxford University Press.

O'Connor, M., Sanson, A. V., Toumbourou, J. W., Hawkins, M. T., Letcher, P., Williams, P., & Olsson, C. (2016). Positive development and resilience in emerging adulthood. In A. J. Arnett (Ed.), *The Oxford handbook of emerging adulthood* (pp. 601–614). New York: Oxford University Press.

Savage, J. (2015). *1966: The year the decade exploded*. Faber & Faber.

Time Magazine. (1967). How young people changed the world. Downloaded from https://time.com/4607270/1967-january-6-anniversary/

Tufts Center for Information & Research on Civic Learning and Engagement. (2016). Election night 2016: 24 million youth voted, most rejected Trump. Downloaded from https://circle.tufts.edu/latest-research/election-night-2016-24-million-youth-voted-most-rejected-trump

Tufts Center for Information & Research on Civic Learning and Engagement. (2020). Election week 2020: Young people increase turnout, lead Biden to victory. Downloaded from https://circle.tufts.edu/latest-research/election-week-2020

Watson Institute of International & Public Affairs at Brown University. (2019). *Costs of war*. Downloaded from https://watson.brown.edu/costsofwar/files/cow/imce/papers/2019/US%20Budgetary%20Costs%20of%20Wars%20November%202019.pdf

7

Climate Change and Expectations for the Future of the Planet

Climate change is going to kill us.

—Male, born 1999

Next we'll turn to one of the more amorphous stressors for Generation Disaster, climate change. It's difficult to fully understand the emotional impact of this topic because unlike more defined threats like traditional disasters and school lockdowns, there's no distinct before, during, and after. Or to be more accurate, there was a "before" period, but the warning signs were largely missed or ignored by the older generations whose actions, like the unrestricted use of fossil fuels, were actually causing the problem. We're currently living the "during," and it's unclear if there will ever be an "after" when conditions improve rather than continue to worsen. In this regard, climate change has more in common with early uncertainties around the pandemic than most of the other issues we're all forced to deal with, though its effects are likely to be felt long after the time when the pandemic has been contained.

So how do people cope with such an undefined form of peril? The situation really runs counter to the kind of acute threat our nervous systems evolved to confront. With more traditional sources of danger, perceiving a threat activates our autonomic nervous system, which mobilizes all available survival resources. We fight or flee, and then assuming we survive, eventually we calm down again. But that process doesn't work so well with a problem like climate change, where we're perceiving a type of danger that we can't effectively beat into submission or run away from. With no direct action we can really take, our usual defense system doesn't ever get to achieve that final step of returning to a baseline state of calm. It stays braced to respond, even though there's nothing tangible to respond to, at least in the traditional ways the fight-or-flight system is prepared for.

Generation Disaster. Karla Vermeulen, Oxford University Press. © Oxford University Press 2021.
DOI: 10.1093/oso/9780190061630.003.0007

This is problematic because one of the main tenets of disaster mental health is that survivors can't start to recover from a traumatic experience until they feel that the threatening event is over and they're safe again (Hobfoll et al., 2007). That's not possible when it comes to climate change, so the issue causes an unusual kind of ongoing stress and anxiety for many people. It's more akin to living with a chronic health condition, or in a community plagued by ongoing violence, than to coping with a more typical acute disaster experience. And the fact that a portion of the population, including some who hold positions of power, continue to deny climate change's significance adds another layer to the stress of the young people who will be the ones really living with its future effects.

Within the United States, many people remain relatively buffered from the direct effects of extreme weather events, and some emerging adults are understandably more focused on immediate stressors like student loans and employment woes. But even those who don't yet personally experience climate change as a major issue are likely to feel concerned to some degree about its impact on natural disaster frequency and intensity, food and water security, and other existential fears about the future. How do members of Generation Disaster experience these worries, and how can they try to manage them? How do they feel about older generations' responsibility for the current situation and politicians' response to it? Do these concerns shape their own behaviors or expectations for the future? This chapter addresses those complex and still unfolding questions.

Climate Change and Mental Health

It's unclear to me where to locate climate change in Bronfenbrenner's Ecological Systems Model. Whether people acknowledge it or not, it certainly impacts the macrosystem for everyone—globally and across age groups. There are also varying degrees of mesosystem and microsystem effects at more individual levels depending on factors like where a person lives (e.g., in a region that's experiencing intensifying natural disasters like wildfires or floods) and what field one works in (e.g., in agriculture, tourism, or other weather-dependent professions). The chronosystem or time-based level is also highly relevant, as it's a lot harder for young people to ignore the existence of a crisis that will worsen throughout their adulthood than it may be for some people later in life, who can choose to view it as an issue that doesn't really impact them personally.

This point is not lost on the younger group, as you'll see in many of their comments throughout this chapter. It's also reflected in an American Psychiatric Association national survey (2019) that asked whether climate change is already impacting the mental health of Americans. Agreement declined steadily by age, with rates of agreement that it definitely or probably is already affecting mental health starting at 59% for those aged 18 to 34 and 57% for those aged 45 to 54. Agreement dropped off to 43% for those aged 45 to 64, then fell again to 33% for those aged 65 and older. A similar pattern was found in a 2020 American Psychological Association survey. While about two thirds of participants of all ages said they experienced at least a little anxiety or worry about climate change and its effects, the level of concern was much higher among the younger participants. Just under half of them said the stress they felt about the topic actually affected their daily lives.

But precisely *how* is the issue impacting mental health? There is extensive literature on the science of climate change, on its physical health effects, and on psychology-adjacent aspects like the impact of media coverage and scientific communication on perceptions about the topic. There's also some work on the impact of participating in environmental advocacy work for emerging adults, who in many cases are leading the efforts to address the issue given its critical salience for their generation (i.e., Matsuba, Alisat, & Pratt, 2017). However, there's actually little published research specifically on climate change's mental health effects in general and apparently none focusing specifically on mental health impacts among emerging adults. In fact, searching PsycINFO for the combined phrases "climate change or global warming," and "emerging adult" yielded precisely zero results as of the end of 2020, and the main academic journal focusing on the group, *Emerging Adulthood*, had yet to publish an article on climate change at that time.

Yet, it's this generation that will be forced to confront the effects of decades of human actions, especially the use of fossil fuels, that will result in global problems like increases in diseases spread by mosquitos and other vectors; increased respiratory illnesses; heat-related illnesses and deaths; and reduced access to necessities like clean water and air, sufficient food, and safe shelter. There will also be more deaths worldwide due to increasingly intense and frequent natural disasters, like floods and wildfires (World Health Organization, 2018). These physical effects are generally well recognized by most people today—apart from a minority who continue to deny them despite irrefutable evidence, often due to economic or ideological motivations (Lewandowsky, Pilditch, Madsen, Oreskes, & Risbey, 2019). Another group recognizes climate change as real but denies that it's anthropogenic (caused by human activity), which allows them to avoid changing their behavior to address the problem.

However, there's far less understanding of the precise connection between climate change and mental health, especially for a generation for whom climate change is just one of many sources of traumatic stress they've experienced throughout their lives. One reason for the lack of empirical research on this relationship is a kind of disconnect in attribution: Virtually all scientists accept that climate change is increasing the intensity and frequency of many kinds of disasters (World Health Organization, 2018). There's also a solid body of research on extreme mental health reactions to disasters, including post-traumatic stress disorder, depression, anxiety, substance misuse, and suicidal ideation, as well as the more common subclinical levels of postdisaster distress that typically resolve over time (Halpern & Vermeulen, 2017). So, we have credible data demonstrating that climate change causes worse natural disasters (A causes B). We also know that those disasters cause negative mental health reactions (B causes C). However, somehow the psychology literature largely fails to connect the dots between A and C into a clear understanding of *how* climate change influences mental health (Hayes, Blashki, Wiseman, Burke, & Reifels, 2018), even when considering disasters as a mediating factor.

It's certainly not that the impact isn't recognized at all. For example, one study that compared meteorological records with responses to a large-scale community survey of stress, depression, and emotional problems found a correlation between rising average temperatures and slight increases in mental health issues in impacted communities, especially among women and low-income residents (Obradovich, Migliorini, Paulus, & Rahwan, 2018). But those authors acknowledged that their study design did "not uncover the causally mediating factors underlying our results. Exposure to more extreme meteorological conditions may produce physiological stressors that precipitate poor mental health, such extremes may initiate inflammatory processes that worsen mental health, or the effects may run entirely through reductions in health maintenance behaviors, like exercise and sleep" (p. 10956). Like these researchers, no one has fully worked out the *mechanism* for how something as global and broadly defined—yet differently experienced—as climate change translates into individual emotional reactions among emerging adults and others.

There's a related temporal skew to the typical research focus when it comes to all forms of trauma, with an emphasis on the "after" phase that largely ignores the "before." Apart from some discussions about how to build individual and community resilience before disasters happen, the field of disaster mental health tends to focus on reactions post-event rather than considering the kind of chronic hopelessness, anxiety, and fatalism people may experience regarding climate change-related threats even before any specific disaster strikes. The result, wrote Hayes et al., of "the risk of overlooking or minimizing the role of climate change within these hazardous events is that this creates a reactive culture of emergency response that inhibits appropriate and effective adaptation planning and preparation for complex emergencies that a changing climate can create" (2018, p. 3).

In other words, focusing exclusively on survivors' reactions *after* a climate change-related event risks creating a kind of learned helplessness about the issue that may discourage efforts to prepare for, mitigate, or prevent these disasters in the first place. This reactive focus may also inhibit any attempts to address pre-event emotional distress. That's particularly problematic for emerging adults, I believe, because far more of them appear to be suffering from general concern about climate change than will ever actually experience an acute disaster related to it. But because these concerns are so ill-defined and difficult to attribute to a specific source, that general sense of dread remains unaddressed if not unrecognized, and it could contribute to an unhealthily anxious baseline for functioning throughout emerging adulthood.

This is difficult to demonstrate empirically because it's so hard to disentangle the various threats the generation is grappling with, but the impression I've received from my students and research participants over the past decade is of a general sense of underlying instability. It's as if their perceptions of climate change's likely effect on their future means that they're standing on a fundamentally wobbly surface, while trying to balance all of the more acute stressors they're shouldering. As one participant in my national survey put it (the dramatic lack of punctuation is from the original):

> My generation faces many challenges. I feel like back then the main issue was race. But now it is gender equality climate change politics baby boom poverty less career options and violence amongst communities along with violence with government officials.
>
> —Female, born 1994

That's a lot to juggle, and that combination of issues makes it difficult to isolate the specific impact of chronic anxiety about climate change from all of the other acute challenges she and her cohort are facing. Worse, that inability to pinpoint the impact of this particular stressor makes it hard to find effective ways to address the issue and thereby restore some sense of stability to emerging adults' foundational beliefs about their very survival.

Loss of the Past, Fear of the Future

Instead of drawing on psychology to describe mental health reactions to climate change, one environmental philosopher created the word *solastalgia* from the Latin word for comfort and the Greek word for pain (Albrecht et al., 2007). Related to "nostalgia," or a yearning for a happier time in the past, solastalgia describes the existential or mental distress related to loss due to environmental change. That could mean the loss of one's homeland if it becomes uninhabitable due to drought or rising sea levels, or the loss of a traditional way of life, like a heritage of farming or fishing that is no longer sustainable.

That description captures one aspect of climate change's emotional impact, but it's essentially backward-looking, reflecting something that was once treasured and now is lost. This aspect is important to recognize, but it seems more salient for older people who experienced a change for the worse and (at the risk of oversimplifying or being reductive about their very real distress) are pining for "the good old days." That differs, it seems, from the concerns of younger people experiencing stress and dread about the crisis they're likely to go through in the future.

This future orientation is better captured by another term that's growing in popular use, though it has yet to be recognized much in the academic literature: "eco-anxiety." This phenomenon was reflected (though not named as such) in many comments I collected in 2019 when I asked a group of my students, all psychology majors in their last year of college, to write about whether climate change worries them. A few described the issue as troubling but not as urgent as other parts of their lives. For example, "With all of the stress I already have with school and other personal things I do not think of climate change much at all" and, reflecting a troubling sense of helplessness, "Climate change is important, just not as important as other things. . . . I figure at this point whatever is going to happen will happen because the damage we have done is irreversible."

For others the issue was much more salient, in very specific ways:

Climate change is the second largest stressor I have besides debt. It's such an intense problem that has a sort of snowball effect which takes a long time to show any problems, but the problems are starting to show. Some specific concerns I have are the increase of temperatures which will eventually melt the ice caps and raise ocean water levels; this will cause any small islands and parts of countries to become submerged in water. Another problem would be the increase of global temperatures affecting mammals and plants alike; if the temperature is high enough, it will end up killing needed plants in the future. Currently the effects can be seen just looking at a thermometer—climate change can make temperatures extremely hot and cold and we've been experiencing those extremes now. As bad as this current winter has been, it actually snowed less than previous years and snow levels may continue to drop. Climate change is an intense problem and needs to be dealt with now to save future generations and this planet.

—Male student

Yes, climate change is something I worry about. It's a little frightening that the earth's temperature is rising, which is causing more ice to melt, which increases the sea level and is a potential threat to arctic animals' survival. I think we are burning through too much fossil fuel too quickly. I believe we need to implement as much renewable energy as possible—windmills, solar power, and geothermal energy. These types I think are necessary to save the future of our planet. I think my cohort is environmentally conscious but at the same time I don't think we put in enough effort to reduce our waste and reduce energy usage.

—Female student

Several students connected the issue to problematic government policies and lack of leadership (again, this was about 3 years into the Trump administration):

Climate change is something that worries me a lot. I'm honestly scared for the future of this planet and of humanity. It is wildly frustrating to me that this issue is one that is not taken more seriously. The planet we live on is dying and nobody is doing anything about it. Or worse, people are actively denying it. We live in a country with a leader who actively perpetuates the idea that climate change doesn't exist because it is cold out. What the fuck is that? That is legitimately, mind-bogglingly insane to think about. People walk around blissfully ignorant to the fact that the world is actively ending. Something needs to be done NOW.

—Male student

Climate change moderately stresses me out regularly based on initiatives I've taken and groups I'm active in. I'm mostly concerned with our country's lack of leadership and knowledge about climate change because we have pulled out of the Paris Climate Agreement and have not signed U.N. initiatives to reduce pollution and switch to renewable resources. I think my generation is very knowledgeable and aware of how serious it is so hopefully we can get someone better elected into office.

—Female student

One young woman even connected eco-anxiety to her thoughts about having children in the future:

> Climate change does worry me and impact my daily life. I recycle as much as I can, but I have been told that many garbage companies "send it all to the same place anyway" so I don't feel like what I'm doing is ever enough to help. Also, I don't know if I'll ever have children because of climate change. Why would I bring a life into the world just for it to be cut short by the consequences of humanity's actions? Reading reports and articles about major shifts happening by 2040 and the loss of life that is expected scares me to death, honestly. I have had nightmares about it and I try not to read any of the apocalyptic articles because I don't want to stress myself out.
>
> —Female student

It's possible that these commenters—all seniors at a liberal arts college where the administration places a lot of emphasis on sustainability—are more conscious about climate change's effects than the general population. However, there were similar levels of concern displayed in my national thousand-person survey of 18- to 29-year-olds, half of whom had not attended college. Expanding on some findings that I summarized in Chapter 5, when participants were asked, "How concerned are you that your community or you personally will be affected by climate change?" 45.7% said they were very or extremely concerned, 35.3% were somewhat concerned, and just 19% were not at all concerned. Those levels were higher than their responses to the question, "How concerned are you that your community or you personally will be affected by a human-caused disaster (terrorist attack, mass shooting, etc.)?" to which 35.6% said they were very or extremely concerned, 44.6% were somewhat concerned, and 19.8% were not at all concerned. Concern about natural disasters like tornadoes, hurricanes, or floods (which of course can be connected to climate change) was even lower: 29.5% said they were very or extremely concerned, 48.1% were somewhat concerned, and 22.4% were not at all concerned. So, climate change elicited the highest level of worry overall—and it's worth repeating that for all three types of threat, only about one in five respondents expressed no concern at all.

Parallel questions enquired about how prepared participants felt to handle each type of threat. Again, climate change fared the worst across all participants, as just 22% said their community was very or extremely prepared, 40.7% said somewhat prepared, and 37.3% selected not at all prepared. That was very close to perceived preparedness for human-caused disasters: 24.8% selected very or extremely prepared, 38.5% said somewhat prepared, and 36.7% selected not at all prepared. Perceptions were somewhat better for natural disasters: 26.6% said they felt very or extremely prepared,

50.1% said somewhat prepared, and 23.3% selected not at all prepared. Once again, it's notable that only about a quarter of respondents or fewer felt adequately prepared to handle these events.

Interestingly, past disaster experience correlated with both concern and preparedness: Participants who said they had personally experienced at least one disaster of any type (33.9% of the entire sample) were significantly more likely to express a higher level of concerns about climate change and natural and human-caused disasters, and they also reported feeling more prepared for each type, with all correlations significant at the $p < .001$ level. This suggests that past disaster experience may be a valuable motivator for people to focus on preparedness, perhaps as a way to increase perceived self-efficacy and control. On the other hand, as discussed in Chapter 5, those who had experienced at least one disaster also reported significantly higher levels of sadness, anxiety, uneasiness, fear, vigilance, anger, and helplessness, so that increased attention to preparedness comes at a real psychological cost.

Another significant difference correlated with political party affiliation. Among Democrats ($n = 396$), 56.4% were very or extremely concerned about climate change, 34.6% were somewhat concerned, and 9.1% were not at all concerned. That contrasted sharply with Republicans ($n = 188$), among whom 27.6% were very or extremely concerned, 32.4% were somewhat concerned, and 39.9% were not at all concerned. Independent voters ($n = 193$) generally aligned closely to Democrats (47.6% very or extremely concerned, 36.3% somewhat concerned, and 16.1% not at all concerned), and those with no party affiliation ($n = 154$) fell between Independents and Republicans (38.3% very or extremely concerned, 41.6% somewhat concerned, and 20.1% not at all concerned). This is consistent with historic patterns of partisan polarization around the issue across age groups, though the divide is starting to diminish among younger Republicans who tend to be more concerned about climate change than their elders (Funk & Hefferon, 2019).

Looking at related political value positions, Republicans were significantly more likely than Democrats to agree with the statements, "I believe individuals should be responsible for their own safety and preparedness," "I believe the world is generally fair," and "Disasters are 'acts of God' and there's nothing we can do to prepare for them." Democrats were more likely to disagree with the statement, "I believe people usually get what they deserve." There were no significant differences between parties in agreement with the statements, "I'm frequently concerned about something bad happening to me or the people I love," "I believe the world is generally safe," "Disasters and accidents can happen to anyone," and "People should help each other out in times of need."

Apart from disaster experience and political affiliation, there were no significant differences in concern levels about climate change by the other demographic variables, including gender and education level. I also asked participants to rank what they feel is the biggest single concern facing us today. Climate change was rated as the number one concern by 32% of respondents, placing it far ahead of the other options: poverty (16.7%), healthcare (16%), racial inequality (14.5%), global relations (10.6%), gender inequality (5%), and a write-in "other" option (5.1%). Only 2.6% of respondents ranked climate change as their least important issue.

Many national survey participants also mentioned climate change within their write-in responses to open-ended questions about challenges and opportunities their generation faces, including the dire comment that opened this chapter. Other examples:

> Climate change used to be something we had time to fix and wouldn't be a real problem until next century. But now we know the effects of climate change are happening now and will get worse in the coming decades.
>
> **—Male, born 1992**

> Climate change is still refuted by the older generation because it won't ever affect them personally but rather their kids and their kids' futures. . . . We are much more open to saving our earth.
>
> **—Female, born 1997**

> My generation's problems stem from a root planted in the distant past, except other generations have had the benefit of mass ignorance and apathy. My generation does not get that opportunity. We have been dealt a bad hand and forced to bet. My generation has to be the one to save Earth and that's our biggest problem.
>
> **—Female, born 2001**

As these qualitative and quantitative survey results demonstrate, worries about climate change are common among emerging adults—not just those on college campuses, and not just those who have directly experienced its effects in the form of a disaster. And let's be clear: These are rational, valid concerns about the future of life on the planet, not overreactions or "global warming hysteria" (Verplanken & Roy, 2013), as some older adults have claimed.

Coping With Eco-Anxiety

So how are members of Generation Disaster supposed to cope with a problem that feels enormous and literally existential, and that they justly feel they inherited (among many other problems) without consent due to previous generations' actions? As one survey participant put it:

> It feels as though we're being stuck with a bill for a party that we didn't attend. We are going to have to be responsible for mitigating climate change, enacting health care reform, reducing income inequality, etc., while older generations don't seem to care.
>
> —Male, born 1992

I wish I could offer effective solutions, but this is a topic that both popular media and mental health professionals are currently grappling with. Plenty of magazines and websites publish service articles with chipper titles like, "Stressed About Climate Change? Eight Tips for Managing Eco-anxiety" (Sarchet, 2019). A lot of the self-help advice takes a problem-focused approach that suggests tangible actions people can take to address climate change's effects. For example, one magazine article (Chen, 2018) suggested five actions to help readers feel less hopeless about the issue: getting involved in an aspect of activism they really care about, investing money responsibly in eco-friendly options, exercising consumer power by purchasing sustainable products, voting for political candidates with credible climate plans, and remaining conscious of the environmental impact of all decisions.

On the professional side, the American Psychological Association's guidance on addressing the mental health aspects of climate change emphasizes building individual resilience by fostering people's self-efficacy and optimism, cultivating active coping and self-regulation, finding a source of personal meaning, boosting personal preparedness, building social connections, and maintaining connections to one's place and culture (Clayton, Manning, Krygsman, & Speiser, 2017). That's all very consistent with the elements of Psychological First Aid, a common disaster mental health response intervention that focuses on restoring people's sense of agency and connectedness so they can return to a sense of normalcy after surviving a distressing event (Halpern & Vermeulen, 2017).

In this case, the American Psychological Association (Clayton et al., 2017) emphasized building those strengths *before* a disaster occurs as a kind of buffer against the more general anxiety caused by concerns about climate change. That's certainly a worthy goal, and the recommended resilience-building effects are likely to generalize to stressors beyond climate change, so these strategies are worth pursuing. However, this strength-based approach doesn't seem to address the more existential or uncontrollable-feeling aspects of the issue. It can be hard for people to even recognize and name these nebulous emotions, let alone know how to handle them.

In one of the few studies to explore this problem among young people, Ojala (2013) looked at Swedish youth from middle childhood through young adulthood, focusing on participants' use of different coping strategies for different types of stressors. These strategies included problem-focused coping, which tries to directly address the root issue in order to reduce negative emotions about it; emotion-focused coping, which tries to regulate or reduce negative emotions without changing the cause of the problem; and meaning-focused coping. This third type, Ojala wrote, is "especially important when the problem cannot be solved at once, or at all, but still demands active involvement. . . . For instance, it can involve finding meaning in a difficult situation, drawing on values and beliefs, and using strategies whereby one acknowledges the threat but re-appraises it in a more positive manner and thereby makes it more manageable" (p. 540).

The young people in Ojala's (2013) study drew on these different strategies depending on which aspect of climate change they were concerned about at a given time. Their problem-focused strategies included steps they were able to take to mitigate the issue directly. That included individual actions like driving less or using more environmentally friendly products, as well as collective actions like encouraging others to make similar changes. At other times, emotion-focused strategies were more helpful to the participants. This included coping methods like deemphasizing the seriousness of the issue to reduce worry, distancing or distracting themselves from the problem, avoiding media exposure, and seeking security through social support. While none of these emotion-focused approaches actually addressed the issue like the problem-focused ones, they did help participants feel less worried, at least temporarily. Finally, the meaning-focused coping strategies included things like positive reappraisal (e.g., concentrating on how much acknowledgment of climate change has grown recently, with the hope that will lead to more action), choosing an optimistic stance, and trusting in technology and science to address the problem.

The main lesson to take from this study is not so much the specific approaches the young people used to manage their eco-anxiety, but the importance of practicing a flexible coping style so people don't become frustrated when any single strategy isn't sufficient. It's somewhat analogous to the classic Serenity Prayer:

> Grant me the serenity to accept the things I cannot change,
> Courage to change the things I can,
> And wisdom to know the difference.

In other words, building a sense of self-efficacy and encouraging problem-focused approaches that actually tackle climate change head on is positive in general for young people, which is probably why they've rallied so strongly behind teen activist Greta Thunberg. That's the "courage to change the things I can" part. However, it's also essential to recognize the limits of what anyone can accomplish directly, and where those limits turn into the "things I cannot change." When someone hits that point, it's important to be able to shift to a strategy that reduces anxiety and despair, even if that sometimes could be perceived as avoidance of the issue, like the student I quoted above who said, "I try not to read any of the apocalyptic articles because I don't want to stress myself out."

Of course, limiting exposure to sensationalistic media or taking the occasional break from thinking about the issue isn't at all the same as denying or ignoring it. No one in this generation has the luxury of pretending climate change won't impact their future, and apart from an ever-shrinking minority of deniers, they know it. Unlike some of the more acute threats discussed in previous chapters, this is a chronic stressor that increasingly affects everyone regardless of gender, race/ethnicity, politics, education level, and so on. Wealthier people may have some ability to shield themselves from climate change's effects, but no one can fully buy their way out of this problem that was created by older generations and left to this group to fix and live with.

It's no wonder many members of Generation Disaster are angry as well as anxious about this issue, and that concern appears likely to color their lives as they move further into adulthood. It is hoped it will also motivate them to actually enact changes to tackle the problem more effectively than members of Generation X and the Baby Boomers have managed, including electing officials who will enact policies that address the issue at the collective level. That goal appeared to play a role in Joe Biden's success in the 2020 election, where one survey found that 78% of young voters said they were somewhat or very concerned about climate change, and 75% somewhat or strongly favored green energy policies (Tufts Center for Information & Research on Civic Learning and Engagement, 2020).

Globally, emerging adults are also entering the field of "climate entrepreneurship," developing innovative technologies to directly tackle various aspects of the problem. This is an explicit goal of the Paris Agreement, which the United Nations says should be cultivated by governments and tech incubators (United Nations Framework Convention on Climate Change, 2018). These young entrepreneurs are harnessing creative thinking and inventive applications of technology to create products and services that not only don't contribute to climate change but attempt to actually reverse its effects—sometimes while making significant profits along the way. No less a proponent of capitalism than *Forbes Magazine* has described "climate change adaptation [as] the greatest entrepreneurial challenge of our time" (Foote, 2018)—a smart strategy to pursue because, not to be too cynical, perhaps tapping into investors' interest in making money will prove to be the most effective way to get older adults to engage in a battle where appeals to simple concern for the future have often fallen short.

I usually like to end each chapter with some cheerful quotes from emerging adults about how their generation is up to the challenge of improving the world, but that proved difficult to do for this topic given how dire the comments about climate change universally were. This was about the most optimistic statement I could find among the thousand survey submissions:

I think the world we will inherit will be rough but we will be able to pull it together.

—**Male, born 2001**

Let's hope that he's correct.

References

Albrecht, G., Sartore, G. M., Connor, L., Higginbotham, N., Freeman, S., Kelly, B., . . . Pollard, G. (2007). Solastalgia: The distress caused by environmental change. *Australian Psychiatry*, *15*(Supplement 1), S95–S98.

American Psychiatric Association. (2019). APA public opinion poll—annual meeting 2019. Downloaded from https://www.psychiatry.org/newsroom/apa-public-opinion-poll-annual-meeting-2019

American Psychological Association. (2020). Majority of US adults believe climate change is most important issue today. Downloaded from https://www.apa.org/news/press/releases/2020/02/climate-change

Chen, R. (2018). Feeling hopeless about climate change? Here are 5 things you can do to help now. *Chatelaine*. Downloaded from https://www.chatelaine.com/living/what-can-i-do-about-climate-change

Clayton, S., Manning, C. M., Krygsman, K., & Speiser, M. (2017). *Mental health and our changing climate: Impacts, implications, and guidance*. Washington, D.C.: American Psychological Association and ecoAmerica. Downloaded from https://www.apa.org/news/press/releases/2017/03/mental-health-climate.pdf

Foote, W. (2018). Climate change adaptation is the greatest entrepreneurial challenge of our time. *Forbes*. Downloaded from https://www.forbes.com/sites/willyfoote/2018/12/10/climate-change-adaptation-is-the-greatest-entrepreneurial-challenge-of-our-time/?sh=65c87e903fff

Funk, C., & Hefferon, M. (2019). Millennial and Gen Z Republicans stand out from their elders on climate and energy issues. Pew Research Center. Downloaded from https://www.pewresearch.org/fact-tank/2019/11/25/younger-republicans-differ-with-older-party-members-on-climate-change-and-energy-issues/

Halpern, J., & Vermeulen, K. (2017). *Disaster mental health interventions: Core principles and practices*. Routledge.

Hayes, K., Blashki, G., Wiseman, J., Burke, S., & Reifels, L. (2018). Climate change and mental health: Risks, impacts and priority actions. *International Journal of Mental Health Systems, 12, 28*.

Hobfoll, S. E., Watson, P., Bell, C. C., Bryant, R. A., Brymer, M. J., Friedman, M. J., . . .Ursano, R. J. (2007). Five essential elements of immediate and mid-term mass trauma intervention: Empirical evidence. *Psychiatry: Interpersonal and Biological Processes, 70*, 283–315.

Lewandowsky, S., Pilditch, T. D., Madsen, J. K., Oreskes, N., & Risbey, J. S. (2019). Influence and seepage: An evidence-resistant minority can affect public opinion and scientific belief formation. *Cognition, 188*, 124–139.

Matsuba, M. K., Alisat, S., & Pratt, M. W. (2017). Environmental activism in emerging adulthood. In L. M. Padilla-Walker and L. J. Nelson (Eds.), *Flourishing in emerging adulthood: Positive development during the third decade of life*. Oxford University Press.

Obradovich, N., Migliorini, R., Paulus, M. P., & Rahwan, I. (2018). Empirical evidence of mental health risks posed by climate change. *Proceedings of the National Academy of Sciences of the United States of America, 115*(43), 10953–10958.

Ojala, M. (2013). Regulating worry, promoting hope: How do children, adolescents, and young adults cope with climate change? *International Journal of Environmental and Science Education, 8*(1), 537–561.

Sarchet, P. (2019) Stressed about climate change? Eight tips for managing eco-anxiety. *New Scientist*. Downloaded from https://www.newscientist.com/article/2220561-stressed-about-climate-change-eight-tips-for-managing-eco-anxiety/#ixzz66K5ZLhDx

Tufts Center for Information & Research on Civic Learning and Engagement. (2020). Election week 2020: Young people increase turnout, lead Biden to victory. Downloaded from https://circle.tufts.edu/latest-research/election-week-2020

United Nations Framework Convention on Climate Change. (2018). *TEC Brief #12: Energizing entrepreneurs to tackle climate change*. Bonn: UNFCCC Secretariat.

Verplanken, B., & Roy, D. (2013). "My worries are rational, climate change is not": Habitual ecological worrying is an adaptive response. *PLoS ONE, 8*(9), ArtID: e74708.

World Health Organization. (2018). Climate change and health. Downloaded from https://www.who.int/news-room/fact-sheets/detail/climate-change-and-health

8

Questioning College

Necessary, Expensive, and No Guarantee of Success

> We can't afford to get a good job unless we go to college. To go to col-
> lege costs money. We don't have that money so we work minimum
> wage to get it. We can't afford housing and basic life necessities on
> minimum wage. If you manage to be lucky and have a rich relative to
> get you through college, you still can't find a job most of the time and
> end up working minimum wage for "experience" in the field. Some
> jobs, like teachers, won't even get paid much over minimum wage
> and yet they still need a college degree to be qualified. We're now all
> drowning in student debt, for the rest of our lives.
>
> **—Female, born 1995, high school diploma**

This chapter shifts slightly away from more traditional disasters' impact on development to consider another experience that is central to emerging adulthood today, whether or not one participates in it: college, and all of the stressors (economic and otherwise) that surround decisions about pursuing and paying for higher education. While attending college is now the norm for American young adults, many I've surveyed, like the woman quoted at the start of the chapter, expressed perceptions that higher education is essential yet inadequate for launching any kind of career. Many people who do attend college now graduate with crippling student loans that drastically limit their career options, yet they believe that without a degree they have no chance of finding decent work. Others don't pursue a degree, which has a different set of implications for the path the rest of their lives may take. It's a decision with far greater consequences than it held for previous generations when many decent jobs were available to those without a college education, and it's yet another source of intense stress for many members of Generation Disaster.

Generation Disaster. Karla Vermeulen, Oxford University Press. © Oxford University Press 2021.
DOI: 10.1093/oso/9780190061630.003.0008

What is it like for today's college students to invest significant time and effort in pursuing a degree they fear will not lead to a living wage, let alone a satisfying career? And what is the transition into adulthood like for those who don't follow the now typical path through college, by either choice or necessity? This chapter, the last in the "Generation Disaster in Emerging Adulthood" section, examines the effects of cultural forces and personal stressors, especially the economy and the impact of taking on student loans, on emerging adults' perceptions of the costs and benefits of attending college.

Dropping Out of High School

First let's examine those emerging adults who don't complete high school, let alone college. The National Center for Education Statistics (NCES), the federal clearinghouse for data related to education, defines high school dropout rates as "the percentage of 16- to 24-year-olds who are not enrolled in school and have not earned a high school credential (either a diploma or an equivalency credential such as a GED certificate)" (NCES, 2019b). The good news is that dropout rates have been declining in recent years for all races (Bureau of Labor Statistics [BLS], 2019). The overall national rate of students dropping out in 2017 was 5.4%—significantly down from 9.1% in 2006, but still comprising some 2.1 million people between ages 16 and 24 who left high school without a diploma.

There are numerous demographic disparities within that group. As of 2017, dropout rates remained higher among Blacks (6.5%) and Hispanics (8.2%) than Whites (4.3%) (NCES, 2019b). The 2017 rates also differed by gender, at 6.4% for males versus 4.4% for females overall. These gender gaps were especially large for Blacks (8.0% for males versus 4.9% for females) and Hispanics (10.0% for males versus 6.4% for females). Interestingly, patterns differed by race/ethnicity for foreign-born and U.S.-born youth, with dropout rates slightly higher for U.S.-born Whites (4.3% vs. 3.5% for foreign born) and Blacks (6.6% vs. 5.1% for foreign born). In contrast, 15.2% of foreign-born Hispanic youth dropped out, compared with 6.3% of U.S.-born Hispanics, perhaps because the foreign-born students were less likely to speak English as their first language, creating an academic challenge. Most disturbingly, dropout rates for all races/ethnicities were vastly higher for youth living in institutional settings, including group quarters, nursing facilities, and adult and juvenile correctional facilities. Overall, the institutionalized youth dropout rate in 2017 was 32.4%—nearly a third of this population—compared with 5.1% of noninstitutionalized peers (NCES, 2019b).

Unsurprisingly, the odds of flourishing in multiple realms of life are stacked against high school dropouts. Apart from the intrinsic disadvantage that comes from not completing what U.S. society has judged to be the minimum standard for an acceptable education, dropping out of high school correlates with many other problems in emerging adulthood and beyond. One nationally representative sample of more than 19,000 emerging adults 18 to 25 years old (Maynard, Salas-Wright, & Vaughn, 2015) examined substance use, mental health, and criminal behavior among dropouts and high school graduates. The dropouts, who were about 10% of the total sample, were significantly less likely to report being employed full time or part-time than the high school graduates; less likely to have family income over $20,000 per year; and more likely to receive food stamps or other forms of government financial aid. After controlling for gender, age, race/ethnicity, and other demographic variables, the authors found that the high school dropouts were significantly more likely to report daily cigarette use, but less likely to report binge drinking than the graduates, perhaps because many of the high school graduates were currently in college, a setting that tends to encourage heavy alcohol use. There were no differences between groups in reporting psychiatric distress or seeking therapy, but the dropouts were twice as likely to report a recent suicide attempt. They were also two to three times more likely to report recent arrests for larceny, assault, or drug possession/sale than the high school graduates (Maynard et al., 2015).

Numerous other studies and government statistics painted a similar picture about the myriad challenges high school dropouts face throughout their lives, starting with largely dismal employment prospects. For example, the BLS (2019a) tracks labor force participation rates, defined as people who are either working or actively seeking work. In October 2018, these rates for people ages 16 to 24 who were not currently enrolled in school were 92.1% for men and 92.6% percent for women with a bachelor's degree or higher, 74% for recent high school graduates who were not enrolled in college, and just 47.2% for recent dropouts. That means that more than half of this group were not attending school, working, or looking for work during the early years of emerging adulthood—hardly a situation likely to launch a successful career. When they are working, it's generally in low-wage jobs with minimal stability and little opportunity for advancement. (More on this is discussed in the next section of this chapter.)

In addition to dropouts' individual suffering, there's also a financial cost to society as they're likely to pay less into the system in the form of taxes than those with higher levels of education, and they're more likely to receive public assistance funding. It seems obvious that not completing high school places dropouts at a grave disadvantage, setting them on a path into emerging adulthood with little potential (with some exceptions) for stability, let alone upward mobility. Effects can also be multigenerational as teen pregnancy is a significant contributor to dropout rates for girls, followed by the risk of unstable marriages or the challenges of single parenthood. This is often associated with poor parenting behaviors, and then their children in turn are at higher risk for dropping out, teen pregnancy, incarceration, and other difficulties as they grow up—all perpetuating a cycle of maladjustment (Centers for Disease Control and Prevention, 2017).

In interpreting these findings, we need to remember that we can see clear correlations between dropping out and subsequent negative consequences, but the direction of causation is not always evident, and the same holds true for the motivation for leaving school. In other words, did someone drop out because they were unable to manage academic work while living in an institutional setting or in deep poverty or homelessness, which made it too difficult to stay in high school, setting them on a challenging trajectory into early adulthood even before they left school? Or did they get into difficult life circumstances as emerging adults because they dropped out and then couldn't find a decent job? While the patterns are different for every individual, what they share is a set of consequences that make the decision to drop out (even if there was no real alternative at the time) very difficult to reverse.

The Devaluation of the High School Diploma

> Living costs went up including education costs and costs of housing. A person is no longer able to work minimum wage and live a minimal life (pay a mortgage and all of their bills). But to get out of minimum wage you must pay to go to school then pay that debt and you're still stuck.
>
> **—Female, born 1991, high school diploma**

What about those who do complete high school, which until quite recently was the highest level of education the majority of Americans achieved? In fact, even completing high school didn't become the norm until 1966 for women and 1967 for men, the years when the median number of school years completed reached 12 for each sex among the overall population—and that median for Blacks and other races wasn't reached until 1978 for both women and men (NCES, 1993). In 1940 less than half of the U.S. population acquired a high school diploma, and now more than 90% do (United States Census Bureau, 2017). Partially making up for a historic imbalance, graduation rates for Black and Hispanic students have recently grown even more quickly than for White students, though a gap remained as of 2017, when 94% of Whites completed high school compared with 87% of Blacks and 71% of Hispanics (United States Census Bureau, 2017).

From a societal perspective, it's difficult to view these growing rates of high school completion as anything but positive: Who could argue that having an adequately educated adult population is not good for a nation? However, from a market perspective it means that the supply of people with a high school diploma has increased tremendously, especially as the growing rate of graduation accompanied a growing population, so there are now some 194 million U.S. residents with a high school diploma or higher (United States Census Bureau, 2017). Exacerbating the imbalance between supply and demand, this growth in the number of people with at least this level of education has been offset by a decrease in decently paying employment for workers whose formal education ended after high school.

Note that I phrased that as a "decrease in *decently paying* employment," not a decrease in jobs. Jobs do exist for those without higher education, but their nature has changed substantially in recent years—and not for the better, from the perspective of many employees. The U.S. BLS categorizes employment in occupations by needed education level, and they reported that 27.7% of jobs as of 2016 required no formal educational credential (meaning not even a high school diploma), and 35.8% required a high school diploma as a typical entry-level requirement. Eleven percent required an associate's degree or some college, 21.3% required a bachelor's degree, and 4.2% required a master's, doctoral, or professional degree.

That means that 63.5% of U.S. jobs, nearly two thirds, should be open to people with no more than a high school diploma—good news for that group, right? Not when you consider the nature of those jobs and, more broadly, how the nature of low-wage work has changed over time. BLS lists these fields, among others, as open to people without a high school diploma: taxi drivers, bartenders, parking lot attendants, hotel cleaners, slaughterers and meat packers, wellhead pumpers, oil and gas roustabouts, miners, and personal care aides. In 2013, the median annual wage for workers in this category was $20,350, which was about 15% below that year's federal poverty level for a family of four.

Fields open to those who completed high school or the equivalent include categories like construction and maintenance, healthcare and personal care, office and administrative support, production, sales and transportation, police and security guards, farmers and ranchers, and food preparers and servers. This group's median annual wage in 2017 was $36,100—above the federal poverty line, but still classified as low-income. And, importantly, those BLS income statistics are based on *full-time employment*, which is no longer a reliable option for many people as more employers shift to "contingent work," which frequently keeps people working just below a full-time level that would qualify them for benefits and opportunities to advance. I return to this trend in detail in the next chapter on economic expectations as it's transforming the world of work for many emerging adults at the start of their careers. Its effects are not limited to those without a higher education, though it does impact them the most.

The Inflation of Higher Education

> Back in the day you could go to school, get your Bachelor's degree, and it would be worth it—you can get a good job. Now a Bachelor's degree is not much better than a high school diploma.
>
> —Female, born 1990, bachelor's degree

> The biggest challenge, from what I have seen, isn't with the actual number of jobs, but with academic inflation and debt. More and more jobs require college degrees, so more people pursue them. Now a B.A. is worth much less than it was years ago, yet college debt is much higher than in years past, which limits opportunities.
>
> —Female, born 1995, pursuing bachelor's degree

As completing high school became the norm for most Americans, more of those graduates started continuing on to college, to the point where that is now the typical path for the majority of emerging adults. Given the statistics presented above, that's a logical decision even if it's exclusively viewed through the lens of employment opportunities, without considering other benefits such as the intrinsic value of education.

When discussing the rise in college attendance, it's important to frame increasing overall numbers within the context of the increasing U.S. population, but the growth rate as a percentage of the age group is still dramatic. According to the NCES (1993), in 1900 only about 2% of 18- to 24-year-olds attended college. That percentage accelerated to 9% by 1940. Attendance dipped slightly among men and increased among women during World War

II, then the surge of returning service members who could attend college on the G.I. Bill after the war increased the rate to 15% by around 1950.

That pattern of growth continued among both men and women, and by 1969 about 35% of 18- to 24-year-olds were enrolled in college, with about a quarter of them attending 2-year institutions. Attendance rates continued to climb through subsequent decades, and in 2018 among those who graduated from high school, 69.1% enrolled in college (BLS, 2019a). More women enrolled in college in 2018 than men, 71.3% versus 66.9%, continuing a trend that actually began back in the 1970s (NCES, 1993). Racial/ethnic disparities for enrollment in 2018 lingered but were not enormous, with rates of 73.4% for Asians, 69.6% for Whites, 65.5% for Hispanics, and 63.6% for Blacks (BLS, 2019a).

As a pro-education college professor, I view this as a very positive trend for our society. Attending college allows students to develop their intellects in general, to dive deeply into the topic they major in, and often to be exposed to a more diverse group of peers and instructors than they had contact with growing up. These are permanent benefits that stay with graduates regardless of their subsequent life paths.

However, my students and research participants remind me regularly that unlike high school, which every U.S. resident has the right to attend for free, attending college carries significant costs—both direct and indirect, financial and emotional. Those costs can vary tremendously depending on the type of institution one attends (2 year vs. 4 year; public vs. private nonprofit vs. private for profit) and where one lives (on or off campus, with or without family). Beyond tuition and living expenses, there are also costs for books, fees, transportation, and more, and it's not always easy to predict these needs in advance, so students often find themselves spending more in a given semester than they expected to or budgeted for. There are also the opportunity costs of attending college rather than working full-time and earning a living, and the less tangible psychological costs in terms of stress and lost sleep for those who need to juggle both school and work or whose choice to pursue higher education conflicts with family values or obligations.

According to the College Board (2019), including tuition, fees, and room and board, the cost of attending a 4-year college in the 2019–2020 academic year averaged $21,950 at public institutions and $49,870 at private nonprofit institutions. Multiply those numbers by 4 years (at least) to get the total cost of a bachelor's degree. This is a drastic increase in cost over what the parents of today's emerging adults would have paid for their education: In 2019 dollars, the average cost for tuition, fees, and room and board for the 1989–1990 academic year was $9,730 at public schools and $25,900 at private nonprofit schools. Again, both sets of figures are in 2019 dollars so that increase is not the result of inflation, but an actual *doubling* of the price of a degree over 30 years.

For some students, especially those with a lower family income, the listed tuition costs may be reduced by grants and scholarships that don't need to be paid back. For example, NCES (2019a) reports that during the 2016–2017 academic year, students whose household income was less than $30,000 per year averaged $11,000 in grant and scholarship aid at public 4-year universities and $23,300 in aid at nonprofit, private 4-year universities. Those figures seem generous, and without them, surely many low-income students would not be able to attend college at all. However, rapidly rising tuition and other expenses typically leave a significant net cost beyond what's subsidized by grants and scholarships—costs that still must be covered by the student or their family. On average, expenses remain of $9,500 per year at public institutions and $20,200 at private ones for this lowest income group.

How is someone from a family earning less than $30,000 per year supposed to dedicate one third to two thirds of their entire household income to paying for college—not just once but for 4 years, assuming the student can graduate on schedule? Which, of course, many of these students can't manage to do because they're working part or full time to cover their expenses, which involves juggling work and inflexible class schedules and fitting in homework whenever they can. That can impact academic performance in general, and it can impede these students' ability to participate in extracurricular activities that look good on a résumé after graduation, like volunteer work and internships (more on this in the next chapter). And all of these added demands can mean delaying graduation, if not dropping out entirely, if a student needs to attend school part time because of work demands. According to the BLS (2019a), part-time students were twice as likely to participate in the labor force as full-time students, 83.4% versus 42%, and students at 2-year colleges were more likely to work than those at 4-year schools, 55.3% versus 45%.

Some students find juggling work and school just too difficult, so they end up dropping out before completing a degree—but often after acquiring student loans they'll still need to pay back, placing them in the worst possible position of owing money for a degree they didn't actually acquire. Other students "stop out," taking time out of school to work with the intention, not always fulfilled, of returning eventually to complete their degree. One study (Terriquez & Gurantz, 2015) of students who took that step found that many did so because they were averse to taking on debt, so they opted instead to take a break from school in order to work and save money in hopes of being able to support themselves once they returned to college. Others reported stopping out because they felt they needed to financially support their families, often because their parents had lost their own jobs due to the Great Recession—thereby directly tying this issue for Generation Disaster to another macrosystem crisis. Presumably, we should expect a similar wave of students stopping or dropping out due to the economic effects of the Covid-19 pandemic, with others choosing not to return temporarily or permanently because they just didn't think it was worth the money to continue remotely when attending classes on campus wasn't possible.

Both of the reasons Terriquez and Gurantz (2015) cited for leaving school—avoiding taking on excessive debt and working to support their families—reflect a level of responsibility and maturity these students should seemingly be praised for, yet their actions often come at the cost of completing their education. As the authors described it:

> People in this age group are not simply passive by-products of their family socioeconomic background. No longer children, young adults make decisions and take actions within the constraints of the social circumstances that determine whether or not they stay in school in the short term. Regardless of whether they come from lower or middle-income family backgrounds, students' own financial decisions can shape whether or not or how long it takes to complete their degrees. (Terriquez & Gurantz, 2015, p. 211)

Even if these students do manage to come back and eventually complete a degree, their education ends up disjointed and out of sync with peers who were able to avoid this kind of disruption, and they may enter the postcollege labor force late, with attendant delays in earnings that cause them to lag behind others their age. Recognizing these downsides, and given the extreme difficulty so many students have keeping up with the financial demands of college, many take out student loans as the only way to avoid stopping or dropping out—and here's where we turn to what countless emerging adults report experiencing as a true personal disaster.

Student Loans: Investment in the Future or Life-Limiting Trap?

> We come out of a college with an education, a shit ton of debt, and then end up working 10 years in a job that has nothing to do with what you went to school for.
>
> —Male, born in 1992, bachelor's degree

Imagine (or remember) finally being a high school senior. You've been told all of your life that graduating from college is essential if you want to succeed. You've received your acceptance letters or emails, researched expenses and financial aid options at each school, and talked to your parents about how much support they can provide, if any. Unless you're very fortunate, there's a gap between what you'll need to pay and what you can afford to pay—possibly a very large gap that exceeds your entire household income. What to do? If you're like two thirds of your peers in the United States, the answer is obvious: Take out a student loan. After all, it's an investment in your future that you'll easily be able to pay off with the lucrative job your associate's or bachelor's degree will guarantee you, right?

Sadly, that's not true for many people. (Note that I focus here on loans taken out by the college students themselves, not those taken out by parents or grandparents. For an excellent overview of the broader impact of education-related debt on families, read Caitlin Zaloom's 2019 book, *Indebted: How Families Make College Work at Any Cost*. I also focus here on funding for undergraduate degrees, but many of the same factors apply even more intensely to graduate programs.)

According to the Institute for College Access and Success (TICAS, 2019), a research and advocacy group focused on higher education policy issues, 65% of 2018 college graduates from 4-year programs held student loans. The amounts owed varied widely by student, and the average has been fairly stable over the past few years, but it's still much higher than it was in the recent past. In 2019 dollars, average student debt by graduation year was as follows:

- 1996: $12,750
- 2000: $17,350
- 2004: $18,650
- 2008: $23,000
- 2012: $29,400
- 2016: $29,650
- 2018: $29,200

So, in the 20 years from 1996 to 2016 the average debt load at graduation more than doubled. Borrowing around 2008 and the following years saw a particularly large spike that coincided with the Great Recession. That hit students on two fronts: At the macrosystem level, as state support for public schools was slashed, these institutions were forced to increase tuition to make up their own budget shortfalls, so attendance costs rose. Additionally, at the microsystem level, many students' families experienced hardships, including parental unemployment and a devaluation of investments, potentially including whatever funds they had managed to save up for education. Parents may have been less able to cover college costs than planned, forcing students to take out loans in order to maintain their enrollment. Prepandemic, these influences had started to ease up for many families as the economy gradually recovered, but the higher costs for tuition and living expenses have not been reversed for today's students (TICAS, 2019), and the increased unemployment for both students and parents caused by the pandemic is likely to force even more to turn to borrowing to cover expenses they can't earn enough to cover.

As a result, many students graduate from college facing loan repayment costs that quickly become unmanageable on the typical salary someone with a newly minted degree can actually attract. (And as I mentioned previously, others are in the even more unfortunate position of having to leave school before graduating and earning that degree, but after they've acquired debt that they're still responsible for.) When the hoped-for career fails to materialize quickly because the job market is saturated with other college graduates, some emerging adults report feeling trapped or enslaved by their debt—even suicidal (Petersen, 2019).

That stress is compounded for some by feeling judged (yes, again) by older generations who fail to understand the spiraling costs of college now compared to when they attended, or who claim the graduates got themselves into this situation by taking out loans to pursue an education in a field that was likely to lead to a poorly paying career path, or who blame the struggling young people for an inability to find decent-paying work related to their major because the older people don't acknowledge the realities of the current job market. Take this example from a former student at my college:

> So many older adults accuse us of being lazy and not wanting to get jobs after college, when the reality is that there are hardly any jobs and the student debt crisis is taking over our generation. The reality of the matter is, college costs ten-plus times more than it did when our parents went to college, and obtaining a higher education was seen as unnecessary for a lot of entry-level jobs. It's ridiculous in this day and age with the cost of college that there are no career opportunities for those who spend exorbitant amounts of money to get an education that they supposedly need to work in their desired field. Everything is more expensive, which is expected and just the way things go over time, but it has become such an impossibly ridiculous standard of living that is really going to mess up our generations to come as far as debt.

> —Female, born 1997

And as that student suggests, these effects threaten to become multigenerational: If this cohort becomes parents while they're still struggling to pay off their own student loans, how can they possibly begin to save for their children's future education, not to mention their eventual retirement? Will they encourage their children to repeat the cycle by taking on debt when it's their turn to consider college, or will they downsize academic expectations for the next generation and encourage their kids to start working rather than continuing their education? Will they even *have* children, or will that, like buying a home, seem like an unobtainable luxury for some, like this next survey participant?

> We have much more challenges than previous generations. The debt, the cost of living, wages, the cost of education, the cost of buying a home, the cost to seek medical help/attention with and without insurance, the cost to live is far too high and it's very hard for my generation to get ahead. It's why we aren't buying homes or cars or having children or having as many children as previous generations. We can't afford it.
>
> —Female, born 1992, pursuing bachelor's degree

For some, trepidation about how loans will impact their future arrives long before graduation. I've had countless classroom discussions with my students about the calculated gamble they chose to make by taking on student debt. They understood the consequences but didn't feel they had any choice, and they were resigned to the possible need to pursue an undesirable job after graduation in order to keep up with loan payments. Similarly, many survey participants wrote about feeling their future options were limited by debt even while they were still enrolled in college, like this one:

> Student loans make many of us feel as if there's no hope of ever being debt-free— how are you supposed to make a living and create a life for yourself with such a large burden hanging over your head?
>
> —Female, born 1990, pursuing bachelor's degree

The older generations who are quick to blame Generation Disaster for getting themselves into debt to pursue a degree need to understand that these young people are not naïve about the true costs of student loans—but sadly, they are not being overly pessimistic about whether those costs will ultimately pay off in terms of employment prospects. It's a different world than it was for previous cohorts and, like so many aspects of life today, a far more stressful and complicated one to try to live in as an emerging adult, whether or not one enters it with a college degree.

Work Opportunities, With and Without Debt

> A college education is very important and with that comes a lot of stress and debt. Some majors require more schooling after a four-year college, costing more money.... Many people do not follow their dreams (such as traveling, and picking the career they truly want) because we are so worried about money.
>
> —Male, born 1997

> The inflation of higher education is so drastic for our generation in comparison to the previous generation. Even if one decides to take the leap, invest in college, then in our generation that person is committing themselves to life of debt and financial struggle, with no actual guarantee of that education helping them in the job market.
>
> —Male, born 1990, pursuing bachelor's degree

First, the good news for those who have chosen to invest in higher education. In July 2019, U.S. unemployment rates for adults ages 25 and older were 3.3% for people with some college or an associate's degree and 2.5% for those with a bachelor's degree or higher, compared with 3.6% for those with only a high school diploma and 4.6% for those with less than a diploma (BLS, 2020). That pattern fits in with the standard story we tell young people that college is the key to success in life, and it remained consistent during the pandemic when July 2020 unemployment rates roughly tripled across the board, to 14.9% for those without a high school diploma, 10.8% for high school graduates, 10.2% for those with some college or an associate's degree, and 7.1% for those with a bachelor's degree or higher. Education is protective in times of economic uncertainty, though it clearly doesn't spare everyone from the risk of job loss.

However, that focus on the entire population distorts the immediate value of a *new* degree, which unfortunately does not guarantee a smooth shift from college into a stable career trajectory. As with high school graduates, the growth in the number of people completing a college degree can essentially be viewed as creating a glut in the supply system that overwhelms demand for newly graduated employees. Looking only at recent graduates, the BLS (2019b) reported that among 20- to 29-year-olds, unemployment rates as of October 2018 for 2018 recipients of associate degrees, bachelor's degrees, and advanced degrees were 9.6%, 12.9%, and 10.4%, respectively—much worse than for older adults without even a high school diploma.

Now, it's not shocking that it might take some time for new graduates to settle into a career path, sometimes following a voluntary period of testing out different jobs and fields. That can be a kind of healthy exploration that reflects one of the potential privileges of emerging adulthood: the ability to try various options out before committing to one for the long term (Krahn, Howard, & Galambos, 2015). However, that period of early employment instability takes on a less positive spin when it's *involuntary*—not the result of deliberate exploration that ultimately leads to an intentional choice of career, but the result of job loss, underemployment, or other undesirable or uncontrollable conditions (Krahn et al., 2015). And any delay in finding stable employment has newly relevant repercussions for a generation as saddled with student debt as so many of today's emerging adults are. It's already prohibitively expensive to establish an independent life after graduating from high school or college, and for those who quickly start to receive loans bills on top of needing funds for rent, transportation, food, health insurance, and all of the other costs of adult living, it can literally be impossible to manage on entry-level wages.

As Petersen (2019) pointed out, this means that there's a growing social and financial divide between those with and without student debt, and that divide can directly influence the options an individual does or does not have in controlling their own future. It's not that those without significant student loans to pay off face a different job market on graduation than those with debts, but they're facing it free of the opportunity-limiting strictures imposed by the need to start making those monthly payments, which the journalist eloquently described:

> Much of the reporting on student loans throws around big numbers ($1.53 trillion in debt!). But for those of us who hold some of that debt—and those with no student debt at all—the cold abstraction of that framing can often feel alienating. To the individual, the $1.53 trillion is not the most pressing problem. The problem is the wedge of your salary that disappears each month. The problem is not being able to find work in the field you took out loans to prepare yourself for. The problem is spending hours of your life on hold with [loan processor] call center representatives who can't answer simple questions. The problem is the growing certainty that you were sold a false bill of goods about the immeasurable value of higher education, and that'll you'll be forever paying down the cost of a broken dream. (Petersen, 2019)

Add the psychological impact of feeling blamed for their struggles by the very same older generations who sold that "false bill of goods" about student debt being a worthwhile investment, and it's little wonder that this issue feels like a very personal disaster for many current emerging adults.

* * *

I don't mean to paint an overly bleak picture here, and I apologize to the debt-holding college student readers who I've probably just sent into panic attacks. It's not all bad! Many people who take on student loans are able to manage their payments on time once they kick in post-graduation, and these loans are the only way many students could possibly pursue the higher education they desire. And I believe the fact that today's young adults are the most highly educated in history is worth celebrating. A Pew Research Center report comparing Millennials (currently ages 25 to 37) to previous generations found that 43% of Millennial women and 36% of men had completed at least a bachelor's degree, compared with 21% and 27%, respectively, of Baby Boomers, and that growth pattern appears likely to continue as Generation Z moves into college age (Bialik & Fry, 2019). Again, that seems like a net gain for society, as we'll need educated people to try to keep our ever more complex world functioning.

However, the same report (Bialik & Fry, 2019) also noted a pattern that is explored in detail in the next chapter: the growing divide between the haves and have-nots, which is often linked to higher education. In 2017, the median income for a household headed by a Millennial with a bachelor's degree or higher was $105,343, compared with $62,358 headed by a Millennial with some college and $49,363 by a high school graduate. This is tangible evidence that a degree makes a significant difference in earning potential, even fairly early in one's career, and it seems to justify the decision to pursue college even if it means taking on debt. Yet many of the respondents quoted throughout this chapter make it clear that for those who end up struggling to keep up with student loan payments, it can feel like a burden they'll never break free from as they move through emerging adulthood, rather than a wise investment that will pay for itself through work opportunities as they were promised by older generations. On the other hand, those who didn't attend college or complete high school may not have student loans to worry about, but they certainly face other barriers to success, including ever more limited job options that provide few opportunities to earn a living wage, let alone to pursue the "American Dream" of upward mobility—a toxic myth we return to in the next chapter.

Regardless of education level, what seems most upsetting to many of the emerging adults I've surveyed is how little understanding or empathy they receive from those older people who they hold responsible for an economy and job market that offer them limited opportunities, whatever decisions they ultimately made about whether higher education was the right choice for them. Many feel they took the advice they were given by parents and others, only to find that shifts in society and the economy mean the rules have changed in ways older generations refuse to acknowledge, let alone try to improve. For example,

The previous generation completely fucked us over thanks to Reaganomics and other unsustainable policies. Then they increased the price of college by over 500% and wonder why we can't just "get a summer job" to pay for college, or why we live with our parents still in our 20s despite rent being higher than it's ever been.

—**Male, born 1995, pursuing bachelor's degree**

My generation cannot afford higher education or housing like past generations could. Past generations think my generation is lazy but really we are living in a world where we have many more obstacles relating to money that we cannot overcome. Older generations had an easier time getting out of poverty than my generation does. . . . We aren't lazy. We aren't "special snowflakes." We are who you raised us to be and we are fighting to have a good life in a broken economy.

—**Female, born 1991, high school diploma**

More on these emerging adults' fight for a good life, their broader economic expectations, and the myth of the American Dream in the next chapter.

References

Bialik, K., & Fry, R. (2019). Millennial life: How young adulthood today compares with prior generations. Pew Research Center. Downloaded from https://www.pewsocialtrends.org/essay/millennial-life-how-young-adulthood-today-compares-with-prior-generations

Bureau of Labor Statistics (BLS). (2019a). College enrollment and work activity of recent high school and college graduates summary. Downloaded from https://www.bls.gov/news.release/hsgec.nr0.htm

Bureau of Labor Statistics (BLS). (2019b). Unemployment rates and earnings by educational attainment. Downloaded from https://www.bls.gov/emp/chart-unemployment-earnings-education.htm

Bureau of Labor Statistics (BLS). (2020). The employment situation—July 2020. Downloaded from https://www.bls.gov/news.release/archives/empsit_08072020.htm

Centers for Disease Control and Prevention. (2017). About teen pregnancy. Downloaded from https://www.cdc.gov/teenpregnancy/about/index.htm

College Board. (2019). Trends in college pricing 2019. Downloaded from https://research.collegeboard.org/trends/college-pricing/highlights

Institute for College Access and Success (TICAS). (2019). Student debt and the class of 2018: 14th annual report. Downloaded from https://ticas.org/wp-content/uploads/2019/09/classof2018.pdf

Krahn, H. J., Howard, A. L., & Galambos, N. L. (2015). Exploring or floundering? The meaning of employment and educational fluctuations in emerging adulthood. *Youth & Society, 47,* 245–266.

Maynard, B. R., Salas-Wright, C. P., & Vaughn, M. G. (2015). High school dropouts in emerging adulthood: Substance use, mental health problems, and crime. *Community Mental Health Journal, 51,* 289–299.

National Center for Education Statistics (NCES). (1993). 120 years of American education: A statistical portrait. Downloaded from https://nces.ed.gov/pubs93/93442.pdf

National Center for Education Statistics (NCES). (2019a). Price of attending an undergraduate institution. Downloaded from https://nces.ed.gov/programs/coe/indicator_coj.asp

National Center for Education Statistics (NCES). (2019b). Status dropout rates. Downloaded from https://nces.ed.gov/programs/coe/indicator_coj.asp

Petersen, A. H. (2019). Here's why so many Americans feel cheated by their student loans. *BuzzFeed News*. Downloaded from https://www.buzzfeednews.com/article/annehelenpetersen/student-debt-college-public-service-loan-forgiveness

Terriquez, V., & Gurantz, O. (2015). Financial challenges in emerging adulthood and students' decisions to stop out of college. *Emerging Adulthood, 3*(3), 204–214.

United States Census Bureau. (2017). High school completion rate is highest in U.S. history. Retrieved from https://www.census.gov/newsroom/press-releases/2017/educational-attainment-2017.html

Zaloom, C. (2019). *Indebted: How families make college work at any cost*. Princeton University Press.

SECTION 3

GENERATION DISASTER MOVING FORWARD

How Will They Shape Our Future Society?

The third and final section discusses how their expectations for the future may shape U.S. society moving forward, including their plans for pursuing careers and starting families—plans that have now been further derailed for many by the pandemic, on top of previously existing economic barriers to typical markers of adulthood that many already grappled with, like settling into a stable career and buying a home.

9

Economic Expectations

> Getting a job is impossible without an education and getting an edu-
> cation is impossible without sinking into debt. With previous gener-
> ations you could get basically any job you applied for and genuinely
> be able to work up from even the most mundane jobs. . . . My gener-
> ation is exhausted. We overwork, overstress, and abuse substances
> to cope. We can't afford therapy no matter how much we all need it
> and no matter how many jobs we work. My friends work 12 hour shifts
> and still can't make rent without three roommates. My sister works
> 18 or more hour shifts as an ER nurse without days off. We are being
> worked to the bone for NO payoff. We are saddled with debt and half
> the time aren't sure when our next real meal will be, if any kind of meal
> at all. Our country is dying and has been dying, the economy is gone
> because we can't afford food let alone to splurge. You have to be born
> rich to survive at this point and it's going to kill us all.
>
> **—Trans man, born 1993**

In this final section of the book, we look toward the future and consider how Generation Disaster's past and current experiences shape their hopes about the next phases of life, starting with their economic and career expectations. Given the depressed economy of their youth, the mortgage crisis that destroyed many families' primary investments, and the current competition for work in a job market that was still recovering from the Great Recession and then crashed again in 2020 due to the Covid-19 pandemic, what are members of Generation Disaster's hopes and fears about their financial prospects?

As we saw in the last chapter, many who attended college are entering adulthood saddled with heavy debts from student loans, while those without more than a high school diploma face limited earning opportunities. Do they think they'll ever be able to find satisfactory work or to retire? If not, how are they reshaping their expectations and coming to terms with restricted hopes for upward mobility? This chapter explores the financial future of this first American

Generation Disaster. Karla Vermeulen, Oxford University Press. © Oxford University Press 2021.
DOI: 10.1093/oso/9780190061630.003.0009

generation who doesn't assume that the norm will be to fare better economically than their parents—a personal disaster of yet another type for those who feel robbed of the opportunity to prosper, no matter how hard they might work. While the data used in this chapter were collected before the economic impact of the pandemic hit, that latest crisis just means that all of these earlier concerns will likely be intensified for most emerging adults until conditions reach some level of long-term recovery—by which point, they may be established on very different career paths than they'd envisioned for themselves.

Has the American Dream Been Canceled?

As I started writing this chapter, I realized I had no idea where the phrase "American Dream" came from, only that it was supposed to capture the essence of equality and potential for success promised in the Declaration of Independence. It turns out that while the concept has been around since the nation's founding, the specific term was coined less than a century ago by a businessman turned writer and historian, James Truslow Adams, in his 1931 book, *The Epic of America*. He described the American Dream as

> that dream of a land in which life should be better and richer and fuller for everyone, with opportunity for each according to ability or achievement. It is a difficult dream for the European upper classes to interpret adequately, and too many of us ourselves have grown weary and mistrustful of it. It is not a dream of motor cars and high wages merely, but a dream of social order in which each man and each woman shall be able to attain to the fullest stature of which they are innately capable, and be recognized by others for what they are, regardless of the fortuitous circumstances of birth or position. (Adams, 1931)

In other words, it was never described as a *guarantee* of success, but a belief that the opportunity to rise is open to everyone who is willing to put in the effort, regardless of where they started on the economic ladder. It's a foundational ethos for the nation, and the fact that it just isn't working in the current economy plainly felt like a broken promise to many of my research participants as they described the struggle to launch their adult work life. Their descriptions are so powerful that I include numerous examples:

> We're stuck at a crossroads where our parents believe if we "work hard" and "do well in school," we'll get a "good job" and the only reason why we're struggling is because we don't "try hard enough," where the reality of it is there is zero guarantee

that our $60,000+ bachelor's degree will be even nearly enough to get a decent job, let alone a good one.

—**Female, born 1997**

I have not even thought about retirement as I am so worried about the lack of job prospects that seem to be in my near future. I don't think the "American Dream" of going to college, getting a good job, getting married and having kids, and being to afford a nice house is attainable to many people anymore. In terms of social justice, we've come a long way, but there is obviously so much more that needs to be done.

—**Unspecified gender, born 1996**

It feels like we got screwed out of a lot of the things previous generations could count on, like being able to graduate and find a job with your degree, or even just to find a supportive unskilled job. We're living at home until we're practically 30 and it sucks. When people call my generation lazy and entitled, it pisses me off because they don't take into account the context of the situation we've inherited. I guess we feel entitled to things because previous generations have been able to be financially comfortable at a MUCH younger age than us. You're damn right I feel entitled to a well paying job, a decent place to live, and a good car; I'm not in grad school for nothing!! My mother only has an Associate's degree and was able to get a job where she worked her way up to a managerial position that pays around $100K a year. I could NEVER make that kind of money with an Associate's degree now. Older generations just don't understand.

—**Unspecified gender, born 1994**

We have many more challenges than previous generations. We are often not paid a living wage, requiring many Millennials to work more than one job and often more than 40 hours per week. We are often unable to pay for college and many entry level jobs want 5+ years of experience, leaving us having to work multiple minimum wage jobs that exhaust our bodies just to be able to barely keep a roof over our heads and ramen on the table. Due to the inability to find jobs that do not require 5+years of experience for entry level positions, a lack of funds to attend college, and a lack of time to figure out how to further our lives since we often have to work more than 40 hours per week to survive, I feel our opportunities are more limited than previous generations. Millennials often end up trapped in our status quo because we don't have the funds or the time to learn new skills or figure out how to move forward. . . . We are often berated by older generations for being lazy. The price of living has skyrocketed since the Baby Boomer era, but our income has not increased to even come close to matching it.

—**Female, born 1990**

Dozens of other write-in responses expressed a similar sense of injustice and, sometimes, outright hopelessness.

Of course, historically emerging adults often go through a period of financial struggle as they enter the workforce, whether or not that follows time in college, and they begin to establish a career path. Wages for entry-level positions are typically low, even in fields where there is great potential for growth as experience increases. (There are some exceptions, like starting salaries at corporate law firms or investment banks, but these positions may require expensive graduate degrees and are only available to an elite few each year.)

Also, as I noted in the previous chapter, young adults may change jobs or entire fields as they explore their options and seek more rewarding work, which may mean returning to school (and often acquiring even more debt) or starting over again at the low end of the pay scale. That intentional exploration can be a positive type of fluctuation if it ultimately leads to a satisfying career path, but it also can reflect a kind of floundering if it's not voluntary or doesn't land the worker in a position with room for advancement (Krahn, Howard, & Galambos, 2015). That's the futile-feeling situation expressed by many of those just quoted—encountering early job frustration and low wages not as a typical developmental hurdle to be overcome with effort and time, but as an inescapable trap imposed by an economic macrosystem they feel they can't change.

Like those quoted, many of the people I've surveyed apparently feel like their entire generation is floundering in their work lives, with little control over their ability to move beyond that typical period of early career financial hardship onto a path toward earning a livable wage. However, it's important to note that this pessimism was not universal across the entire thousand-person national sample. Consider the responses to these two questions:

Compared to previous generations, do you think your generation has better or worse career opportunities?
- Somewhat or much worse: 35.3%
- About the same: 29.4%
- Somewhat or much better: 35.3%

How confident are you that you'll be able to have a satisfying career in your chosen field?
- Not at all confident: 8.9%
- Not very confident: 17.3%
- Somewhat confident: 25.0%

- Very confident: 14.1%
- Not sure: 34.7%

At the group level, exactly equal numbers saw their generation's career prospects as better versus worse than in the past, while at the individual level about a quarter doubted their ability to achieve the career they'd like. That's depressing for those who hold those negative expectations, but those are not the views of the majority. In fact, when asked to describe their generation's opportunities relative to earlier groups, many commenters cited better career prospects for women and minorities, and dozens mentioned the value of technology in increasing job options. Take these examples:

> People in my generation I think are more willing to take risks and make their own path, without fear of society telling them it's wrong. There are more creative career opportunities now in terms of social media and the Internet.
>
> **—Female, born 1990**

> We can use the Internet and the gig economy to make a living. We have the ability to launch small-scale businesses and enterprises that can reach a large number of people. We are also more supportive of each other.
>
> **—Female, born 1990**

> I think we have greater opportunities than previous groups did. There are more jobs now and more non-traditional roles for men and women to have. I think people are more open to see women doing work that was once considered only for men and vice versa. . . . Stereotypes of my generation as being lazy and not wanting to work need to change; we aren't lazy, we do want to work—we just work in a different way than do previous generations. We want [to be] rewarded with praise and time off and want a good work/life balance; different things are important to us and that is what employers need to focus on and learn.
>
> **—Male, born 1995**

> I would say we have a lot of opportunities. Starting businesses is something my generation is thriving at and I think it's wonderful. I also think this generation is working hard towards equality, which is opening up more opportunities for ALL people.
>
> **—Female, born 1990**

What is behind this sharp divide in perspectives between those who do and don't perceive promising career prospects? There's no single explanation, but a major factor brings us back to the core assumption of the American

Dream: the belief that everyone has the same shot at success if they want it. In reality, access to opportunity has never been truly equal for minorities, women, members of certain religious or cultural groups, people with disabilities, or others who face barriers to capitalizing on that egalitarian ideal. And, in fact, the American Dream concept can be used to blame individuals for their lack of success: If our national belief is that anyone can pull themselves up by their bootstraps (whatever that means) if they just work hard enough, that allows us to claim that anyone who *doesn't* prosper must just be lazy or unambitious, rather than forcing us to acknowledge that the ideal of equality isn't quite so balanced in practice.

Even more problematic, that emphasis on the individual's responsibility for their own success can actually affect the entire macrosystem if it's used by policymakers to shift resources away from creating laws that might increase equality and opportunity, as public policy expert and former Secretary of Labor Robert Reich pointed out:

> So, why is America still perpetuating the fallacy of the self-made individual? Because those in power want you to believe it. If everyone thinks they're on their own, it's easier for the powerful to dismantle unions, unravel safety nets, and slash taxes for the wealthy. It's in their interest to keep the American Dream deeply rooted in our psyche—the assumption that you determine your destiny. So we don't demand reforms that are necessary—paid family and medical leave, for example, or early childhood education, accessible childcare, and policies that lift every family out of poverty. (Reich, 2019)

Absent those supports, it's a lot harder for those starting out with fewer advantages to actually achieve the upward mobility they've been promised by the myth of the American Dream. Instead, the rich tend to get richer and the poor tend to stay poor. That's not a new phenomenon, but multiple aspects of the current economy and job market make that pattern even more difficult to break for Generation Disaster than in the past, confirming the realistic basis of the pessimistic perspective of those starting out at the lower end of the socioeconomic spectrum or with other barriers to growth. Let's examine these primary factors, focusing mostly on how they have changed over the course this cohort's lives.

Spiraling Income and Wealth Inequality

I describe the harm caused by today's unpaid internship system and the gig economy later in the chapter, but first let's look at current national patterns of income relative to the past, especially a phenomenon Harvard-based researchers Chetty et al. (2016) described as the "fading American Dream." Using historic tax records to analyze the proportion of children who earned more at age 30 than their parents did at the same age, adjusted for inflation, they identified a clear downward trend from those born in 1940 to the 1980s (shortly before the oldest members of Generation Disaster were born in 1990). Approximately 90% of those born in 1940 fared better than their parents had, supporting the American societal expectation of upward mobility as the standard pattern. However, the likelihood of achieving that income mobility trailed steadily downward over the following decades, to the point where just 50% of children born in the 1980s outearned their parents at age 30. The decrease was especially steep among middle-class families and in regions where stable industrial jobs have dried up.

While Chetty et al.'s (2016) findings indicate that half of the population still does manage to fare better financially than their parents by the time they're moving into full adulthood, that means that half currently *don't*, which is a troubling change in the standard the American Dream myth taught us to expect. And the authors' economic models projected that an overall increase in the national gross domestic product wouldn't be sufficient to benefit those most at risk of stagnation or downward mobility. That's because of the way growth is currently distributed across the U.S. population, with a small share of high-income households benefiting the most from any general improvements to the economy. In other words, economic gains for the country tend to remain in the hands of those already at the higher end of the socioeconomic spectrum, belying the aphorism popularized by President John F. Kennedy that "a rising tide lifts all boats." Instead, as one British politician quipped, accurately if not amusingly, "They used to say a rising tide lifted all boats. Now the rising tide just seems to lift the yachts" (Leroux, 2013).

And this brings us back to the biggest stressor for those aspiring to become or stay middle class or higher: the growing gap between the rich and everybody else. The psychological impact of this divide was captured vividly by this survey participant:

Our Social Security is being threatened. Our economy only helps the rich. The rich get tax cuts while everyone else suffers. There's no money coming down to help and we are all clawing to earn a good living while the ultra rich complain that their taxes are too high and they can't afford their second Lamborghini. . . . We are really hard workers, but we are frustrated. We are looked down upon by all other generations and called names, while they are happily retired and we're drowning in student debt. No wonder suicide rates are high, we have no control over our destiny and the ones that do are going to die soon anyway, so they don't have to/won't be around to suffer the consequences like we will.

—Female, born in 1995

That's a remarkably bleak assessment by this young woman of her current situation and future prospects, but is it an accurate perception of inequalities in the economy? Some of the commenter's perceptions may be exaggerated, but her core points unfortunately reflect real changes that have occurred during her lifetime. Consider a recent shift in income disparities by class, using data from the World Inequality Database (2020) to look at pretax national income in current dollars. In 1990 those in the bottom half of the U.S. population made an average of $9,489; the middle 40% made an average of $31,399; and those in the top 10% made an average of $109,306. In 2014 those averages were $16,219, $65,352, and $303,907, respectively.

That means for those in the bottom half, average income increased by 71%. For those in the middle 40% it increased by 108%, and for the top 10% it nearly tripled. The disparity in income growth was even more extreme for the highest earners: In 1990 the top 1% made $410,591, which grew to $1.31 million in 2014. Looked at another way, in 1990 the top 10% made 11.5 times the average income of the bottom 50%. In 2014 they made 18.7 times as much. For the top 1%, the multiple went from 43.3 to 80.8 times average income relative to the bottom half. So yes, the income divide between the very rich and the rest of the population is growing, and income growth for those in the middle is at a rate closer to the poor than to the rich.

Paralleling the rise of income inequality in the United States, the distribution of wealth has also become remarkably imbalanced. Wealth refers to the assets individuals own, like property and investments, minus their debts, including mortgages, student loans, and credit card balances. Wealth is important because it can allow people to increase their net value outside of their income in order to prepare for a time when they no longer receive the regular influx of a salary or wages, whether that's chosen in the form of retirement, unplanned in the form of a layoff, or unavoidable due to a disability or caregiving demand that prevents a person from working. Many assets can also be passed along to one's heirs as a gift or inheritance, so it's a method of supporting the next generation and retaining wealth within a family. If, that is, one can actually afford to acquire any assets after covering the growing costs of living—a goal that is increasingly out of reach for those who didn't start life off already blessed with these financial advantages.

The current wealth divide in the United States is staggering. According to the World Inequality Database (2020), as of 2014 adults in the middle 40% of the wealth distribution owned 27.2% of the country's assets, while those in the lowest 50% actually had a slightly negative net personal wealth as their debts exceeded their assets. In contrast, the richest 10% of Americans possessed 73% of the nation's wealth. Like income, this gap is even more extreme at the very top, where the richest 0.1% now own more than the bottom 80%, and the very richest 400 individuals own more than the bottom 150 million Americans combined (Ingraham, 2019).

Let's consider how this growing divide in wealth is likely to impact today's emerging adults, extrapolating from U.S. Federal Reserve (2020) data demonstrating changes over time in how relevant demographic factors correlate with the accumulation of assets. The Fed defined these as including real estate, consumer durables, corporate equities and mutual fund shares, pension entitlements, private businesses, and other assets.

Education: Education correlates increasingly strongly with wealth accumulation. In 1990, people with a college degree or higher owned 54.2% of the national total of $24.9 trillion in assets. The rest was distributed across lower education levels: 19.1% was held by those with some college, 18.3% by high school graduates, and 8.5% by those without a high school diploma. As of the third quarter of 2019, the nation's $122.6 trillion in assets had skewed even more sharply by education: People with a college degree owned 70.1% of the asset pie; some college, 16.7%; high school diploma, 9.0%; and no high school diploma, just 4.3%.

So, wealth increasingly tracks education level, with very little currently remaining among those with a high school degree or less. That's bad news for those without a college degree. While it should be good news for those who did pursue higher education, that advantage will be offset for those who obtained a college education only by acquiring substantial student loans, as described in the previous chapter. The resulting debt places these young adults in the negative net wealth category at the start of their careers—a position that's increasingly difficult, though not impossible, to climb out of given the current employment market.

Race: Historic wealth disparities linger discouragingly between racial/ethnic groups. A 2016 national survey by the Federal Reserve (Dettling, Hsu, Jacobs, Moore, & Thompson, 2017) found that median family wealth for Black and Hispanic families was a fraction of that for White families: respectively, $17,699, $20,700, and $171,000. This wealth gap mirrors disparities in household income, which is much higher on average for White families than Black or Hispanic ones. Black households are about twice as likely to have zero or negative net worth than White ones, about one in five versus one in 10, with Hispanic households falling in between the other groups.

Repeated Fed surveys over time also found that White families' net worth bounced back much more quickly after the Great Recession ended in 2010, while Black and Hispanic families took several years longer to return to a wealth growth phase. Given the different starting points for each group, this isn't surprising because of the role assets can play as a buffer against any financial crisis, individual or collective. Those with a smaller asset cushion to begin with are more likely to lose everything and have to start re-creating wealth from scratch (perhaps after first working to emerge from a debt position), while those with more to start with are likely to retain at least some assets they can rebuild from. Undoubtedly we'll see this same pattern repeated as a result of the Covid-19 pandemic's impact on the U.S. economy. Also, please note that the higher pre-recession net worth for Whites wasn't necessarily due to any superior American Dream–style bootstrap pulling: Those families were much more likely than the other groups to have received an asset boost in the form of an inheritance or other major gift, with 26% of Whites getting this unearned advantage compared with fewer than 10% of the Black and Hispanic families.

These discrepancies between racial/ethnic groups may partially explain why the benefits of higher education are not evenly distributed when it comes to household wealth. That 2016 Federal Reserve study (Dettling et al., 2017) found that the value of a college degree varied widely by ethnicity: The median net worth of Black and Hispanic families headed by someone with a bachelor's degree was well below $100,000, in comparison with $397,100 for those headed by a White person with a bachelor's degree. However, the value of that degree grew twice as much between 2013 and 2016 for the Black and Hispanic households, a far bigger increase than for the White households, indicating at least some narrowing of the wealth gap relative to education and race.

Age: Assets are also increasingly dominated by older people. Now, it's natural that those farther along in their earning and investing lives would have more to show for it so we would always expect to see wealth concentrated among older adults, but that skew has become much more pronounced over the past 30 years. In 1990, those aged 70 and older held 17.2% of the country's assets; those 55 to 69 had 32.6%, those 40 to 54 had 33.3%, and those under 40 had 16.9%. That means about two thirds of all assets were owned by people between 40 and 69, with the rest evenly distributed at both ends of the age spectrum. But as of the end of 2019 the distribution had tilted sharply to the older side, with two thirds of all assets now held by those 55 and older: age 70 plus, 24.8%; 55 to 69, 42.9%; 40 to 54, 23.7%. Those under age 40 now hold just 8.6% of the wealth—half what they did three decades ago (Federal Reserve, 2020).

Part of that upward shift reflects the population swell of Baby Boomers becoming senior citizens, but it's still wildly disproportionate relative to the overall U.S. population distribution: Those people age 70 and older who hold almost a quarter of the country's assets comprise just 11% of the population, while the 8.6% of assets owned by those under 40 is divided among 52% of the population.

Compound Interest Versus Compound Worries

That tiny sliver of the pie available to those at the younger end of the spectrum is especially problematic because of the basic tendency of wealth to grow over time. Barring crises like periodic stock market crashes or the 2008 housing market collapse (whose impact I'm certainly not minimizing), assets tend to appreciate over time as property values rise, stocks appreciate, and savings collect compound interest. Money begets money, which means the earlier someone has access to it, the more valuable it's likely to become for them and their children—ideally at a time when assets can best be leveraged to provide a boost to the next generation.

Those fortunate to inherit wealth at an early age, or who have a safety net of parents or others willing to support or subsidize them, benefit from many possible financial and emotional advantages. To name just a few, they may have been able to afford to attend higher quality institutions and to graduate from college and even graduate school free of debt so they're not starting their careers in a negative asset position. They may have more freedom to explore different fields in pursuit of a satisfying career, or to choose a path they know is unlikely to become lucrative, like the arts or social services, because they don't need to be driven primarily by how much they'll earn. If they decide to have children they may choose for one parent to stop work temporarily or permanently to raise the kids themselves, or they may be able to afford high-quality child care that suits their schedule and enriches the child's early development. Rather than paying rent each month, they may be able to invest in buying a house, whose value is likely to increase over time (assuming they don't overmortgage it), allowing them to sell and trade up to a nicer house whose value will appreciate still further, or to downsize and invest the profit. They can save for their children's education and for their own retirement. And while it's difficult to measure empirically, they also benefit psychologically from the knowledge that they're not one layoff, or even one car breakdown, away from financial catastrophe. They may actually be able to achieve that American Dream of increased prosperity, but largely because they started off from a relatively privileged place.

For those without such advantages, financial security initially comes down to their ability to earn an income that covers daily expenses and that just maybe provides some extra funds they can save in order to start acquiring assets like a home or retirement fund. As one Federal Reserve report put it, "Wealth tends to increase with income because of higher levels of saving among higher-income families, and because of the feedback effect on higher incomes from the returns generated by accumulated assets" (Dettling et al., 2017). Again, money begets money.

But what if the best income a person can earn isn't even sufficient to cover basic expenses, like the situations described by these survey participants?

We simply cannot afford to live. We can't afford kids, to buy houses, to pay off school or prepare for retirement/emergencies. . . . It just sucks. I'm someone who went to school, got married, started a family and works a full-time job and two part-time jobs. My husband works full time and is in the Air Force Guard with no student loan debt. And yet we still can't put money into savings and barely get by with student loans and debt.

—Female, born 1992

I have a few friends who graduated with their bachelor's degrees last May and still haven't been able to find a job in their field. My best friend has a dual degree in math and business and works as a waitress at Buffalo Wild Wings because she can't even get an interview with any corporations. They want people with more experience. Meanwhile, she hasn't had any help from her parents since high school and has all of her own bills to pay including rent. It's very worrisome, because my generation is told we will have no opportunities without going to college, but then we do everything they say and we still get shorted, and that didn't happen with our parents' generation. It's no wonder that once we make it into our chosen field, we feel entitled to respect and enough money to survive. Older people would too if they were entering the workforce today.

—Female, born 1997

This brings us to some of the characteristics of today's work environment that are making it especially difficult for many members of Generation Disaster to launch careers that might deliver that promise of upward mobility, even if they did go to college and do work as hard as possible—if, as the woman just quoted observed, they did everything they were told to by their elders and still feel shorted by the opportunities available to them, given the economic macrosystem that happened to be in place as they became emerging adults.

Opportunity Blockers

Before delving into some specific challenges for Generation Disaster, I want to make it clear that it's not impossible for people to overcome these career barriers and climb to a higher socioeconomic status, though this is another area where majority status is correlated with more positive outcomes and where those starting off with more advantages are likely to remain more advantaged and vice versa.

Looking at the most extreme possible increase in household income, from those who grew up in the poorest 20% of the population (the lowest quintile or fifth) and reached the top 20% as adults, Chetty, Hendren, Jones, and Porter (2019) found that 11% of White Americans born into the worst poverty were able to achieve that leap. (To be clear, that's not 11% of the entire population, but 11% of those coming from that poorest 20% in childhood, so fewer than 2% of the overall population were able to make that most extreme climb toward prosperity.) Then, by descending adult income quintile, 16% of the poorest children became upper middle class, 20% became middle class, 25% lower middle class, and 29% remained in the poorest quintile as adults. A similar pattern applied to Blacks but with far fewer able to rise to higher levels: Just 3% of the poorest Black children became rich adults; 6% became upper middle class, 16% became middle class, 38% lower middle class, and 37% remained poor as adults. Hispanics fared between Blacks and Whites, and Asian Americans achieved the highest rates of growth, with 44% rising from childhood poverty to upper middle-class or rich adult household income.

Majority status also appears to have a protective effect for those born at the top: Among Whites, 41% who were born into the richest fifth of families remained in the top 20% as adults, and another 24% slipped just one quintile to upper middle class. Nine percent ended up poor—very close to the 11% of Whites who traveled in the opposite direction from poor to rich. In contrast, Blacks were far more likely to experience downward mobility in household income. Among those born rich, just 18% stayed in that top quintile as adults, while 20% became upper middle class, 24% became middle class, 21% became lower middle class, and 17% became poor as adults. That means six times as many Blacks went from childhood wealth to adult poverty than vice versa. And all of the mobility trends were more advantageous for White men than for White women or for men or women of all other races. (If you're interested in viewing other changes, the New York Times [Badger, Miller, Pearce, & Quealy, 2018] offers an interactive tool that lets you use these data to make your own comparisons by race and gender.)

Still, despite their historic and ongoing advantage, White men are not immune to the recent changes in labor market structure that make the hope of climbing the wealth ladder seem so impossible for many emerging adults who are currently trying to start out from the bottom rungs. (In fact, the shock of some White men at their loss of assumed privilege is driving a small portion toward political extremism and, in some extreme cases, violence against women or those who they believe are oppressing them, but that's a subject for another book. As a starting point, see sociologist Michael Kimmel's 2017 *Angry White Men: American Masculinity at the End of an Era*, which discusses some men's sense of "aggrieved entitlement" about their perceived loss of power.)

Looking at the psychological impact of today's job market conditions, one economist (Graham, 2017) who studied the relationship between income inequality and well-being found that poor Whites were even less optimistic that hard work would lead to opportunities to improve their lives than poor Hispanics or Blacks, despite their actual advantages in relative access to economic improvement. The researcher suggested that may be because poor and lower middle class Whites identified more strongly with traditional blue-collar jobs that are rapidly vanishing, while poor minorities have more of a history of piecing together work from multiple sources, which has provided some level of resilience in adapting to the current job market.

If that interpretation is accurate, it seems like a pretty underwhelming silver lining to a long record of unfair access to decently paying work for Black and Hispanic Americans, but it would explain why many Whites seem to have been taken more by surprise by their recent economic vulnerability to downward mobility. That may also explain why compared with respondents of color, White participants in my national survey said they perceived statistically significantly worse career opportunities for themselves than for previous generations, and they expressed significantly lower expectations that they would have a satisfying career, be able to afford a home, or be able to retire comfortably than previous generations.

In contrast, the Black participants reported significantly more *positive* expectations in all of those areas relative to previous generations, while Hispanic respondents were slightly more positive, but not at a statistically significant level. That seems to reflect the trends in education, income, and wealth described above: Minority groups haven't fully closed the historical gaps with

Whites yet, but they know they're making progress, while many middle class and poorer Whites feel like they're losing ground relative to both minorities and the wealthiest segments of all Americans. To further torture the old cliché, if the rising economic tide now only lifts the yachts, some less privileged Whites are like boats that feel the tide has suddenly turned against them personally and unfairly.

So, let's recognize that these barriers to growth cut across race and gender, though not equally. The real dividing point for opportunity is the socioeconomic class a person was born into and/or their access to opportunities that allow them to begin adulthood with more resources, which then provide access to even more opportunities in an upward cycle. However, initiating that positive cycle is far more difficult than it's ever been for those starting off without useful advantages that help them start to climb over current barriers to mobility.

Let's consider two characteristics of today's working world that further stack the deck against many emerging adults' ability to launch careers that might ultimately lead to the accumulation of some personal wealth: internships and the gig economy.

Unpaid Internships: With distant roots in the apprenticeship system of the Middle Ages, today's internships are an increasingly common part of the college experience or the first step in seeking work after finishing college (or possibly after high school, though that's less common). We saw how the cost of attending college serves to filter emerging adults into different levels of career opportunity in the previous chapter. Similarly, students' ability to pursue an internship during the academic year, over the summer, or in the period shortly after graduation provides another chance for some to learn needed skills and to differentiate themselves from the competition for entry-level positions in professional fields with limited job openings. But that opportunity is not open to everyone, and it carries a direct cost for those who don't have funding to pay all of their expenses since time spent at the internship means hours not working elsewhere, earning wages to cover tuition and living expenses.

At their best, these temporary positions can provide a genuinely valuable professional experience for the intern, building both skills and connections, and overseeing these programs in a meaningful way absolutely requires some resources on the part of the employer. However, some less well-intentioned employers have been quick to capitalize on internship programs to obtain free labor. In fact, employer use of unpaid interns as a source of labor became so rampant in the first decade of the twenty-first century that interns began filing lawsuits against entertainment and media companies, arguing that their effort merited compensation (Waxman, 2018). Some won their suits, but in 2018 the Department of Labor released new guidelines outlining seven factors that loosely characterize unpaid internships in a manner that favors employers' ability to claim that the intern is the primary beneficiary of the relationship so they don't need to be compensated like a regular employee (U.S. Department of Labor Wage and Hour Division, 2018).

And given that typical lack of compensation, not everyone can afford to participate in these potentially career-boosting, but unremunerative, programs. Some internships do pay a modest hourly rate or a stipend, but that's rarely as much as students could make working the same hours in retail or another part-time job. On top of the opportunity costs of lost wages, there can be significant out-of-pocket costs as well. If people have relocated for a summer internship they'll have to cover travel and living expenses, or commuting costs for something closer to home. They may need to buy a new wardrobe. Additionally, if they're doing the internship for college credit, students often have to pay tuition fees to their institution for the privilege of working for free somewhere else. Realistically, it could costs thousands of dollars in direct expenses to participate in an internship, not to mention the amount of lost income because that time wasn't spent at a paying job, and there's no guarantee that investment will ultimately pay off in a career-building job offer.

For lower income students it's like the gamble on college all over again: Will investing time and effort in pursuing an internship ultimately pay off in valuable connections and experiences, making it worth the potential direct costs, as well as the opportunity costs due to the lost wages a paying job would have provided for the same time spent working? Or will this turn out to be another experience they're assured by older people is a necessary investment in their future that won't actually work out as promised, like college itself for many who feel oppressed by debt? For those already taking on burdensome amounts of student loans it may not feel—or actually be—worth the risk of accruing even more debt in exchange for an uncertain payoff. Instead, internship positions go to those who can afford the time and expense, shutting out those who would actually benefit the most from the ability to make connections and get a foot in the door. And so, in this hypercompetitive market, those without that experience enter the job search feeling even further at a disadvantage, like these survey participants:

We are expected to have experience before we can get positions that give experience. We have to take low wage jobs and pay student loans and rent and every other bill and get shamed for having roommates or moving back home.

—Female, born 1990

Oversaturation of the market has made it a really competitive environment to live. I am expected to have multiple, multiple means of relevant experience, but I cannot take on some opportunities due to lack of pay. I cannot live if I am not paid, and I live simply. . . . We have more opportunities; we have more competition for those opportunities. It is a race to stand out and over-perform so that we can then perform adequately in our desired field.

—Male, born 1996

Older generations consider us lazy for not being able to find jobs and establish ourselves in the economy and world their negligence created. I find it laughable that they think my generation is spoiled, because if we are, it's because they spoiled us. But it is not being spoiled to want a job instead of an unpaid internship. They would never have worked for free and now they are asking us to do that. Unpaid work is a huge challenge to middle class and poor people because they cannot afford to not be paid for a year. Entry level was authentic 30 or 60 years ago, now they expect you to enter the workforce with a year's experience. This is unfair and takes advantage of young workers. Older generations also paid much less for tuition and could have a side job to pay for it. Now it would be impossible to pay off $20,000 to $50,000 a year on a minimum wage salary. This economic obstacle creates immense debt for students and prevents them from saving to retire and from buying homes. These challenges show our generation has it worse economically than previous generations.

—Unspecified gender, born 1996

The Gig Economy: If unpaid internships are a major amplifier of privilege for this generation, the rise of the gig economy as they entered emerging adulthood is the great equalizer for those without access to the resources that can kick-start a professional career, including higher education. However, in this case that equality means a lowering of most boats, with the constant risk of sinking for many of the most vulnerable. (That is the final nautical analogy in this chapter, I promise.)

What exactly is the gig economy, and who participates in it? Not surprisingly, it's often women and those with less education who end up in the least stable positions (and note that this pattern applies across age groups, not just for emerging adults). According to Bureau of Labor Statistics (BLS; 2019) figures regarding education and more traditional, nongig forms of employment in 2018, for people age 25 and older:

- Those with less than a high school diploma had median weekly earnings of $553 and an unemployment rate of 5.6%.

- Those with a high school diploma had median weekly earnings of $730 and an unemployment rate of 4.1%.
- Those with a college diploma or higher had median weekly earnings of $1,198 and an unemployment rate of 2.2%.

So there is a clear, positive, linear relationship between education and income, and a negative relationship (in the statistical sense, meaning a higher level of one variable correlates with a lower level of the other) between education and unemployment. Still, there is a job market for those with less education, if a low-paying one.

However, those BLS statistics are described as "earnings for full-time wage and salary workers," which brings us to the real issue with today's work opportunities at all levels of education: the shift away from steady, reliable jobs to what economists refer to as "contingent employment" and the rest of us know as the gig economy. That can take many forms, but BLS defined these workers as "people who do not expect their jobs to last or who reported that their jobs are temporary. They do not have an implicit or explicit contract for continuing employment."

These are the categories defined by the BLS (2018) as "alternative employment arrangements":

Independent contractors: Workers who are identified as independent contractors, independent consultants, or freelance workers, regardless of whether they are self-employed or wage and salary workers. As of 2017, there were 10.6 million independent contractors, who made up 6.9% of total U.S. employment. Their median weekly earnings were $851.

On-call workers: Workers who are called to work only as needed, although they can be scheduled to work for several days or weeks in a row. The 2.6 million on-call workers in 2017 made up 1.7% of total U.S. employment. Their median weekly earnings were $797.

Temporary help agency workers: Workers who are paid by a temporary help agency, whether or not their job is temporary. As of 2017, there were 1.4 million temp agency workers, who made up 0.9% of total U.S. employment. Their median weekly earnings were $521.

Workers provided by contract firms: Workers who are employed by a company that provides them or their services to others under contract, are usually assigned to only one customer, and usually work at the customer's worksite. As of 2017, just under 1 million contract firm workers made up 0.6% of total U.S. employment. Their median weekly earnings were $1,077, reflecting the fact that these positions tend to be concentrated in professional occupations requiring more education or experience than the other contingent categories.

Focusing purely on weekly earnings, some of these positions don't seem too bad compared with traditional employment, where the overall median earnings in 2017 were $884 per week. However, there are a number of disparities within the population of contingent workers (BLS, 2018):

- Men are more likely than women to work in the two most lucrative categories, independent contractors and workers with contract firms.
- The majority of contingent workers in all categories were between 25 and 54 years old. Those 55 and older were more likely to work as independent contractors than any other type of arrangement.
- The youngest workers, ages 16 to 24, were most likely to work in the worst paying categories, temp agency worker and on-call worker.
- Temp agency workers were the most likely to have only a high school diploma or less education (47.6%), but those with limited education were represented in all categories, making up 37.3% of on-call workers and about 32% for both independent contractors and workers with a contract firm.

Again, just looking at earnings and employment rates, people *are* finding work in these alternative arrangements, including those with less education. But that positive focus conceals a number of disadvantages of this type of work. First, it's less likely to be full time than traditional arrangements, generally defined as 35 or more hours per week. While 83.1% of all U.S. employees usually worked full time in 2017, full-time rates for the contingent workers in 2017 were as follows: worker with contract firm, 84.1%; temp agency worker, 76.9%; independent contractor, 70.5%; on-call worker, 55.4% (BLS, 2018).

Of course, some people want to work part time because of other demands like family or school obligations or health limitations. The BLS estimates that in 2016, of the total U.S. workforce, 14.1% voluntarily worked part time, while just 3.1% were involuntarily part time because they couldn't find full-time positions. However, whether it's by choice or not, part-time workers or those considered contractors often aren't eligible for important employer-provided benefits that can help them not only earn a consistent income, but also possibly begin to accrue some assets. Since in the United States all but the most basic benefits are offered at the discretion of the employer, this creates another form of inequality between those at the top and those lower down the employment ladder.

For example, take Uber, the ride-sharing company that's practically synonymous with the gig economy. Prepandemic, the benefits available to corporate employees included health insurance, dental insurance, gym membership, life insurance, 401(k) plan, military leave, maternity and paternity leave, fertility assistance, family medical leave, professional development plan, reduced or flexible hours, tuition assistance, vacation and paid time off, mobile phone discounts, employee discounts, and free lunch or snacks. That's all on top of salaries that averaged around $91,000 for managers and $129,000 for software engineers.

In contrast, Uber drivers are considered contractors rather than employees, so they're not eligible for any of those benefits. Not only do they have to provide and maintain their own vehicles, but also they have to pay for their own healthcare and don't receive overtime pay or sick days (Kerr & Morse, 2019). Uber drivers' hourly pay can vary widely based on location, time of day, and other variables, but one analysis estimated that after Uber took its cut of fees and the driver paid expenses like gas and car insurance, they earned an average of $8.55 to $11.77 for each hour they worked. That means an average annual income of $36,525 for full-time drivers, with no employer-provided health insurance or retirement plans, let alone access to fertility assistance or gym memberships (Reed, 2019). There's literally no such thing as a free lunch for these gig workers, unlike their corporate counterparts.

Uber may be an extreme example of disparities between employees and contractors, but a similar lack of access to basic benefits is apparent among many of the contingent workers in the BLS survey (2018). As of 2017 at least two thirds of them had health insurance coverage, though for many that came through a family member, government program, or private purchase. They were far less likely to have employer-provided health insurance than the 53.4% of workers in traditional arrangements, compared with 41.3% of workers with contract firms; 28.2% of on-call workers; and just 12.8% of temp agency workers.

The same pattern applied to whether workers were eligible for retirement benefits: While 50.8% of workers in traditional arrangements had the option to join an employer-provided pension or retirement plan, only 35.4% of on-call workers and just 12.7% of temp agency workers had access to the same perk. Actual rates of participation in saving for retirement through employer-provided options were even lower: 46.3% for traditional workers, 30.1% for on-call workers, and just 6.6% for temp agency workers (BLS, 2018). It's not surprising that those working in the lower paying categories were the least able to set aside savings for retirement, but it still raises serious concerns about how they will be able to support themselves once their already marginal earnings come to an end.

Not everyone dislikes gig work: Among independent contractors, 79.1% said they preferred their current working arrangement, and just 8.8% would prefer a traditional position (BLS, 2018). But satisfaction was far lower among the more unstable and less well compensated categories: On-call workers were evenly split, with 43.8% preferring their current arrangement, and 43.0% preferring a traditional arrangement; 38.5% of temp agency workers liked their arrangement, but 46.4% would have preferred a traditional job.

The fact that satisfaction was higher among those who earn more brings us back to the point made previously in the chapter: Changing jobs or exploring nontraditional fields or types of work can be healthy, especially early in life, if it's by choice and it eventually leads to a satisfying work life. But if it's involuntary and forces a person (at any age) to cobble together a number of badly compensated gigs with no benefits or potential for advancement, it's likely to be a source of tremendous frustration, like for these survey participants:

> Most of us are buried under student loan debt, with many of us unable to one day afford purchasing a home (with a good number unable to even move out of our parents' house), car, or save for future emergencies. We are consistently underpaid and now entering the era of the "gig economy," which further puts us at a disadvantage. This further makes us unable to responsibly save for retirement. . . . The only entitlement we may have is that we feel we are entitled to the same opportunities and privileges that previous generations received, exploited, and have now ruined. My generation is fortunately more aware of the issues and has the opportunity to do something about it now that we've reached an [age] where we can run for office.
> —**Female, born 1991**

> I think we have more opportunities to be creative and work in jobs that we enjoy, instead of just trying to get by. . . . More jobs are going freelance as companies don't want to provide benefits for employees. So people are often working multiple jobs in order to get by. Those jobs are lower paying, and things like the housing market have skyrocketed. . . . I think that we're incredibly hardworking, which is what the older generations don't understand. Many of us are working multiple jobs and extended hours just to make a decent wage.
> —**Female, born 1992**

> The gig economy is going to ruin my generation's ability to save money, and we are going to raise children who will absolutely face ecological disaster. . . . Far fewer opportunities exist for us. Companies will shrink, they will outsource work, they

will hire more temporary, contract, and gig employees and eschew offering retirement and healthcare to employees. . . . We face an incredibly exploitative economy,
imminent ecological disaster, and a government hell-bent on changing laws to
ensure that people have as little say in policy as possible. Economic inequality is
rapidly increasing. Healthcare is increasingly expensive. There will be no Social
Security program when we are ready to retire, and yet people from my generation
are far less likely to have retirement savings at all compared to previous generations. We won't own property, have children, have healthcare, or have retirement
savings. We will scrape by to pay rent.

—**Female, born 1994**

The frustration, betrayal, and despair of these commenters is palpable and,
I believe, justified. To be clear, they may not represent their entire generation
since, as I noted above, equal numbers of survey participants overall thought
their generation had better career opportunities relative to earlier generations
as felt they had worse opportunities (35.3% on each side, with the remaining
29.4% saying they were about the same). But the more optimistic views tended
to be held by those coming from more privileged households, at statistically
significant levels: Among those who said they were currently wealthy or upper
middle class ($n = 155$), 42.6% thought their career opportunities were better
than in the past, and 32.9% though they were worse. The opposite pattern was
found among those who said they were lower middle class or living below or
close to the poverty line ($n = 345$): 33% perceived better opportunities versus
40% worse. Those in the middle class ($n = 454$) were slightly but not significantly optimistic, with 35.7% perceiving better opportunities, and 33.5% perceiving worse. This seems to provide yet more evidence of the theme that has
run throughout this chapter: People with resources tend to be buffered from
fiscal (and other) stressors, while those starting with less as emerging adults
are far more vulnerable to external forces like economic shifts, so they must
really struggle to establish a stable foothold on the career ladder.

Let's end by looking at Generation Disaster's expectations for an economic
milestone that's far off in the future, but that many are already concerned
about, preparing for retirement. I return to the dream of home ownership in
the next chapter.

Retirement

We are less likely to have retirement unless our government
does something about the excessive spending and debt we have

accumulated over the years, that is falling on the shoulders of my generation, and it's gonna ruin us, as well as the fact that the cost of living
keeps going higher and the quality of life is getting worse.

—**Male, born 1990**

Retiring generally feels like a distant fantasy to people in their teens and 20s,
not an immediate concern, so I was surprised by how frequently the subject came up in the write-in responses to the national survey. A few of the
retirement-related comments were actually about earlier generations, like
this one:

The last generation did not save for retirement as they should have, and because of
that they aren't leaving the work force, leaving less jobs for the current generation
and then blaming them for it. They also have a hard time grasping the concept of
inflation.

—**Male, born 1992**

That sense of older workers intentionally holding on to positions they should
be vacating to make room for younger people came up repeatedly, and it
seemed to be yet another source of grievance that many participants held
against Baby Boomers. These comments also seemed somewhat unsympa-
thetic about the very real financial losses many older adults unexpectedly
took on their investments during the Great Recession, forcing them to post-
pone retirement.

Many other commenters focused on how impossible a prospect retirement
ever felt for them. To quantify this, I asked, "Compared to previous generations, do you think members of your generation are more or less likely to
be able to afford to retire comfortably?" Responses for the entire group were,
frankly, bleak:

- Somewhat or much less likely: 55.5%
- About the same: 26.4%
- Somewhat or much more likely: 18.1%

There were also differences by subgroup, with women and those with less
education feeling significantly less likely to be able to retire comfortably. In
partial contrast to the findings above about perceived career opportunities
correlating with participant socioeconomic status, higher current household socioeconomic status had less of a buffering effect on expectations for
retirement relative to previous generations: Even among those who identified

as upper middle class or wealthy, slightly more than half (50.3%) reported thinking they'd be less likely to be able to retire comfortably. That was about the same as for those in the middle class (51.5% less likely). And once again, those who described themselves as living below or close to the poverty line or in the lower middle class reported the most dire expectations about the future, with almost two thirds (65.7%) saying they expected to be less likely to retire, and just 12.5% thinking they're more likely to be able to do so than past generations.

I find these gloomy retirement perceptions especially troubling because they demonstrate such a long-term sense of hopelessness: More than half of a cohort who are barely beginning their careers already envision the end of their working lives, decades in the future, as unlikely to allow them to achieve what seemed like a basic right to their grandparents. Remember, these are their comparisons to previous generations, so the pessimism doesn't just reflect resentment about the current wealth gap that has concentrated assets so disproportionately among older adults. Instead, it's like these young people have learned that the normal trajectory Americans have been told to expect if they worked hard—upward economic mobility, or at least stability, culminating in a comfortable retirement—had suddenly reversed itself, and they're the ones who will take the fall for what they perceive as the irresponsible or avaricious fiscal policies and practices of previous generations. I don't know if this should be viewed as a kind of learned helplessness resulting from all of the other blows the cohort has already absorbed, but whatever the cause, it's disturbing to see how pessimistic many members of Generation Disaster are about both short-term and long-term economic prospects.

It's also important to note that these negative financial expectations across all measures were the worst for those in the older half of Generation Disaster (who roughly make up the younger half of the Millennial generation), apparently reflecting the impact of the timing of the Great Recession. These older participants, who were aged 24 to 29 when they responded to the survey in 2019, were less optimistic than those aged 18 to 23 about their opportunities relative to previous generations to establish a successful career, afford a home, and retire comfortably. Those differences were all statistically significant differences at the $p < .001$ level.

Sadly, those are probably realistic perceptions for a subset who entered the job market at a low point, just as opportunities remained limited across time for young adults who entered the workforce during the Great Depression. To requote a passage from an excellent overview of the multiple forces stacked against this particular group:

"A lot of workers were just 18 at the wrong time," says William Spriggs, an economics professor at Howard University and an assistant secretary for policy at the Department of Labor in the Obama administration. "Employers didn't say, 'Oops, we missed a generation. In 2008 we weren't hiring graduates, let's hire all the people we passed over.' No, they hired the class of 2012." (Hobbes, 2017)

In the first draft of this chapter, written in early 2020, I wrote that "The younger half of Generation Disaster may have it somewhat better as hiring had started to recover by the time they'll begin entering the workforce," but those gains have effectively been wiped out by the Covid-19 pandemic, and the rate of another recovery can't be predicted at this time. I fear many on the younger end now face the same kind of disadvantaged start to their working lives due to this more recent economic and societal disaster. And even when things do stabilize again, the very nature of much of the labor market has perhaps irrevocably shifted to a shape that older generations never had to navigate, making the odds of finding a stable, salaried position with benefits and room for advancement increasingly unlikely for those members of Generation Disaster who are unfortunate to be just starting out during this period of uncertainty—as if they didn't already have enough challenges in their lives.

* * *

It's not all bad, thankfully, and some emerging adults have found the shift away from traditional types of work liberating:

We have fewer opportunities to improve our lives than previous generations, but more [opportunities] to do what we love.

—Male, born 1990

The more challenges, the more opportunities. In that regard I think we have the same number, but somewhat different opportunities as previous generations regarding social issues. Many of the same issues are still in need of improvements such as racial discrimination, gender discrimination, and caring for the Earth generally, but within those issues we have new topics that open the door for discussion and improvement. Regarding economic opportunities, they are largely the same in the sense that there are always jobs available for innovative, industrious, and hardworking individuals, but the types of jobs have changed significantly because of the impact that technology has had, especially in the information age. The value of a degree has diminished while the cost has increased, taking away the silver bullet status that some gave college degrees for improving economic opportunity.

—Male, born 1990

Others emphasized their eagerness to work, provided their effort is fairly compensated:

We have a harder time getting good paying jobs out of college, college is morbidly expensive and often puts us into debt, buying a house or having a family seems out of reach due to costs, the cost of living has increased exponentially while wages have not followed. Although technology has increased our access to everything and made life simpler in most aspects, our everyday opportunities such as having good paying jobs and owning our own homes and living comfortably without having to work our bodies to the bone has significantly decreased compared to previous generations. . . . We just want everyone to be able to live comfortably and happily with equal rights and opportunities for all. We aren't afraid of hard work or effort, we just want to be paid accordingly.

—Female, born 1992

Many participants mentioned how economic stressors, in combination with other worries like climate change, are influencing their choices about other adult milestones like finding a partner and starting a family:

I would say opportunities are about the same. While older generations are retiring later and holding jobs in fields we could be entering, technology has opened up new careers and younger generations are more fitted to those types of fields and careers. . . . We have much more challenges than previous generations. The debt, the cost of living, wages, the cost of education, the cost of buying a home, the cost to seek medical help/attention with and without insurance, the cost to live is far too high and it's very hard for my generation to get ahead. It's why we aren't buying homes or cars or having children or having as many children as previous generations. We can't afford it.

—Female, born 1992

We delve into these family issues next.

Again, not all survey participants shared such dire perspectives about their professional and financial futures as some of the people I've quoted. Still, even if they're a minority among their generation, the raw anguish of some of these commenters about the limited career opportunities they perceive, and how those limits are likely to restrict their access to other traditional rewards of adult life, merit attention and concern. They're mad as hell, but when it comes to the economy, they don't seem to see any alternatives or hope for macrosystem changes that will enable them to take control over their financial futures, and very few explicitly connected the economy to political actions like voting in their comments.

As upsetting as this chapter's contents are, I hope the words of these distressed young people convince readers that members of Generation Disaster are not just whining about the usual early career challenges each cohort faces. Their opportunities to establish a stable path into the working world really have changed from the past. That's been demonstrated to be especially true for those who were unfortunate enough to enter the field at the height of the Great Recession, and most likely will be the same for those getting started during and shortly after the pandemic. Those who started out without the advantages of family wealth or connections genuinely may never recover from that rocky economic start, no matter how hard they work. Older people would do them a service by not blaming those who likely will not be able to achieve the American Dream—which was only ever accessible to a portion of the population anyway—because of the circumstances they've inherited from us.

References

Adams, J. T. (1931). *The epic of America*. Boston: Little, Brown.

Badger, E., Miller, C. C., Pearce, A., & Quealy, K. (2018). Income mobility charts for girls, Asian-Americans and other groups. Or make your own. *New York Times*. Downloaded from https://www.nytimes.com/interactive/2018/03/27/upshot/make-your-own-mobility-animation.html

Bureau of Labor Statistics (BLS). (2018). Spotlight on statistics: Workers in alternative employment arrangements. Downloaded from https://www.bls.gov/spotlight/2018/workers-in-alternative-employment-arrangements/home.htm

Bureau of Labor Statistics (BLS). (2019). Unemployment rates and earnings by educational attainment. Downloaded from https://www.bls.gov/emp/chart-unemployment-earnings-education.htm

Chetty, R., Grusky, D., Hell, M., Hendren, N., Manduca, R., & Narang, J. (2016). The fading American Dream: Trends in absolute income mobility since 1940. National Bureau of Economic Research Working Paper 22910. Downloaded from https://opportunityinsights.org/wp-content/uploads/2018/03/abs_mobility_paper.pdf

Chetty, R., Hendren, N., Jones, M. R., & Porter, S. R. (2019). Race and economic opportunity in the United States: An intergenerational perspective. The Equality of Opportunity Project. *Quarterly Journal of Economics*. Downloaded from https://opportunityinsights.org/wp-content/uploads/2018/04/race_paper.pdf

Dettling, L. J., Hsu, J. W., Jacobs, L., Moore, K. B., & Thompson, J. P. (2017). Recent trends in wealth-holding by race and ethnicity: Evidence from the survey of Consumer Finances, FEDS Notes. Board of Governors of the Federal Reserve System. Downloaded from https://www.federalreserve.gov/econres/notes/feds-notes/recent-trends-in-wealth-holding-by-race-and-ethnicity-evidence-from-the-survey-of-consumer-finances-20170927.htm

Federal Reserve. (2020). Distributional financial accounts. Downloaded from https://www.federalreserve.gov/releases/z1/dataviz/dfa/

Graham, C. (2017). *Happiness for all? Unequal hopes and lives in pursuit of the American Dream.* Princeton University Press.

Hobbes, M. (2017). FML: Why Millennials are facing the scariest financial future of any generation since the Great Depression. *Huffington Post Highline.* Downloaded from https://highline.huffingtonpost.com/articles/en/poor-millennials-print/

Ingraham, C. (2019). Wealth concentration returning to "levels last seen during the Roaring Twenties," according to new research. *Washington Post.* Retrieved from https://www.washingtonpost.com/us-policy/2019/02/08/wealth-concentration-returning-levels-last-seen-during-roaring-twenties-according-new-research/

Kerr, D., & Morse, A. (2019). Uber, Lyft business could be upended by California gig-worker bill. *CNET.* Downloaded from https://www.cnet.com/news/uber-lyft-business-could-be-upended-by-california-gig-worker-bill/

Kimmel, M. (2017). *Angry white men: American masculinity at the end of an era, revised edition.* Bold Type Books.

Krahn, H. J., Howard, A. L., & Galambos, N. L. (2015). Exploring or floundering? The meaning of employment and educational fluctuations in emerging adulthood. *Youth & Society, 47,* 245–266.

Leroux, M. (2013). It's plain sailing for one manufacturing industry. *Sunday Times.* Downloaded from https://www.thetimes.co.uk/article/its-plain-sailing-for-one-manufacturing-industry-p35ws3tpkbh

Reed, E. (2019). How much do Uber and Lyft drivers make in 2019? *The Street.* Downloaded from https://www.thestreet.com/personal-finance/education/how-much-do-uber-lyft-drivers-make-14804869

Reich, R. (2019). The myth of the rugged individual. *American Prospect.* Downloaded from https://prospect.org/economy/myth-rugged-individual/

U.S. Department of Labor Wage and Hour Division. (2018). Fact sheet #71: Internship programs under the Fair Labor Standards Act. Downloaded from https://www.dol.gov/whd/regs/compliance/whdfs71.pdf

Waxman, O. B. (2018). How internships replaced the entry-level job. *Time.* Downloaded from https://time.com/5342599/history-of-interns-internships/

World Inequality Database. (2020). USA. Downloaded from https://wid.world/country/usa/

10

Family Expectations

> We're often described as entitled, spoiled, etc., but many of us are stressed by things such as student debt and having to find a job in a bad job market. Our student debt is so insanely high that it's become common for us to live with parents or other family members. We also have to deal with pressures of getting married and having kids, and honestly, not all of us want a traditional relationship.
>
> **—Female, born 1993**

> We don't make as much money and pay much more for things; we have no health care and no money to get insurance, we will likely never be able to afford houses and it is now nearly impossible to live without roommates and almost impossible to gain financial security.
>
> **—Male, born 1999**

This final chapter on Generation Disaster's expectations for the future will bring things back to the microsystem to consider how members envision the development of their personal lives moving forward in an era when emerging adults have more choices than ever, but each choice comes at some cost. How have their life experiences shaped this group's expectations for their own future families, including hopes for finding a lasting partner and having (or not having) children of their own? What are their views about marriage? Building on themes from previous chapters, how are those expectations shaped by the rocky economy, by their perceptions about the general safety of the world, and for some, by fears about climate change's impact that make them question whether it's fair to produce another generation at all? How have expanded rights and reproductive technologies shaped these expectations for LGBTQ (lesbian, gay, bisexual, transgender, queer/questioning) individuals or those who might choose to become single parents, as well as those for whom more traditional routes to parenthood are available but no

Generation Disaster. Karla Vermeulen, Oxford University Press. © Oxford University Press 2021.
DOI: 10.1093/oso/9780190061630.003.0010

longer the only option? We focus on how the cohort's hopes and plans for their personal lives are influenced by the worldview they've formed in response to their complex environment and by major societal shifts around these customary, but no longer automatic, markers of adulthood that are causing some to take alternative paths around traditional approaches to family formation—whether by choice or because they feel circumstances beyond their control have forced them to.

This is probably the least disaster-specific topic in the book, though I've already included numerous participant quotes in previous chapters that mentioned how interconnected stressors like climate change and despair about achieving financial stability make some people question their access to traditional family structures. But many of the shifting behaviors I'll discuss here generally reflect the broader developmental patterns that are at the very core of the concept of emerging adulthood: the recognition that today's young people take on these tasks over a more prolonged and flexible time frame than was ever the norm in the past. As we'll see, that offers many potential benefits, but involves trade-offs as well.

There is an extensive body of well-researched literature on the topic of changing patterns of romance, marriage, and parenthood among emerging adults. If readers are interested in much deeper dives into this important aspect of development, try these books:

- Arnett (2014), *Emerging Adulthood: The Winding Road From the Late Teens Through the Twenties*
- Willoughby and James (2017), *The Marriage Paradox: Why Emerging Adults Love Marriage Yet Push It Aside*
- Konstam (2019), *The Romantic Lives of Emerging Adults: Getting From I to We*

Readers can also learn about diverse aspects of family formation through numerous scholarly articles published in the journal *Emerging Adulthood* and other developmentally focused academic journals. I won't attempt to be comprehensive here about these broader themes, but focus on how today's emerging adults' formative environments shaped their expectations for establishing their own families—however that's defined for each individual— as they move through this period. As we've seen throughout the book, these influences include exposure to 9/11, school shootings, and other disasters, but I can't overestimate how strongly economic forces have played a significant part in all aspects of life for Generation Disaster, including affecting fundamental decisions like whether they'll be able to afford children at any point.

Changing Family Compositions

According to widely respected guidance for emerging adults:

> First comes love,
> Then comes marriage.
> Then comes baby
> In a baby carriage.

No, of course that life advice comes from the classic K-I-S-S-I-N-G nursery rhyme that has been used to taunt embarrassed, crush-holding children for decades (NurseryRhymes.org, n.d.). But it does reflect the sequence of events that was traditionally regarded as proper for most young people in the United States, at least throughout much of the twentieth century: First they paired up with a partner, then they got married, then they procreated. Presumably they moved in together at the time of marriage (that part got left out of the rhyme, as children are apparently less interested in real estate transactions than in romance), but certainly not before putting a ring on it. Frequently, the newlyweds were moving into their shared place directly from their respective parents' homes, hence the tradition of wedding guests giving gifts like silverware, toasters, and other domestic items needed to set up a first household (Yglesias, 2019). Any divergence from this path—a path which, of course, was only open to people in heterosexual relationships—might have been viewed as a sign of failure (i.e., the "old maid" who couldn't attract a husband or the "barren woman" who couldn't bear children) or as cause for suspicion about the individual who didn't follow the norm (i.e., the "confirmed bachelor" who never seemed very interested in finding a wife).

Today there's vastly more variability in possible sequences of pursuing these traditional developmental milestones of establishing a home, finding a partner, making it legal, and reproducing. People not only can shift around the order in which they undertake each of these actions but also can opt in or out of each element entirely with far less stigma than in the past. The once strictly heteronormative steps of marriage and having children are now open to LGBTQ individuals, and there are many more ways of reproducing through technology that are open to people of any gender and relationship status, provided they can afford them. On the other hand, effective birth control and access (in most places in the United States) to safe and legal abortions mean that people who don't want to have a child at a given time can make that decision, when in the past they may have had to proceed with an unwanted pregnancy and the subsequent demands of raising the child.

To be sure, these societal shifts toward more flexibility don't apply to every individual emerging adult. Many people still opt for (or face pressure to conform to) more traditional patterns due to their own or their families' religious or cultural beliefs or other values that influence their preferences about family formation. However, it's clear that both laws and cultural norms have changed in a direction that supports choice in each of these realms, and the results are already dramatic. Consider these statistics, all from the U.S. Census Bureau (2020), on the changing demographics of various aspects of family structure in America.

Marriage Trends

- The median age at first marriage dipped slightly in the first half of the twentieth century, from about 26 years for men and 22 years for women in 1900, to a low of 22.5 for men and 20.1 for women in the late 1950s. Since then it has risen steeply to 29.8 for men and 28.0 for women in 2019, including marriages of same-sex couples.
- Across all adults (which for the purposes of marriage statistics, the U.S. Census disturbingly defines as those ages 15 and above), currently about 55% of American men are married, down from 70% in 1960. About 35% of U.S. adult men have never married, up from about 25% in 1960.
- Among all women, half are now married, down from two thirds in 1960. About 30% have never married, compared with 19% in 1960.
- Current marriage rates vary by race. They're highest for Asians (62.0% for women, 61.6% for men); then Whites (53.9% for women, 56.2% for men); then Hispanics (49.0% for women, 47.2% for men); and lowest for Blacks (32.7% for women, 37.5% for men).
- Divorce is far more common than in the past. Currently about 10% of all men and women are divorced, compared with about 2% in 1960.

Living arrangement trends

- Reflecting the trends of delaying marriage, younger adults are far less likely to live with a spouse today than in previous decades. In 2019, just 9.0% of women and 5.5% of men aged 18 to 24 lived with a spouse, compared with 46.3% of women and 31.2% of men this age in 1967.
- Those aged 25 to 34 in 2019 were more likely than the younger group to live with a spouse, including 44.8% of women and 35.6% of men—but that's still a dramatic drop from those living at this age with a spouse in 1967, when that included 82.7% of women and 82.6% of men.

- While fewer people are marrying, many more are cohabitating with a partner (though it seems likely that living together outside of marriage was underreported in the past when it was highly stigmatized, so I suspect the historic census figures may be lower than the reality was at the time). In 1967, 70% of all U.S. adults aged 18 and older lived with a spouse, and only 1% reported living with an unmarried partner. In 2019, just over 50% of all adults lived with a spouse, and about 8% lived with an unmarried partner.
- Among 18- to 24-year-olds, 10.7% of women and 6.8% of men lived with a partner in 2019, up from 0.1% of men and an undetectable share of women this age in 1967. Similarly, 15.3% of women and 14.3% of men aged 25 to 34 currently live with a partner, up from the 0.2% of women and 0.3% of men this age who acknowledged cohabitating in 1967.
- One out of four U.S. parents living with a child under 18 are now unmarried, compared with 7% in 1968. However, that doesn't mean all of their children live in a single-parent home, as 35% of these unmarried parents cohabitate with a partner.

Reproduction trends

- While historically the U.S. population has included more children than older adults, that ratio is projected to even out around 2035 and then to flip. By 2060, it's estimated that adults aged 65 and older will make up about one quarter of the total population, while just one fifth will be children under 18. This reflects two simultaneous patterns: expanding life spans and declining birth rates.
- Overall the percentage of women who eventually have a child has actually grown a bit in the recent past, up from about 80% in the early 1990s to 86% in 2016. However, that's down from 90% in 1976.
- Central to the emerging adulthood experience, many women are delaying parenthood until later than in the past: The median age of first birth is now 26.9, compared with 22.7 in 1980.
- There's a further divide in age at first birth by education level, with college-educated women now having children an average of seven years later than those without a degree.

It's clear that the time frame for accomplishing all of these traditional milestones is growing longer on average, and many adults are not completing some steps at all. On the other hand, LGBTQ individuals and others now have access to aspects of family formation they were previously barred from pursuing, at least with legal recognition. I don't want to impose my values on these changes, but it's easy (at least from my perspective) to assume this is all good: Thanks to these evolving norms, today's emerging adults have more options available to them, and they're far less constrained in their life choices than any previous generation has been. But here is the million-dollar question that may recast that rosy view in a more pessimistic light: Do these decisions truly reflect *choices* for some members of Generation Disaster?

The answer to that question directly parallels the point made in previous chapters about the impact of changing jobs repeatedly during emerging adulthood: If those changes are voluntary and lead to an upward career trajectory, their effect is likely positive, resulting in the individual ultimately flourishing in work, even if it takes them a while to reach that outcome. However, if those job changes are involuntary and lead to lateral or negative moves, they may generate a sense of floundering and downward economic mobility (Krahn, Howard, & Galambos, 2015). Similarly, if emerging adults are pursuing non-traditional paths toward family formation by choice, they're likely to appreciate the greater flexibility produced by these less rigid societal expectation. Some may welcome a newly acquired legal ability to marry and/or have children, while others may be grateful they have socially acceptable and biologically feasible alternatives to those customary paths.

However, my research makes it evident that many young people would actually *like* more traditional timing for steps like buying a home (or at least moving out of their parents' house) and having children, but they simply can't afford to make those leaps into adult responsibilities, so they're delaying taking them on. On the surface this appears to be a voluntary and mature choice. This subset of the generation is doing the fiscally responsible thing by not taking on the unrealistic mortgages many of their parents embraced, or having kids they know they can't afford to raise the way they would like to. Their financial prudence is laudable, but what is its cost emotionally? Let's look at the impact of these shifting patterns and how they connect to influences like the lingering effects of the Great Recession on all members of Generation Disaster as they negotiate these personal milestones of emerging adulthood.

Boomerang Blues: Living With Parents in Emerging Adulthood

While many of the emerging adults who don't live with a spouse or partner currently reside alone or with roommates, a lot of them are living in their parents' homes rather than establishing their own households during their 20s. Some have never moved out at all, and others may have left the parental home for a period while attending college and/or starting to work before returning to the nest. This group is sometimes referred to as "boomerang children."

According to U.S. Census Bureau statistics, rates of this kind of intergenerational coresidence haven't changed all that much over time for the younger segment of emerging adults. In 2019, there were 55.6% of 18- to 24-year-old men who lived with their parents, compared with 58% in 1967. During the same period, rates for women in this age group grew from 41.9% to 52.2%. Despite some increase among women, it seems fairly normative over time for those at the younger end of emerging adulthood to live with parents as they're finishing school and trying to launch a career. However, this takes on a different significance when the situation extends later into, and even beyond, emerging adulthood. In 1967, some 9.1% of men and 5.3% of women aged 25 to 34 years old lived with their parents. As of 2019, these percentages had more than doubled to 19.4% of men and 12.3% of women. On top of this general trend, an additional wave of adult children moved back in with their parents during the pandemic, leading to the highest rate of cohabitation since the Great Depression (Fry, Passel, & Cohn, 2020). As of the time of writing, it's unclear how many of them will remain at home and how many will move out again once it's economically feasible.

Sometimes this coresidence continues because adult children don't have the maturity or independence to strike out on their own—the so-called failure to launch phenomenon that's another source of "kids today" indignation among some older people. (Read McConville's 2020 book *Failure to Launch* for a practical guide to helping young people in this situation.) For others, coresidence provides practical, financial, and emotional benefits for both sides, making it a kind of positive symbiotic arrangement—provided roles can be successfully renegotiated so that parents acknowledge the younger generation's adult status, and the children accept their parents' financial and behavioral expectations for living in their home (Casares & White, 2018). One study of Finnish emerging adults even found lower mortality rates among 20- to 24-year-olds who lived with their married parents than in other arrangements (Remes & Martikainen, 2012). Coresidence can be especially beneficial for emerging adults with young children of their own, especially single parents. They can share child care and other responsibilities with their parents, who may relish the opportunity to spend time with their grandchildren (Guzzo, 2016).

Clearly, coresidence during emerging adulthood is not automatically a bad thing when it's a mutual choice for both generations, and it really reflects a return to historic norms that only started to change in the latter part of the twentieth century (Seiffge-Krenke, 2013). However, for many members of

Generation Disaster, the trend of remaining in the parental home well into their 20s is not by choice. They *want* independence from their parents; they simply can't afford to pay for their own places given rising housing costs in most areas, the weight of all of the debt they carry from student loans, and the stunted job prospects they face. That's the situation captured by these comments from my national survey:

> There are not enough job opportunities for a growing amount of people graduating college. Being able to make enough money to buy a house, or even to move out of your parents' house is not possible for many people.
>
> —Female, born 1998

> The gap between the rich and poor is greater than it's ever been. The middle class is becoming poor. Wages have been stagnant for decades as inflation and cost of living is rising fast. College debt is causing more people to live at home with parents and delay life events.
>
> —Male, born 1992

The tone of these comments makes it evident that some of the people who remain in a parent's home well into emerging adulthood aren't doing so due to any kind of laziness or resistance to taking on the responsibilities of living independently. These young people are clearly frustrated by the numerous ways in which their financial situations are limiting their ability to pursue many of the positive milestones that have traditionally marked full entry into adulthood. As these commenters observed, many can't even start that process with the initial step of moving out and solidifying their individuation from parents, let alone have realistic expectations of ever being able to buy a home.

The Dwindling Dream of Home Ownership

> We don't make as much money and pay much more for things; we have no health care and no money to get insurance, we will likely never be able to afford houses and it is now nearly impossible to live without roommates and almost impossible to gain financial security. We are far from entitled; we have much, much less financial stability, less money, less ability to live, we are only called entitled because we know our worth.
>
> —Male, born 1999

While it now seems like a foundational part of the American Dream, the pursuit of home ownership really only became widespread for the middle class after World War II when the government supported mass construction of affordable housing for veterans and their families (Kelleher, 2019). That subsidization, and the growing accessibility of automobiles, fed the expansion of suburban neighborhoods, which were soon filled with the many babies who would grow up into the Boomers.

But these early years of suburban growth weren't all backyard barbecues and neighborhood kids playing catch, or at least not for everyone. Suburban development fostered "White flight" out of many cities, leaving behind Black residents who were often prevented by housing restrictions and biased mortgage lending policies from pursuing the same investment in home ownership as their White peers. Since a home is often a family's main asset, these practices that prevented many Blacks from buying homes back when they were more affordable greatly fueled the current wealth gap discussed in the previous chapter—and, appallingly, many banks have been caught still practicing discriminatory or predatory lending practices against minority applicants in recent years, so that unequal access to investing in property continues (Harriot, 2018).

For all races, aspiring homeowners' unrealistic perceptions that property values would inevitably appreciate, fueled by banks and mortgage lenders who were happy to extend irrational levels of credit, led to the 2008 collapse of the real estate market that was described in Chapter 2. That experience made many people wary about investing in property, or at least about overextending themselves. (See Belsky, 2013, for a detailed history of attitudes toward home ownership before and after the 2008 mortgage crisis.) These days, with that painful lesson still fresh, not everyone wants to buy a home. However, as many of the comments throughout this chapter indicate, it still feels unfair to many emerging adults that home ownership doesn't even seem like an eventual possibility given the imbalance they face between income and costs of living, compounded for many by the need to pay student loans.

To find out about expectations in this area, I asked my national survey participants, "Compared to previous generations, do you think members of your generation are more or less likely to be able to afford to buy a home?" Results were very similar to their pessimistic expectations about retirement. For the entire thousand-person group, responses were

- Somewhat or much less likely: 53.3%
- About the same: 27.3%
- Somewhat or much more likely: 19.4%

While this response is based on participants' current expectations, not their actual purchasing ability at any point in the future, it closely mirrors the "fading American Dream" study (Chetty et al., 2016) described in the previous chapter that found that just 50% of children born in the 1980s outearned their parents at age 30. Again, it's as if our culturally engrained expectation of at least matching the success of our parents now only applies to half of the population.

And those prospects were perceived as even worse for subsets of participants, in largely predictable ways that also paralleled their retirement expectations. These respondents were statistically significantly less likely to think they'd ever be able to afford a home than previous generations:

- Females
- Those who had a high school diploma as the highest education level completed
- Those with a lower household income

This negative perception is somewhat countered by actual home ownership statistics. At the start of 2019, according to the U.S. Census Bureau, 35.4% of Americans under age 35 owned a home, which is barely less than the 37.1% in 1994. Moving forward, we'll need to factor in the economic impact of the new catastrophe of the Covid-19 pandemic. That caused many people to lose their jobs, motivating the moves back in with parents, but it also inspired a wave of suburban house purchases as people who could afford to buy a home fled cities, seeking more space and driving up housing stock prices in some markets. However, that increase in housing costs may have been partially offset by reduced rents in some urban markets that might allow remaining renters to save funds toward a future down payment, so it's difficult to predict the final impact of the pandemic on emerging adults' long-term purchasing prospects. Still, it seems likely that a homeownership gap will grow among this generation to mirror the income and wealth gaps described in the previous chapter, further perpetuating the divide between haves and have-nots.

Cohabitation Versus Marriage

Another shift that characterizes today's emerging adults is the growing frequency of romantic partners living together "outside of wedlock"—a term that now feels almost as dated as its even more judgmental counterpart, "shacking up." Of course, not all members of the generation embrace living together with a romantic partner as personally desirable. For example, Rogers, Willoughby, and Nelson (2016) found that 18- to 29-year-olds who had never married were less likely to view cohabitation as acceptable if they primarily viewed the period of emerging adulthood as a time to prepare for future family roles, rather than as a time to take risks. This may partly explain why only about 15% of unmarried couples aged 25 to 34 (U.S. Census Bureau) actually do currently live together. Still, one national survey found that 78% of people aged 18 to 29 said it was acceptable for an unmarried couple to live together even if they didn't plan to marry, reflecting a higher rate of approval of the practice among emerging adults than in any older age group (Horowitz, Graf, & Livingston, 2019).

For some couples, cohabitation may be an interim step toward marriage, especially while the partners focus on financial security. A Pew Research Center study (Horowitz et al., 2019) asked specifically about reasons why cohabiting participants who would one day like to get married were not yet engaged or wed to their current partner, and more respondents cited practical reasons than emotional ones. While 47% said their partner was not ready to make that kind of commitment and 44% said they themselves were not ready to make that commitment, 56% said it was because they were not ready financially, and another 53% said their partner was not ready financially. Similarly, 44% said they were not far enough along in their career to get married. (Also, 39% said they were not sure their current partner was the right person for them; let's hope they were not completing the web-based survey while that partner could view their responses.) Overall only about 4 out of 10 respondents who were cohabitating but not yet engaged said they wanted to get married someday; 24% did not ever want to marry, and 35% weren't sure, reflecting a shift away from marriage as the default endpoint for romantic relationships.

Horowitz et al. (2019) also found that young people were the most likely to see living together as a helpful step toward marriage: 63% of those aged 18 to 29 thought that couples who lived together first were more likely to have a successful marriage, while 10% thought they had a worse chance at success, compared with 48% and 13% of participants of all ages holding those views, respectively. Are these optimistic beliefs accurate? The evidence is mixed. Holmes, Brown, Shafer, and Stoddard (2017) summarized a number of studies that found negative effects of cohabitation prior to marriage, including lower quality marital communication and satisfaction and higher risk of divorce. However, those outcomes appeared to be associated with a less consciously planned approach to living together, sometimes described as "sliding into" cohabitation out of economic or pragmatic motivations. In contrast, researchers including Rhoades, Stanley, and Markman (2009) found that couples who moved in together as an intentional step toward marriage did not face similar risks.

This is an important distinction for emerging adults to keep in mind if they're considering moving in with a romantic partner: Are they intentionally choosing to cohabitate as a sign of lasting romantic commitment (whether or not they expect that to ultimately end in marriage), or are they sliding into it so they can afford to move out of their parent's house or for other largely instrumental reasons? Even if it's the latter, couples may decide it's a good enough motivation to proceed, but it is hoped they'll do so consciously and with full recognition of the emotional and financial costs if things don't work out and they need to disentangle their lives.

Those who do take the plunge of committing to marriage, whether or not that follows living together, are doing so later than ever before. As noted above, the median age at first marriage as of 2019 was the oldest in history: 29.8 for men and 28.0 for women. That means that getting married is no longer a typical experience during emerging adulthood. Still, about half of all Americans do eventually get married—and now that includes same-sex unions, including the 61% of LGBTQ couples living together who are legally married (Geiger & Livingston, 2019).

This shift toward delaying marriage is a continuation of a trend that has been emerging over the past few decades, so I'm in no way suggesting that it's specific to Generation Disaster or directly related to 9/11 and the other stressors this group grew up with. I did not ask my national survey participants about their attitudes toward relationships or marriage, but demographically they did match the overall trend: Just over 40% said they were in a long-term partnership, legally married, or in a domestic partnership, while 50.9% were single and 8.8% were in a casual relationship. Those in the more committed groups skewed strongly toward the older half of the group, with 74.0% of the long-term partnerships and 88.9% of the marriages reported by those born between 1990 and 1996.

It's also important to note that this timing trend doesn't seem to reflect any fundamental rejection or devaluation of the institution of marriage. Many emerging adults still view getting married as generally desirable; they just don't want to do it quite yet. Willoughby and James (2017) described this as "the marriage paradox" in their book of that name. Younger people are also more supportive of same-sex and interracial marriages than older generations. In one survey (Parker, Graf, & Igielnik, 2019), 47% of Generation Z and Millennial participants said they thought gay and lesbian couples being able to marry was good for society, while 15% thought it was bad; 53% said people of different races marrying each other was good for society, and just 4% said it was bad. Those rates of support for same-sex and interracial marriages were considerably higher than those reported by Baby Boomers, which were 27% and 30% respectively.

So overall, it doesn't appear that there's real erosion in how emerging adults view marriage as ultimately desirable; they're simply not in a rush to take that step. And why should they—if the delay is their personal preference and they do so with full awareness of the potential consequences—when reduced stigma and (for straight couples) access to birth control means they're now free to experience multiple relationships before committing to one, if they choose to pursue that particular form of exploration during this stage? This is one area where Generation Disaster arguably has an advantage over the Baby Boomers, however much the older group may deserve credit for launching the sexual revolution that ultimately led to today's less rigid expectations. If and when today's emerging adults do choose to marry, it can be for motivations like love and companionship rather than to meet family expectations—or because previously it was the only socially acceptable way to have sex.

However, like every choice in life, selecting one option means sacrificing the alternatives, and that certainly applies to putting off or opting out of marriage. Some people who delay marriage past emerging adulthood in order to focus on their careers later express regret over missed relationships (Willoughby & James, 2017), and those who want to procreate may be surprised by how quickly fertility issues can arise with age, as we'll see in the next section. Above all, this comes down to our key question of whether members of this generation are genuinely *choosing* to delay marriage, if they proceed with it at all, or if they're not pursuing that end because they believe they can't afford it or are driven by some other motivation or fear they don't feel they can control, in which case it's not really a choice at all.

Then Comes Baby?

Which brings us to the final major aspect of family formation many emerging adults consider, the decision about whether and when to have children. Like marriage, there are more options around this life experience than ever before. Straight couples who don't want children can prevent their conception, while same-sex couples and individuals who choose to become single parents can use reproductive technology to conceive a child if they don't want to adopt. Medical advances also can overcome many, though not all, fertility issues, though that often involves substantial financial and emotional costs.

Again like marriage, the general trend is toward delaying parenthood for those who do ultimately choose it, especially for people with higher levels of education. Postponing parenthood while one completes college and establishes a career can be beneficial for future children as it means they're likely to grow up in a household with higher socioeconomic status, which often correlates with multiple systemwide advantages like safer neighborhoods and access to higher quality schools than less well-off parents can provide (Pew Research Center, 2015).

Indeed, as high school dropout rates decrease and attending college increases, children are more commonly being born to parents with higher levels of education. For example, according to data from the U.S. Department of Education (ChildTrends.org, 2019a):

- In 1974, 27% of White mothers, 58% of Black mothers, and 62% of Hispanic mothers of children aged 6 to 18 had not completed high school. By 2018 those rates had fallen to 4%, 9%, and 31%, respectively.
- The percentages of children aged 6 to 18 whose mothers completed a bachelor's degree or higher also rose dramatically during that time period, from 9% to 46% for White women, from 4% to 27% for Black women, and from 4% to 16% for Hispanic women.

While this is generally a positive trend overall, it reflects yet another area where there's a growing divide between the haves and have-nots, with continuing racial disparities as well as educational ones. These differences are present even among the very youngest portion of emerging adulthood: While the overall birth rate in 2017 among 18- and 19-year-old women was 35.1 per thousand in the population, it was about 50% higher for ethnic minorities—52.1 and 52.7 births per thousand Black and Hispanic women, respectively, compared with 33.2 births per thousand White women (ChildTrends.org, 2019b). Overall, 86.8% of these young mothers were unmarried.

Unfortunately, children born to young, single parents face many obstacles (but note that these statistics generally include all teen mothers, not just the 18- and 19-year-olds, so the negative effects may be somewhat less intense for the older teens than for a 15- or 16-year-old mother). According to the Centers for Disease Control and Prevention (n.d.), teen mothers are more likely to drop out of high school, with graduation rates of just 50% by age 22 compared with about 90% for young women without children. As we saw in the previous chapters, lacking a high school diploma severely restricts work opportunities, setting the young family on a difficult financial trajectory. Then as the children born to teen mothers grow up, they're more likely to have academic problems and health problems, be incarcerated during adolescence, and face unemployment as a young adult. They're also more likely to drop out of high school and become teen parents themselves, perpetuating the cycle.

As teen pregnancies have decreased over recent decades, the average age when a woman bears her first child has crept up steadily. Between 1936 and 1945, among women having children 29% were still teenagers at the time of their first birth (though they were far more likely to be married already than current teen mothers, as earlier marriage was also the norm then), and just 8% were over 30 when they bore their first child. Between 1966 and 1975, 19% of women had their first child before age 20, and 24% were over 30 when they first gave birth—triple the rate of the earlier cohort. By 2016, 30% of first births were to women over age 30 (Agree, 2018). That was also the first year that the fertility rate for 30- to 34-year-old women exceeded that of 25- to 29-year-olds.

Overall, it appears that aspiring parents are taking charge of the timing when they take this momentous step (again, assuming this is an active choice rather than the result of financial fears or other barriers), but it should be noted that there are potential downsides to delaying parenthood, even if that's done in order to achieve financial stability or pursue other intentional goals before having kids. Physically, older couples may find it more difficult to conceive, and pregnancy may be more complicated for older women. We're also seeing the emergence of a cross-generational shift that will increase as long as the trend toward later parenthood continues: The age gap between grandparents and grandchildren is growing. Consider the difference just between two generations in a row bearing children at age 30 compared to age 20, which means the older parents become grandparents at age 60 versus age 40. That's not necessarily a bad thing, especially as increasing life spans for older people mean they may have the same number of years to get to know their grandchildren as in the past, but it does potentially change the nature of the relationship for both generations—and for the mothers and fathers in the middle who may find themselves simultaneously providing caregiving for young children and aging parents (Agree, 2018).

Regardless of the timing of a birth or adoption, financially it may be difficult for one or both parents to take time off of work to adjust to the new addition, especially since the United States is the only major country that doesn't federally mandate any paid parental leave (though a handful of states have enacted state-level leave laws, and some employers choose to provide it as a benefit). Lacking this guaranteed paid leave, many new parents have to choose between taking time off without pay to care for a new baby or adopted child (not to mention for birth mothers to recover from the delivery) or continuing to work in order to earn money. The resulting "career-and-care-crunch of competing work and family responsibilities" (Mehta, Arnett, Palmer, & Nelson, 2020, p. 437) is one of the defining characteristics of the post-emerging adulthood period, now starting to be referred to as "established adulthood."

That adjustment may be somewhat easier for couples where one partner can work while the other stays with the child for some time, but single parents and those who can't afford to lose any wages may have to return to their jobs almost immediately. This also has a psychological cost. Babies and adoptees may not have adequate time to attach to caregivers, and new parents may feel distress and guilt at such early separation. It's yet another example of how economic disparities can impact major life choices, with potential multigenerational effects.

The Paradox of Choice

Clearly, there have been major changes in the options emerging adults face for family formation and many other aspects of life, for women in particular. As one demographer summarized it, these shifts were

a product of dramatic changes in the second half of the 20th century in women's roles, especially greater access to the labor force and to higher education. Employment and marriage were no longer seen as tradeoffs for women. All women, including married women and mothers, began working for pay in greater numbers; investments in women's education pushed marriage and childbearing to later ages, especially for those with a college education; and the stigma of non-marital childbearing declined. . . . Transformations in norms about sexuality and family life accompanied changes in women's roles. As more effective birth control became available, gender roles more fluid, and family responsibilities more volitional, alternatives to lifelong marriage commitments such as divorce, remarriage, and cohabitation became acceptable. (Agree, 2018)

Even if some current emerging adults don't fully recognize how rapidly societal standards changed in the decades before their birth, they do seem to appreciate the resulting effects on their own lives. When I asked my national sample, "Compared to previous generations, do you think your generation has experienced more or less gender equality?" half (50.7%) said they felt they had somewhat or much more equality, 23.0% said somewhat or much less, and the rest said equality was about the same. They were even more cognizant of the rise in gay rights. Asked, "Compared to previous generations, do you think your generation is more or less open to the rights of members of the LGTBQ community?" 72.6 said they were somewhat or much more open; 20.0% said about the same, and just 8.4% thought their generation was somewhat or much less open.

So they recognize the societal increases in equality, and their actions make it clear that they're taking advantage of the multiple paths to family formation that are now available. I doubt that many emerging adults would choose to go back to the more rigid expectations of their grandparents' time when there was much less flexibility to diverge from the love/marriage/baby track, whether or not that really suited an individual's preferences. Yet remnants of some of those outmoded patterns linger, for better or worse, particularly when it comes to gendered patterns around work and family demands within heterosexual couples.

Not to be overly simplistic about these norms, but modern women are told they can "have it all"—love, family, and career. Most continue to hold jobs, by preference or necessity, after having children, stretching some thin in terms of time, energy, and emotions. And some men may have internalized traditional but no longer feasible ideas about single-handedly supporting a family, and about what their role in the home should be. One study (Coyle, Van Leer, Schroeder, & Fulcher, 2015) examined childless college students' expectations for how they would handle future work-family conflicts like balancing careers and kids. They found that young women anticipated more conflicts when family demands would impact their work, while men had the opposite expectations, that their work was more likely to cause conflict within their families.

This reflects a highly traditional, even stereotypical "breadwinner-caregiver model" where men are assumed to be the primary providers of resources while women are primary family caretakers (Coyle et al., 2015). The young women in that study also expressed more plans to change their behaviors to adapt to conflicting demands than the men did. This was a small ($N = 121$), homogeneous, college-based sample, so it doesn't necessarily reflect the broader generation, but it does capture the ongoing influence of traditional gender roles on future family expectations, and the expectation that women will do most of the work adapting to competing demands in order to sustain family functioning. This reflects the kind of "invisible labor" that is still disproportionately performed by mothers in many households with heterosexual parents (Ciciolla & Luthar, 2019), though the limited research on same-sex couples suggests a more egalitarian division of labor in the home for both male (Tornello, Kruczkowski, & Patterson, 2015) and female (Goldberg & Perry-Jenkins, 2007) parents.

In a sense, this reflects the price of "having it all," especially for women (straight or gay). Yes, they can now pursue higher education and career ambitions, but if they also want to have children, sacrifices will need to be made—of sleep, at the very least. At the same time, modern men (again, straight or gay) may be grappling with evolving roles and opportunities, including an unexpectedly stunted earning ability for those starting off without family advantages or access to opportunities. For both sexes, there's no longer a script to follow like there essentially was in the past, even if they might have rebelled at needing to conform at those more rigid expectations if they'd actually been subjected to them.

It's difficult to prove this point, but I wonder if stress about having so many options is behind some of the anxiety current emerging adults experience as they make important decisions like whether to marry or reproduce. Some of the comments survey participants have posted display a kind of nostalgia for the simpler, if less flexible, times of the past, like these two women:

> Cost of living has increased dramatically, as has the cost of education and healthcare. But the wages have not increased nearly as much. Previous generations were able to have one parent working a 40-hour-a-week job and with that job they could purchase a home and live comfortably with their wife and kids. With our generation now with the low minimum wage it takes at least four adults working and living together to be able to afford a junky apartment.
>
> —Female, born 1997

> We have a really hard time with college and jobs and being able to afford everything. Back in the day, older generations had an easier time affording things. One parent could work while the other stayed home to care for kids. Nowadays, it is so difficult to make ends meet.... The older generations do not understand how hard we have it and they like to call us lazy but we have it harder than them. We have to fight to survive and make ends meet to have a family.
>
> —Female, born 1996

That last comment literally frames the choice to have a family of one's own as requiring a fight for survival, and it seems to be a fight many members of Generation Disaster are seriously debating whether or not to engage in. Each individual will need to weigh the costs and benefits for him- or herself, but it seems that concerns about being able to afford to raise children financially, compounded by existential concerns about forces like climate change and disasters, are making many young people question whether reproducing is irrational or unfair to hypothetical offspring. It will be interesting to see what decisions this cohort ultimately makes about family formation as they move further into adulthood.

Lockdown Drills in Kindergarten: The Next Generation

The final point I address in this chapter is Generation Disaster's safety concerns for their own children, now or in the future. This brings us full circle, back to the security-driven parenting many members experienced during their post-9/11 childhoods, and to their own early exposure to school security measures and other reminders of danger. How are those experiences now shaping their perceptions about whether the world will be safe for their own kids?

To my regret, I didn't think to ask my survey participants about this specifically, but some raised their concerns in open-ended responses like these:

I'm scared for my daughter to start school because some kid might come shoot it up.

—Female, born 1990

The world seems to be less safe. Children can't play outside alone without someone trying to kidnap them. In my grandparents' era, there was a more carefree feel to the world. Now we feel the need to protect our children from every little thing.

—Female, born 1991

So much more has happened in this generation. So much has changed. It's not like it used to be back then where you can let the kids stay outside all day long till the streetlights came on. Now we worry about kidnapping bad drivers careless people pedophiles overall bad people.

—Female, born 1990

Again, these comments seem to reflect a kind of nostalgia for the supposedly idyllic days of yore—which, no offense to the writers, I'll counter is not an entirely accurate perception of the past. Parents have always worried about their children and tried to protect them from harm; they just didn't have the technology to monitor them constantly like modern caregivers do. My childhood throughout the 1970s was filled with earnest warnings about "stranger danger" (though to be fair, I was also able to play outside until the streetlights came on). These public service announcements tried to convince my peers and me to fear anyone we didn't know and to trust those we did—which of course is in total opposition to the reality that most abductions and acts of child maltreatment are conducted by relatives, then and now.

This was followed by the utterly bonkers "satanic panic" movement in the 1980s, a widespread moral panic promoting the belief that organized groups of devil worshippers were abusing and murdering thousands, if not millions, of children in elaborate rituals throughout the United States. Concerned parents, police officers, and therapists inadvertently implanted false memories of being abused in countless children, thereby generating actual trauma in kids who had previously been unharmed. Despite the fact that there was never a shred of physical evidence of these allegedly widespread acts of ritual violence, many accused people faced lengthy criminal trials that destroyed their reputations, and the psychological damage to children and families was immeasurable (Wright, 1995).

Now, that's an extreme example of the kind of concern parents have had for their children's well-being in past generations, but it's a reminder that previous eras were never perceived at the time as perfectly safe for kids. In this regard, I don't think members of Generation Disaster who express concern about their children's well-being are any different from their own ancestors. (And, in words I never thought I would have to write, the satanic panic of my youth is now rivaled by an even more bonkers conspiracy theory, QAnon, which the New York Times summarized as "a sprawling set of internet conspiracy theories that allege, falsely, that the world is run by a cabal of Satan-worshiping pedophiles who are plotting against Mr. Trump while operating a global child sex-trafficking ring" [Roose, 2020]. The fact that they felt compelled to include the word falsely in that description reveals a lot about life in 2020–2021.)

But seriously, it's a caregiver's job to do what they can to protect their daughters and sons, though exactly what they're protecting them from does change over time. And that's where I'll argue that this cohort differs from earlier ones: not necessarily in the intensity of their fears, but in their complexity. I acknowledge that this is another of those cross-generational comparisons that can't fully be supported with firm evidence because of a lack of parallel historical data. I was not able to find any research on what previous cohorts of parents feared most for their kids at the time—and like the point I made in Chapter 5 about mental health comparisons across time, even if we did have those data, it's entirely possible that we modern readers would fail to grasp the full impact of earlier sources of anxiety that are no longer relevant. For example, even in a time of global Covid-19 pandemic, it's probably hard for us to really understand the terror many parents would have experienced annually throughout much of the twentieth century about their kids contracting polio or other then-untreatable infectious diseases that are no longer a threat. Should we take the historic concern of a parent in 1952, when more than 20,000 children in the United States became permanently paralyzed due to polio (Routh, Oberste, & Patel, n.d.), any less seriously than today's parents' fears about school shootings, which their kids are far less likely to experience?

The main point is this: If you're afraid, realistically or not, that your child is at risk of being harmed by a particular cause, it almost doesn't matter what that cause is. I'm definitely not claiming that those entering into parenthood today—or choosing not to because of their trepidations—have concerns that are any more or less valid than in the past, but it's plausible that their own complicated relationship to feelings of security and anxiety may intensify their fears as they start to extend their families to the next generation. In other words, if they're entering parenthood with a history of elevated stress and anxiety because of everything they've been exposed to up to that point, it's likely that they'll now channel some of that fear toward their offspring.

In analyzing survey responses, two comments addressing the idea of children and security really stood out to me. First there was this stark one:

> [9/11] makes you look at the world differently. It scares me bringing a child into this world and having no way to protect them and know you can keep them safe.
>
> —Female, born 1997

So, parents never feel fully up to the task of keeping their kids safe, but this woman directly ties her fears about child safety to the attacks of 9/11, which occurred when she herself was less than 5 years old. That's quite a lingering impact for an event she probably can't even remember, and it exemplifies the power of these kinds of historic turning points in our culture, including 9/11 for this generation.

Again, I'm not claiming that parents haven't had these kinds of collective, existential worries in the past. When Pearl Harbor was attacked in December 1941 and the United States entered into World War II, my paternal grandparents had one young son and my grandmother was 6 months pregnant with my father. I'm sure they questioned the wisdom of bringing children into the world during wartime, but they were following the standard script of the time for a young married couple, producing what would ultimately be four healthy children. I wonder how many Silent Generation and Baby Boom children might not have been born if their parents had as many options as Generation Disaster do—an unanswerable question.

Then there was this comment, reflecting the complexity of life today for emerging adults:

[Our challenges include] jobs, additional stress, and anxiety towards the current realities of the world, such as safety concerns, climate change, high costs to education and health care, the increasing wealth gap. Many of us are worried about how to make ends meet, and not following traditional steps of settling down, get married, buy a home, and have children, etc. I think previous generations look down on us for this.

—Female, born 1993

This one perfectly encapsulates so many of the themes that have woven throughout this book. They boil down to concerns about money and safety that are influencing the generation's major life choices for careers and family formation, all compounded by feeling judged by older adults. If people don't follow "traditional steps of settling down, get married, buy a home, and have children, etc." because they know they just can't afford it and/or they're too afraid about the security of the world to pursue these future-oriented actions, should we really view those decisions as choices, or are some members of this generation being deprived of these achievements of adulthood that were virtually guaranteed (at least for straight couples) in the past?

And my final, related question for this chapter about family expectations: Why do we keep judging actions like living with parents well into adulthood, or not reproducing, as selfish or immature? This seems like the counterpart to the tendency to blame young people for not managing to achieve the American Dream when the deck was so fully stacked against them that upward mobility was a virtual impossibility. In this case, members of Generation Disaster are sacrificing what some might really *want* for themselves. They're making rational, fiscally responsible choices, yet older adults criticize them for not following in their own traditional paths—even if they themselves might have chosen a different route if they'd had the option at the time. It's yet another area where older groups need to do more to try to understand everything this cohort is trying to cope with, including the personal toll it takes for them to make responsible choices about their future families.

References

Agree, E. M. (2018). Future directions for the demography of aging: Proceedings of a workshop. In M. K. Majmundar & M. D. Hayward (Eds.), *National Academies of Sciences, Engineering, and Medicine; Division of Behavioral and Social Sciences and Education; Committee on Population*. Washington, DC: National Academies Press. Downloaded from https://www.ncbi.nlm.nih.gov/books/NBK513078/

Arnett, J. J. (2014). *Emerging adulthood: The winding road from the late teens through the twenties*. Oxford University Press.

Belsky, E. S. (2013). The dream lives on: The future of homeownership in America. Joint Center for Housing Studies, Harvard University. Downloaded from https://www.jchs.harvard.edu/sites/default/files/w13-1_belsky_0.pdf

Casares, D. R., & White, C. C. (2018). The phenomenological experience of parents who live with a boomerang child. *American Journal of Family Therapy, 46*(3), 227–243.

Centers for Disease Control and Prevention. (n.d.). About teen pregnancy. Downloaded from https://www.cdc.gov/teenpregnancy/about/

Chetty, R., Grusky, D., Hell, M., Hendren, N., Manduca, R., & Narang, J. (2016). The fading American dream: Trends in absolute income mobility since 1940 (National Bureau of Economic Research Working Paper 22910). Downloaded from https://opportunityinsights.org/wp-content/uploads/2018/03/abs_mobility_paper.pdf

ChildTrends.org. (2019a). Parental education. *ChildTrends*. Downloaded from https://www.childtrends.org/indicators/parental-education

ChildTrends.org. (2019b). Teen births. *ChildTrends*. Downloaded from https://www.childtrends.org/indicators/teen-births

Ciciolla, L., & Luthar, S. S. (2019). Invisible household labor and ramifications for adjustment: Mothers as captains of households. *Sex Roles: A Journal of Research, 81*(7–8), 467–486.

Coyle, E. F., Van Leer, E., Schroeder, K. M., & Fulcher, M. (2015). Planning to have it all: Emerging adults' expectations of future work-family conflict. *Sex Roles: A Journal of Research, 72*(11–12), 547–557.

Fry, R., Passel, J. S., & Cohn, D. (2020). A majority of young adults in the U.S. live with their parents for the first time since the Great Depression. Pew Research Center. Downloaded from https://www.pewresearch.org/fact-tank/2020/09/04/a-majority-of-young-adults-in-the-u-s-live-with-their-parents-for-the-first-time-since-the-great-depression/

Geiger, A. W., & Livingston, G. (2019). 8 facts about love and marriage in America. Pew Research Center. Downloaded from https://www.pewresearch.org/fact-tank/2019/02/13/8-facts-about-love-and-marriage/

Goldberg, A. E., & Perry-Jenkins, M. (2007). The division of labor and perceptions of parental roles: Lesbian couples across the transition to parenthood. *Journal of Social and Personal Relationships, 24*(2), 297–318.

Guzzo, K. B. (2016). Do young mothers and fathers differ in the likelihood of returning home? *Journal of Marriage and Family, 78*(5), 1332–1351.

Harriot, M. (2018). Redlining 2.0: How banks block black homeowners. *TheRoot*. Downloaded from https://www.theroot.com/redlining-2-0-how-banks-block-black-homebuyers-1823083306

Holmes, E. K., Brown, G., Shafer, K., & Stoddard, N. (2017). Healthy transitions to family formation. In L. M. Padilla-Walker & L. J. Nelson (Eds.), *Flourishing in emerging adulthood: Positive development during the third decade of life* (pp. 70–97). Oxford University Press.

Horowitz, J. M., Graf, N., & Livingston, G. (2019). Marriage and cohabitation in the U.S. Pew Research Center. Downloaded from https://www.pewsocialtrends.org/2019/11/06/marriage-and-cohabitation-in-the-u-s/

Kelleher, K. (2019). The homeownership obsession: How buying homes became a part of the American dream—and also a nightmare. *Curbed*. Downloaded from https://www.curbed.com/2019/11/13/20944014/why-buy-house-homeownership-history

Konstam, V. (2019). *The romantic lives of emerging adults: Getting from I to we*. Oxford University Press.

Krahn, H. J., Howard, A. L., & Galambos, N. L. (2015). Exploring or floundering? The meaning of employment and educational fluctuations in emerging adulthood. *Youth & Society, 47*, 245–266.

McConville, M. (2020). *Failure to launch: Why your twentysomething hasn't grown up . . . and what to do about it.* G.P. Putnam's Sons.

Mehta, C. M., Arnett, J. J., Palmer, C. G., & Nelson, L. J. (2020). Established adulthood: A new conception of ages 30 to 45. *American Psychologist, 75*(4), 431–444.

NurseryRhymes.org. (n.d.) *K-I-S-S-I-N-G.* Downloaded from https://www.nurseryrhymes. org/k-i-s-s-i-n-g.html

Organization for Economic Cooperation and Development. (2019). Parental leave systems. OECD Family Database. Downloaded from http://www.oecd.org/els/soc/PF2_1_Parental_leave_systems.pdf

Parker, K., Graf, N., & Igielnik, R. (2019). Generation Z looks a lot like Millennials on key social and political issues. Pew Research Center. Downloaded from https://www.pewsocialtrends.org/2019/01/17/generation-z-looks-a-lot-like-millennials-on-key-social-and-political-issues/

Pew Research Center. (2015). Parenting in America: Outlook, worries, aspirations are strongly linked to financial situation. Downloaded from https://www.pewsocialtrends.org/2015/12/17/parenting-in-america/

Remes, H. M., & Martikainen, P. T. (2012). Living arrangements and external causes of deaths in early adulthood. *Journal of Adolescent Health, 50*(2), 164–171.

Rhoades, G. K., Stanley, S. M., & Markman, H. J. (2009). Couples' reasons for cohabitation: Associations with individual well-being and relationship quality. *Journal of Family Issues, 30,* 233–258.

Rogers, A. A., Willoughby, B. J., & Nelson, L. J. (2016). Young adults' perceived purposes of emerging adulthood: Implications for cohabitation. *Journal of Psychology: Interdisciplinary and Applied, 150*(4), 485–501.

Roose, K. (2020). What is QAnon, the viral pro-Trump conspiracy theory? *New York Times.* Retrieved from https://www.nytimes.com/article/what-is-qanon.html

Routh, J. A., Oberste, M. S., & Patel, M. (n.d.). Poliomyelitis. In S. W. Roush, L. M. Baldy, & M. A. Nelson (Eds.), *Manual for the surveillance of vaccine-preventable diseases* (Chap. 9). Downloaded from https://www.cdc.gov/vaccines/pubs/surv-manual/chpt12-polio.html

Seiffge-Krenke, I. (2013). "She's leaving home . . ." Antecedents, consequences, and cultural patterns in the leaving home process. *Emerging Adulthood, 1*(2), 114–124.

Tornello, S. L., Kruczkowski, S. M., & Patterson, C. J. (2015). Division of labor and relationship quality among male same-sex couples who became fathers via surrogacy. *Journal of GLBT Family Studies, 11*(4), 375–394.

United States Census Bureau. (2020). Families and living arrangements. Downloaded from https://www.census.gov/topics/families.html

Vespa, J. (2017). The changing economics and demographics of young adulthood: 1975–2016. United States Census Bureau. Downloaded from https://www.census.gov/content/dam/Census/library/publications/2017/demo/p20-579.pdf

Willoughby, B. J., & James, S. L. (2017). *The marriage paradox: Why emerging adults love marriage yet push it aside.* Oxford University Press.

Wright, L. (1995). *Remembering Satan.* New York: Vintage Books.

Yglesias, M. (2019). Stop the scourge of wedding presents. *Slate.* Downloaded from http://www.slate.com/articles/life/weddings/2013/06/wedding_present_etiquette_let_s_do_away_with_wedding_registries_and_give.html

11
Conclusion

I have learned so much while researching and writing this book. Some of those lessons have come directly from students who were in my classes or working on my research team, and many more have come from the thousands of anonymous study participants who were willing not only to complete a survey, but to take the time to write the heartfelt and sometimes heartbreaking responses to open-ended questions that I believe are the most valuable part of this work.

It's a tired cliché to compare anything to an iceberg, but it's so true in this situation: The developmental effects of growing up in the post-9/11 world, amid so many other acute disasters, are the tip of the issues I first observed among my students. But that was only the visible apex: Just beneath the surface this generation has endured chronic stressors like climate change and the steady fear of school shootings, driven home by participation in school lockdowns and disproportionate media coverage of these rare but awful events. And that layer rests on an even broader base of unjust social conditions that feel so entrenched that many members of Generation Disaster can't seem to see any way to alter them—systemic racism, for sure, and especially the problems of the income and wealth gaps, whose impact I thoroughly underestimated when I began this project.

It's beyond troubling to imagine how much worse that particular issue will grow as a result of the pandemic, which was still raging globally as I completed the book. Many emerging adults who were already working faced the loss of their jobs, especially those who were marginally employed in gig work or in low-paying fields like hospitality and retail, while others were forced to tolerate frightening risks of exposure in order to keep getting paid. Anyone who graduates, drops, or stops out of school during this time will be battling for work in a catastrophic job market that's likely to be even worse than the situation faced by the Millennials, whose career trajectories were so derailed by the Great Recession. The pandemic is yet another form of calamity that's impacting everyone in society, but with distinct and likely lasting developmental consequences for emerging adults that I won't attempt to predict—but do intend to study.

Generation Disaster. Karla Vermeulen, Oxford University Press. © Oxford University Press 2021.
DOI: 10.1093/oso/9780190061630.003.0011

Even before it was exacerbated by the outbreak, the power of underlying and, for some members of the cohort, all-encompassing economic stress was the most important lesson I learned from this work, and it also feels like the most intractable problem to me. As many participant quotations in the chapters later in the book showed, this generation is not afraid of hard work. They welcome it, in fact, but they want to be compensated fairly, which seems like a reasonable expectation. How many early career Gen X and Baby Boomers would have tolerated the expectation of providing free labor in the form of an internship, or being paid by the task with absolutely no security or benefits like those working in the gig economy? Probably not many, yet those are the workforce conditions we've created for today's emerging adults.

And then there's the question of higher education. Should we change the narrative we tell young people that college is the only route to success and worth any debt they have to take on to pursue a degree? As a college professor who values education deeply, it pains me to no end to acknowledge that some people might be better off without pursuing an advanced degree, but that's the reality that I've had to confront after doing this research and hearing firsthand from my students how much they'll need to sacrifice well into the future to pay off their loans—and that's from students at a public college whose tuition is a fraction of that charged at private institutions.

On the personal side of typical adult developmental milestones, the incredibly widened variety of options for pursuing goals like forming a family still seems generally positive to me, especially as it accommodates LGBTQ individuals, those who don't want a traditional family structure, and anyone else who benefits from more societal acceptance of alternative paths. However, there are clearly trade-offs as well for those who might want those traditional rewards of adulthood like having children and buying a home, but who feel like these outcomes are not available to them because of circumstances beyond their control, especially economic constraints. Those are not just stressors, but deep losses of essential human experiences for many emerging adults.

***

I hope this book has validated for readers who are members of Generation Disaster that their struggles are real, and that at least some older people recognize that fact and respect them for surviving the intense cumulative load of stressors they've had to deal with throughout their lives. And I really hope that it convinces older readers to pause and reflect on how their elders treated them in their youth and to consider other ways of thinking about this cohort. At the very least, let's recognize their courage, strength, and immense capacity for adapting and moving forward. Their world is so much more complicated than the one in which I became an emerging adult in the early 1990s that despite all of this research, I cannot fully fathom how profoundly different their experiences have been.

"Resilience" is a big buzzword these days in the field of mental health and in the world in general. It's defined variously as the ability to bounce back quickly from a negative response to a difficult situation or the ability to ride out the difficult situation without having a strong negative response to it. Whichever definition you prefer, I hope you'll acknowledge that members of Generation Disaster are, on the whole, unbelievably resilient. They're stressed, sometimes anxious or depressed, and often pessimistic about aspects of their futures, but those reactions are in no way disproportionate to the challenges of the world they've inherited. Like the survey participant quoted in Chapter 5, some feel they're "literally just trying to survive." Others are thriving. And most are probably vacillating between floundering and flourishing, making their way through this early stage of adulthood as best as they can.

I know it's not realistic to encourage older adults to retire from their lucrative jobs or powerful political positions to make way for the next generation, or to voluntarily redistribute their assets to narrow the wealth gap. But one thing we can easily do is to stop judging this group and start listening to them. That's what I learned to do when I started teaching, and I am now 100% Team Generation Disaster. They're not perfect, of course, but they deserve our empathy and respect, and they deserve every chance to demonstrate what they're capable of when simply given the opportunity.

As usual, I finish this chapter with a few voices of emerging adults in their words. These two relatively positive examples came from my national survey:

We are more consumer-conscious, we care more about the environment, we are more open, less racist, and generally motivated to do things in life that makes us happy. We are the generation that can implement a lot of changes on both a small and large scale, such as healthcare, protecting the environment, reducing poverty, etc.

—Female, born 1993

We are more open-minded and understanding. We are willing to work hard in underpaid positions to make ends meet. We have a great sense of humor and are more interested in politics. Many women in my generation have flourished in their ability, education, and careers. We are underestimated, but we are rising. Our voices will be heard soon.

—Female, born 1994

I end the book with this reflection by a student who was in one of my spring 2020 courses. She wrote this while she was completing our class remotely from her parents' home, 2 months after the pandemic closed our campus. It was her final week of college before she would graduate (without a commencement ceremony or any of the other traditional rites that mark that accomplishment) into a strange new environment and a terrible job market. Her impassioned blend of guarded optimism and realistic concern about the future reflects the views of so many emerging adults I've met, so it seems appropriate to give her the final word.

The world that we knew before is forever changed and society will be forever changed because of [the pandemic]. I think people will have PTSD after being in quarantine, or until there is a vaccine for the virus. I believe people may be too afraid to go out to eat when we are told that the public world is open again, too anxious to open doors for others since we will be less than six feet apart from each other, and won't be able to give a stranger a smile because their face will be covered with a mask. All of our futures will be forever changed after this, and I hope it changes our healthcare system. 2.5 million people lost their health insurance in the span of two weeks the past month in this country during a global pandemic. Healthcare should be a human right and I hope our government sees that since we were obviously not prepared for this pandemic, considering that fact that we have close to three-quarters of a million confirmed cases in our entire country as of right now. Some good things to look at are that March was the first month without a school shooting in this country for a while, nature is slowly being restored, yet almost everyone I know my age is having a mental breakdown about either finding a job after they graduate next month or because they recently got laid off from their previous job. I also think the pandemic will affect my generation moving forward in the sense that it will make us realize that life is so fragile and can be taken away from us at any moment. We will more than likely try to enjoy the moment more and be more thankful for our loved ones and friends once we can be reunited again. I believe this to be true since the pandemic makes you realize that love is the most important currency we have right now, since if we do not rise up together we will fall apart, and at the end of the day we just have to hold on to hope for a better tomorrow, since without hope we have nothing. With that, mental illness may be on the rise from having to adapt to quarantine life and then having to adapt to what the world will look like after it, and that makes me both scared and excited to see what the future holds for the citizens of this country as well as for my generation as we try and move into adulthood.

I'm also excited to see what the future holds for us all as this group comes into their full powers. I wish the members of Generation Disaster all the best—if you're one of them and would like to share your own story, please do so at https://www.generationdisaster.com.

Index

For the benefit of digital users, indexed terms that span two pages (e.g., 52–53) may, on occasion, appear on only one of those pages.